FLASHBACK LOS ANGELES

POSTCARD VIEWS: THEN AND NOW

MICHAEL OLDHAM

Schiffer Publishing Ltd

4880 Lower Valley Road • Atglen, PA 19310

DEDICATION

To Aunt Beverly and Uncle Rich

Library of Congress Control Number: 2014934290

Type set in Bodoni

ISBN: 978-0-7643-4586-9
Printed in China

Published by Schiffer Publishing, Ltd.
4880 Lower Valley Road
Atglen, PA 19310
Phone: (610) 593-1777; Fax: (610) 593-2002
E-mail: Info@schifferbooks.com

CONTENTS

INTRODUCTION

Flashback Los Angeles, Postcard Views: Then and Now was primarily created to be a pictorial experience. Therefore, the pages are dominated with visuals — postcards (the "then" views) and photographs (the "now" views).

Save for the captions found directly under the then/now views, this book's writing is purposely breezy. Many of its words come either from my knowledge gained by enjoying Los Angeles-filled books or from paying visits to the area since the time my parents took the family on drives from Orange County in the 1960s. In short, this book is a guide-like tour in its writing style.

Flashing back in time through the pages of a book is one type of visual experience. My ultimate goal in writing *Flashback Los Angeles*, though, is to inspire readers to go out and see the views displayed in these pages for themselves. Why? Because no picture replaces the experience of seeing and touching an old and proud building. Also, because it is actually a healthy thing to feel a tinge of sadness when you see a modern building in place of a now-demolished historic one. Both experiences keep the public interested in saving still-standing historic structures around for future generations.

"HOUSEKEEPING" NOTES:

All photographs ("now" views) were taken by the author in either 2008 or 2012. The postcards ("then" views) are from the author's personal collection.

Not all photographs could be lined up with the postcard views for a variety of reasons. Some postcard views were taken high up inside buildings that did not offer easy access to the author. Physical obstacles, such as foliage and building structures, often times blocked a "now" photo from being able to line up with a "then" view. Even camera lens differences between the postcard photographer and the author's cameras sometimes prevented a more perfect line-up of the "then" and "now" views.

It should be noted that some cities in this book, such as Beverly Hills, are not technically part of Los Angeles. However, we have included such cities in this book since they are located inside Los Angeles County.

SELECTED BIBLIOGRAPHY:

Pitt, Leonard and Dale Pitt. *Los Angeles A to Z: An Encyclopedia of the City and County*. Berkley, Los Angeles, London: University of California Press, 1997.

CHAPTER 1

BEVERLY HILLS

THEN

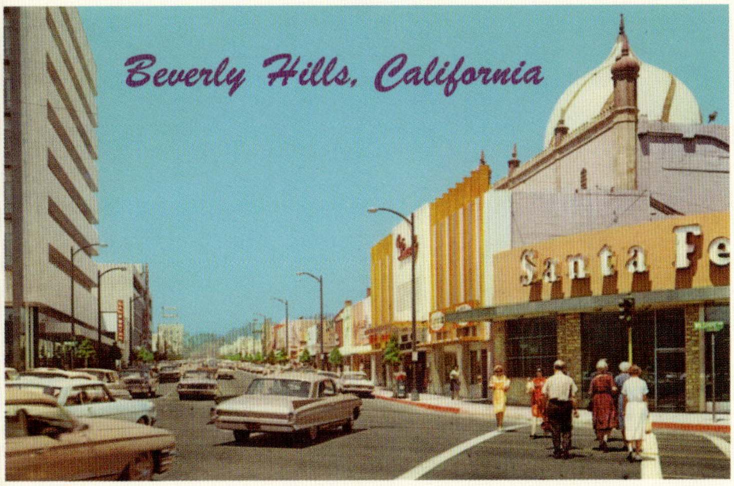

Beverly Hills.

NOW

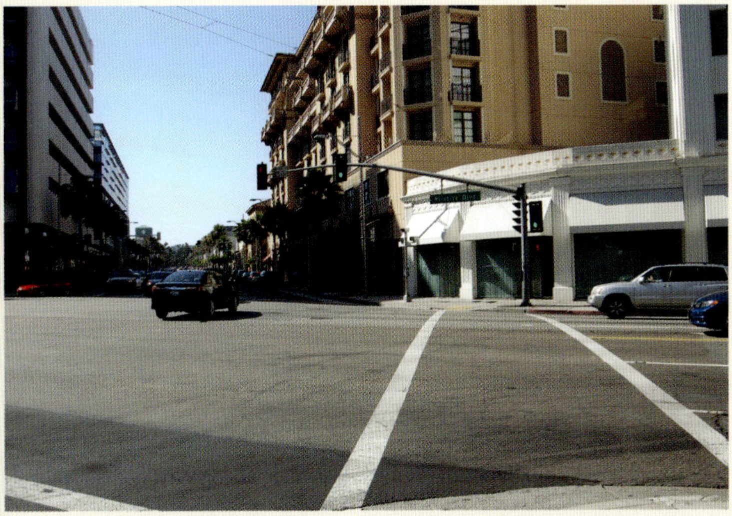

Beverly Hills looking north from Wilshire Boulevard onto North Beverly Drive.

Beverly Hills is known as the "Movie Star Capital." The city invokes thoughts of movie stars, manicured lawns, and high-end retail shops.

THEN

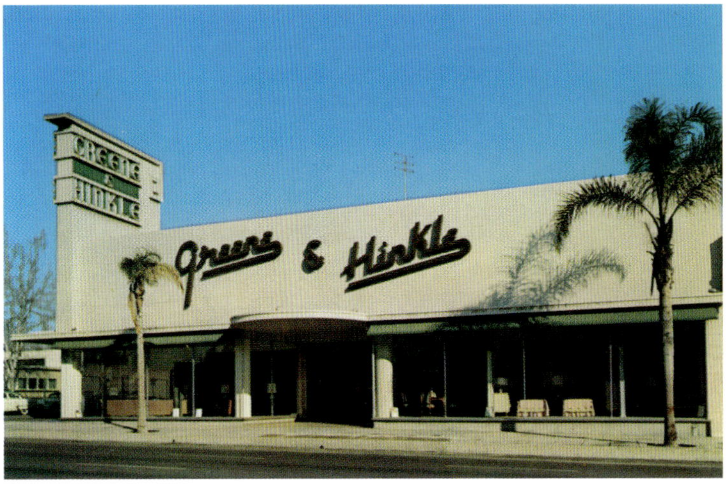

Greene & Hinkle.

NOW

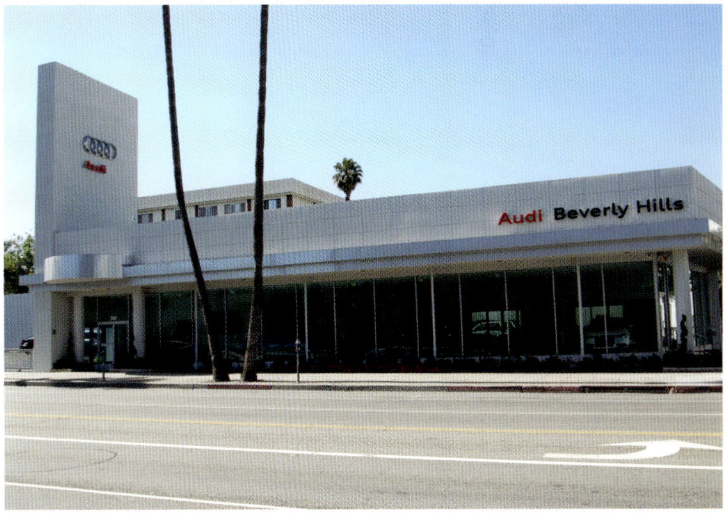

The Greene & Hinkle store was located at 8825 Wilshire Boulevard. The building remains, but the store is gone.

Greene & Hinkle was a decorating and home furnishings company. Modernist chairs, floor coverings, and draperies were among the items the store had in its offerings. The former Greene & Hinkle building continues to furnish Wilshire Boulevard.

THEN

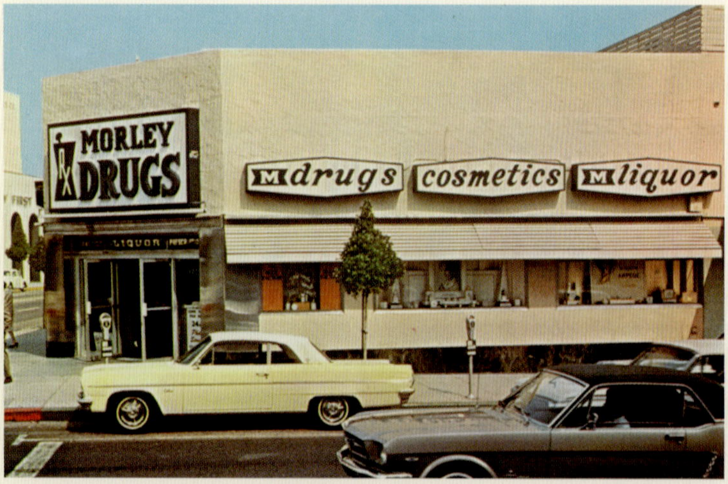

Morley Drug Store.

NOW

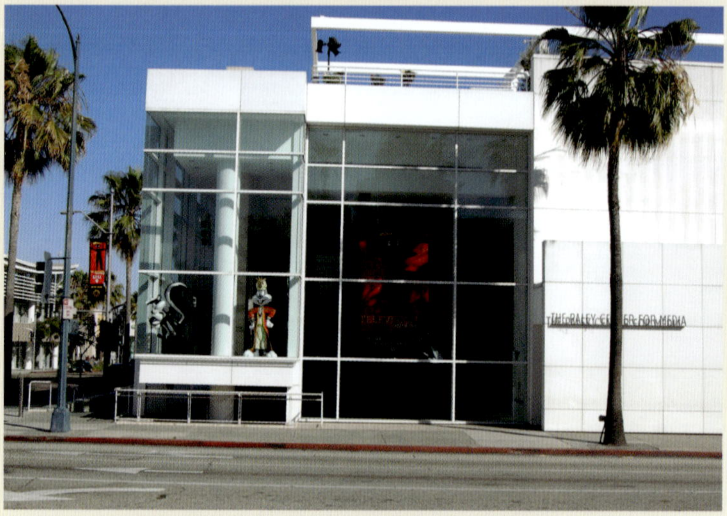

Morley Drug Store was located at 470 North Beverly Drive. Both the building and the store are no longer.

Despite its glamorous reputation, Beverly Hills still needed common shops, such as a drug store.

THEN

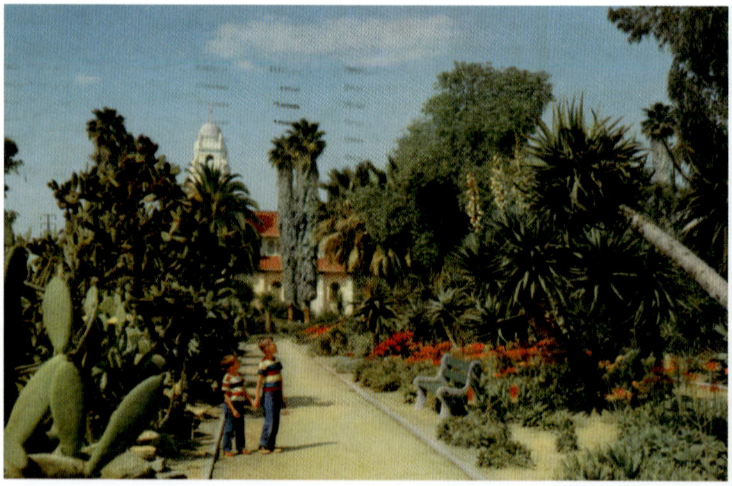

Beverly Park Gardens.

NOW

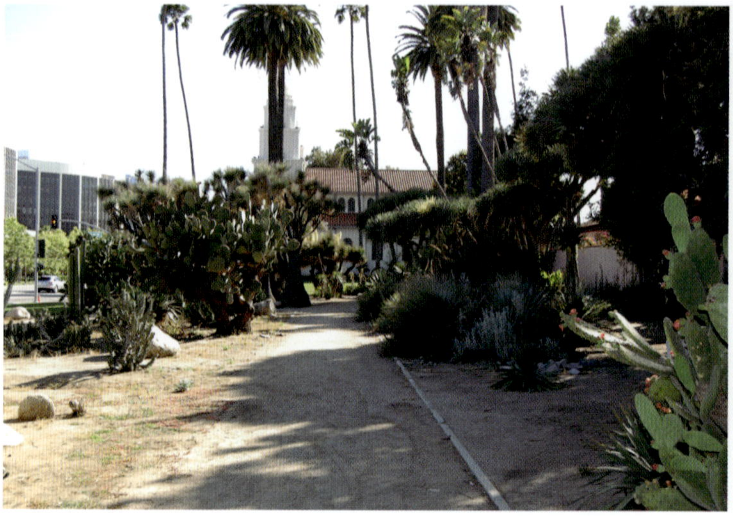

Beverly Park Gardens, looking west along the path that runs parallel to Santa Monica Boulevard. The church in the background is on the northwest corner of Santa Monica Boulevard and Bedford Drive.

The beautiful park areas of Beverly Hills seem to go almost unnoticed by tourists hoping to see a celebrity.

THEN

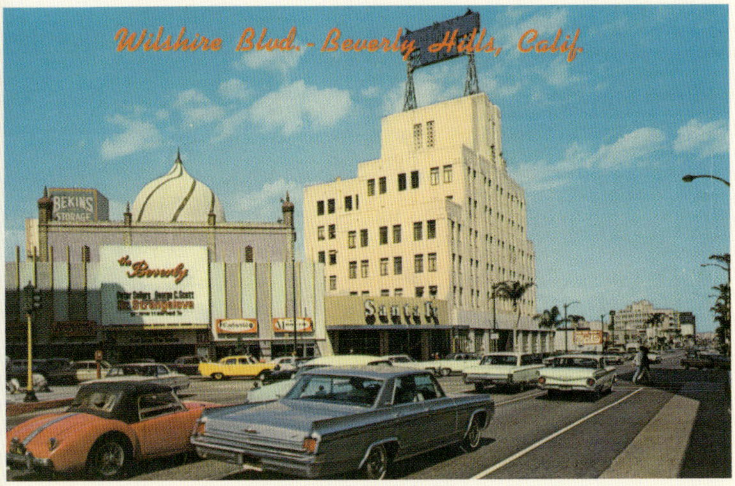

Wilshire Boulevard.

NOW

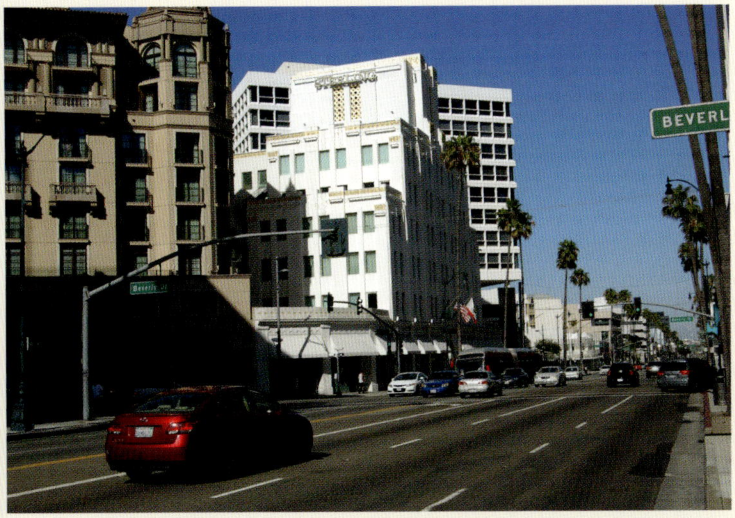

Wilshire Boulevard, looking east just before it divides Beverly Drive into North, on the left, and South, on the right.

Big-name department stores and hotels sit along busy Wilshire Boulevard. Fancy cars often zoom by the Beverly Wilshire Hotel, which has fronted the boulevard for decades.

THEN

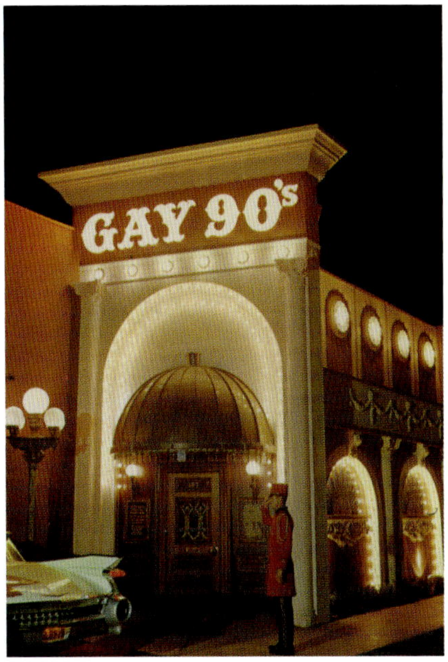

Gay 90's nightclub.

NOW

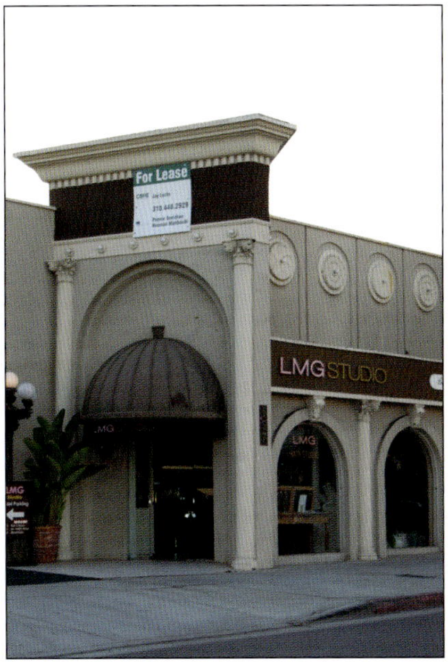

Gay 90's nightclub was located at 157 North La Cienega Boulevard. The building remains, but the nightclub is no longer.

The Gay 90's nightclub referred to itself as "A Saloon Created For The Carriage Trade." It offered a "Gleaming Fire Pole," "Beauteous Genteel Feminine Cupbearers," and "Professors of the Piano." Restaurants and nightclubs, such as The Gay 90's, made the famed "Restaurant Row" area of Beverly Hills legendary.

CHAPTER 2

CENTURY CITY

THEN

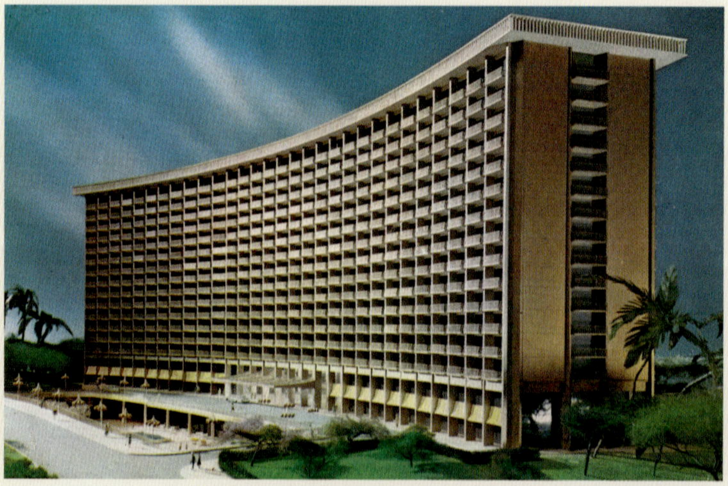

THEN

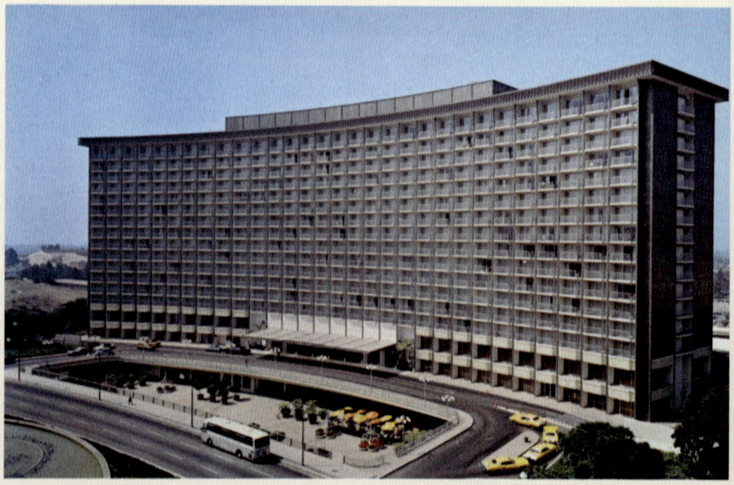

The Century Plaza Hotel.

NOW

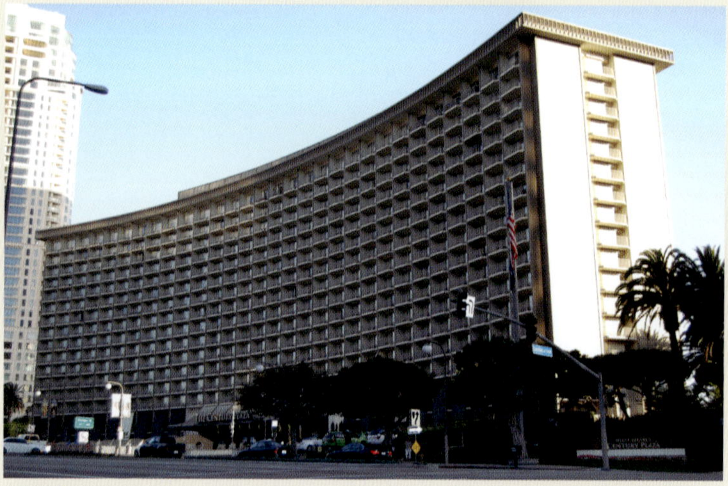

The Century Plaza Hotel is located at 2025 Avenue of the Stars.

The business district of Century City is where one can gaze at tall buildings of glass, steel, and concrete. The Century Plaza Hotel is one such structure, and it is the city's figurative heart. Shopping awaits just a stone's throw away at the city's famed Century City mall.

THEN

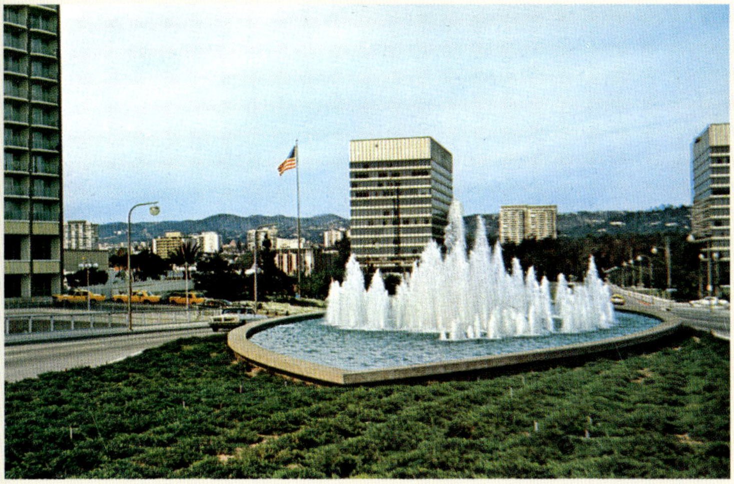

THEN

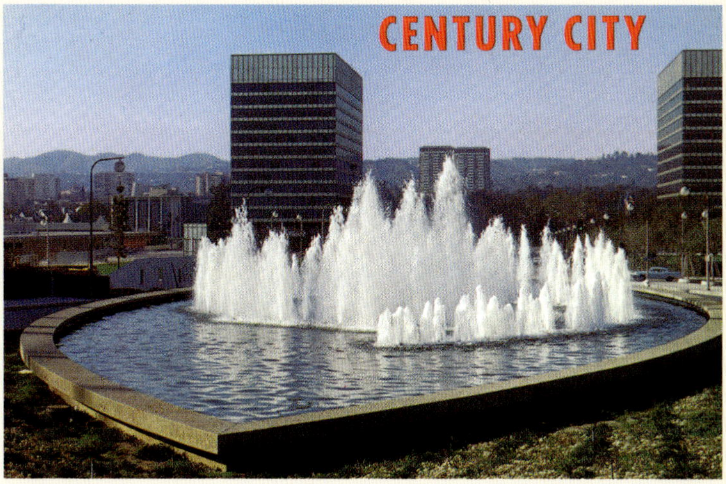

Fountain in front of the Century Plaza Hotel.

NOW

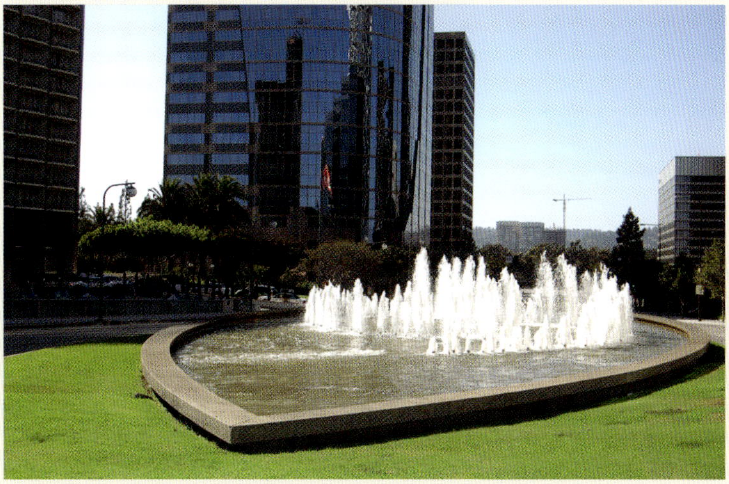

Fountain in front of the Century Plaza Hotel.

The fountain splits the Avenue of the Stars. Its waters spout in front of both the Century Plaza Hotel and another relatively new Century City landmark building, 2000 Avenue of the Stars.

THEN

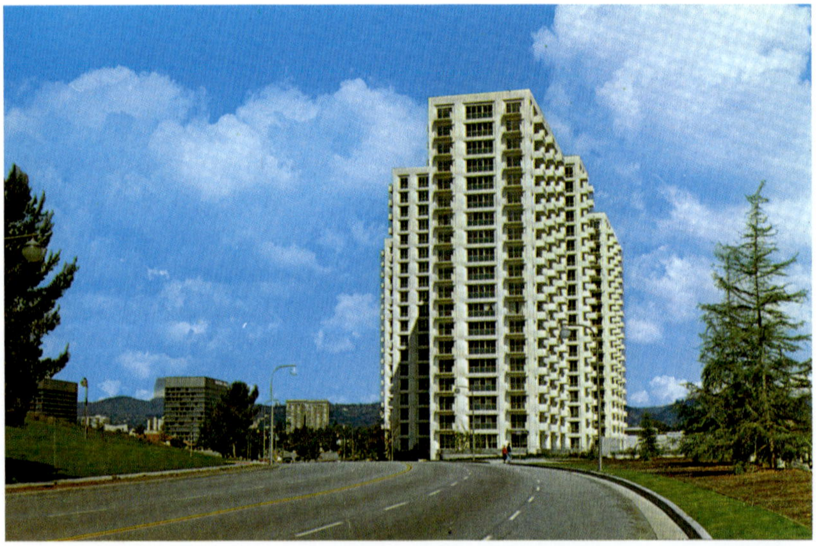

Looking north on Century Park East.

NOW

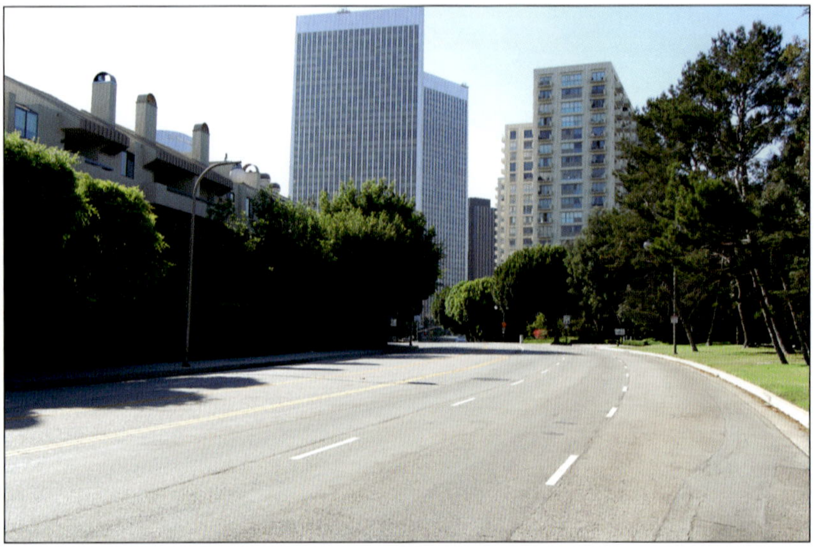

Looking north on Century Park East.

Over the years, Century City has seen developments reach for the sky. Still, it is rare to see pedestrians walking around Century City at night, save for the occasional dog walker who lives within its boundaries.

CHAPTER 3
DOWNTOWN

THEN

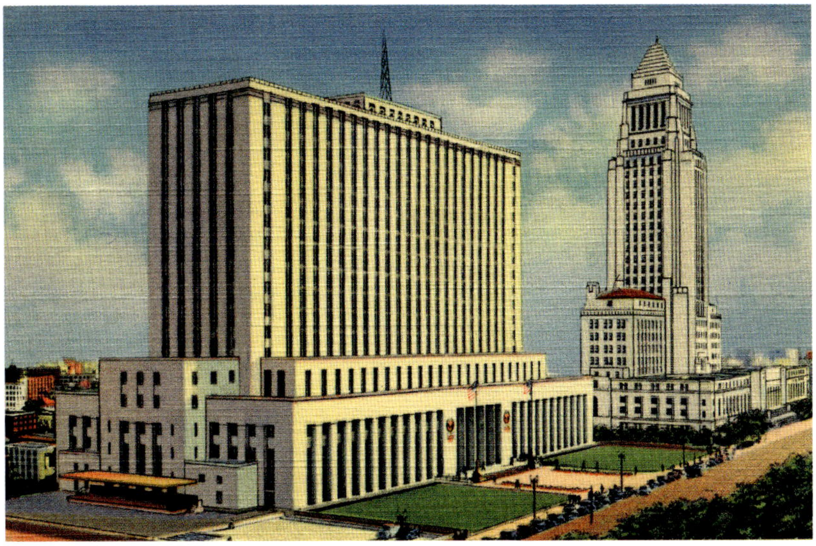

Looking south on Spring Street towards City Hall.

NOW

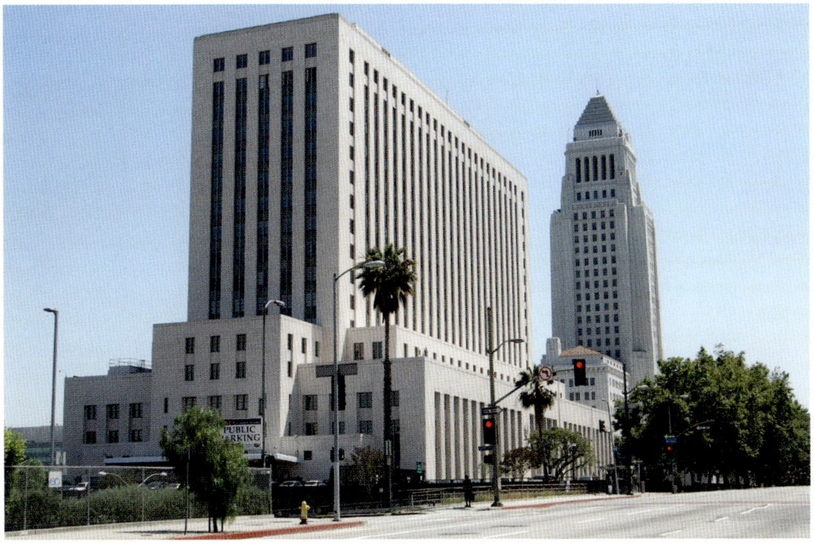

Looking south on Spring Street towards City Hall.
Arcadia Street is nearest cross street shown here.

Los Angeles touches so many lives, but few residents have touched its city hall. It does take effort, given downtown's multitudes of one-way streets and parking challenges.

THEN

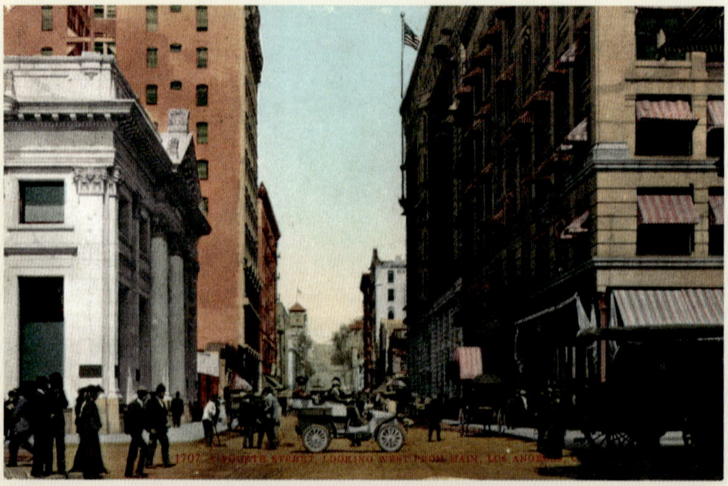

Fourth Street looking west from Main Street.

NOW

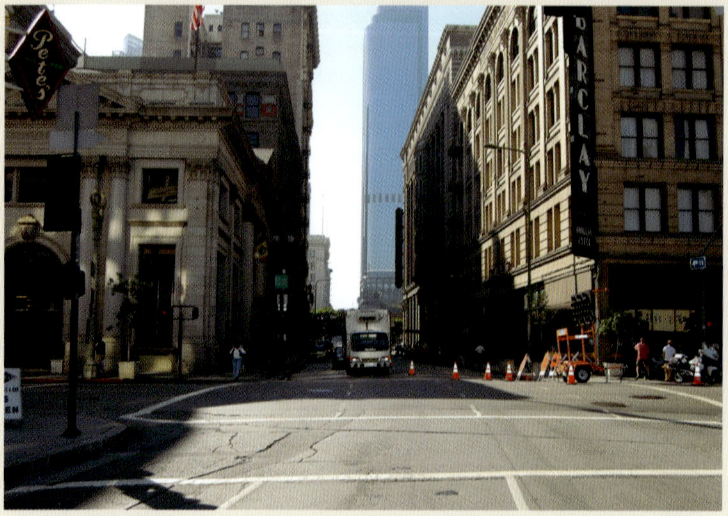

Fourth Street looking west from Main Street.

The ancient, foreground buildings are a contrast to the modern glass and steel in the background.

THEN

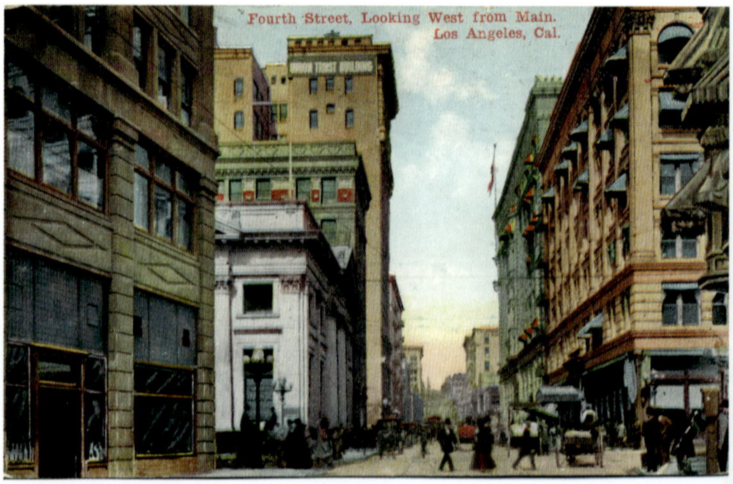

Fourth Street looking west from Main Street.

NOW

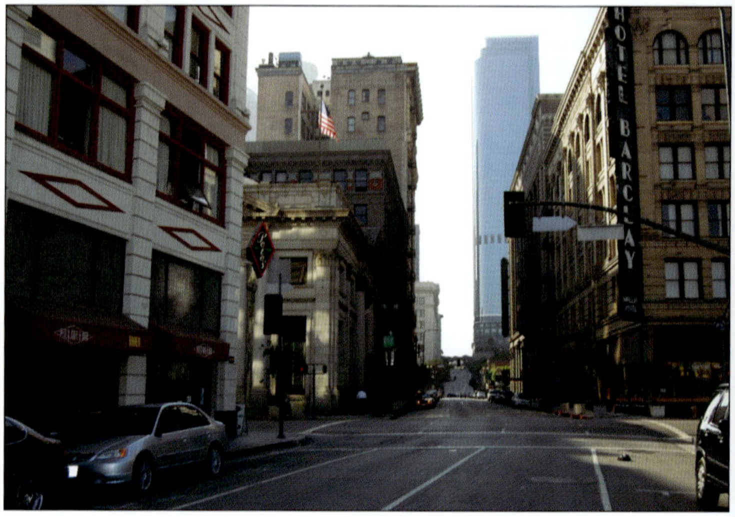

Fourth Street looking west from Main Street.

It is refreshing how many of the historic buildings from downtown's historic core remain standing.

THEN

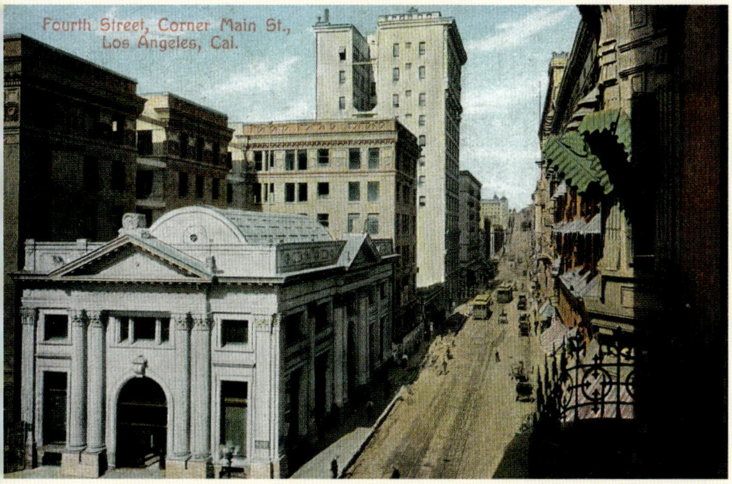

Looking west on 4th Street from Main Street.

NOW

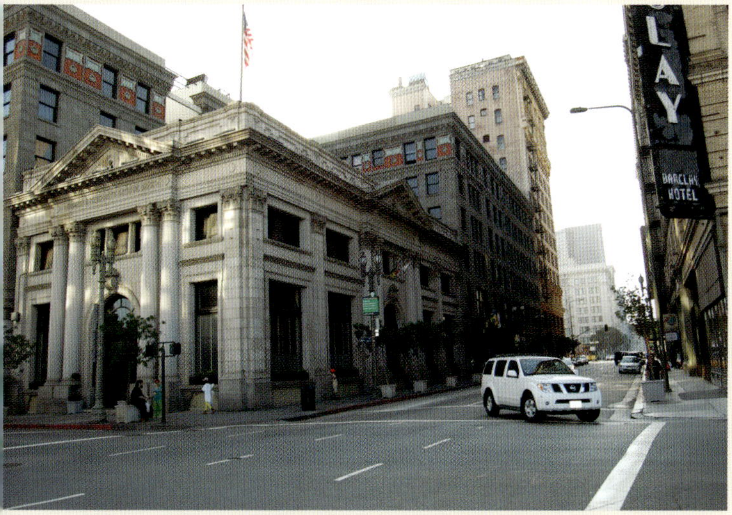

Looking west on 4th Street from Main Street. East 4th Street becomes West 4th Street at this intersection.

In the "now" view, a modern car is driving with its back to the Farmers and Merchants Bank building.

THEN

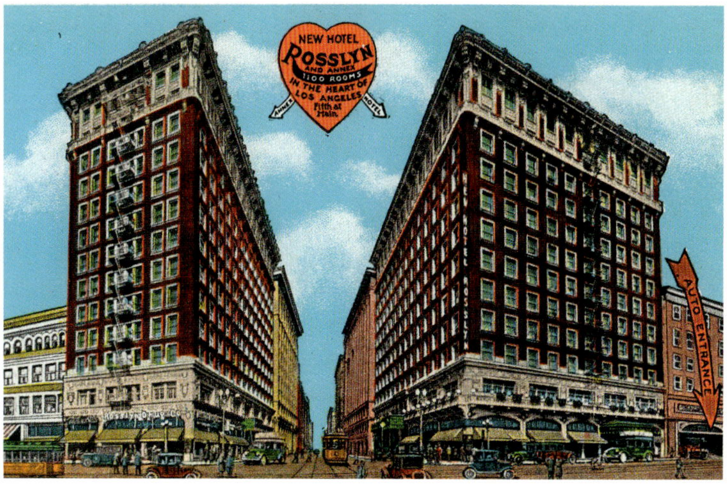

Hotel Rosslyn.

NOW

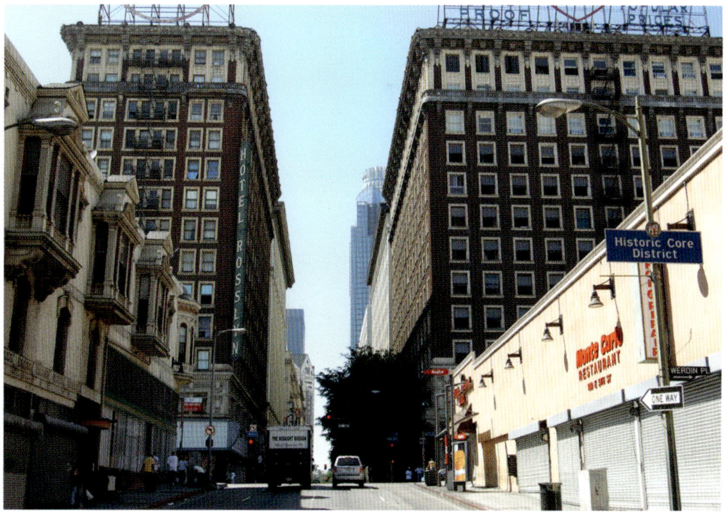

Hotel Rosslyn was located where 5th and Main streets meet. The building remains, though it is no longer the Hotel Rosslyn.

In person, most of the buildings in downtown's Historic Core District have a "wow" factor to them.

THEN

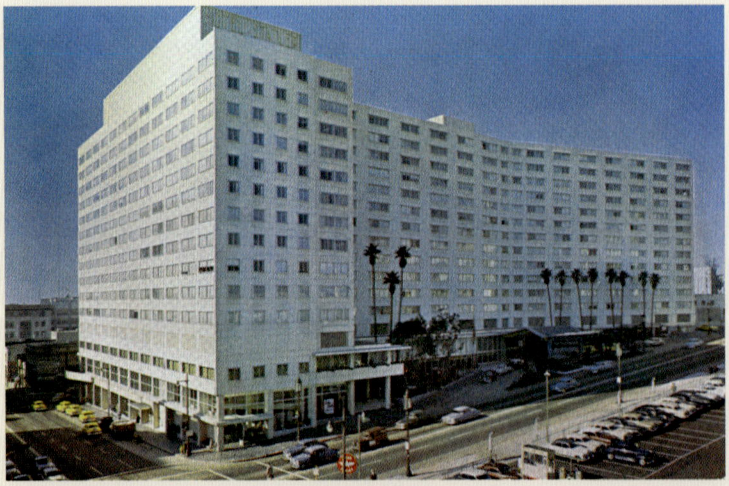

Hotel Statler.

NOW

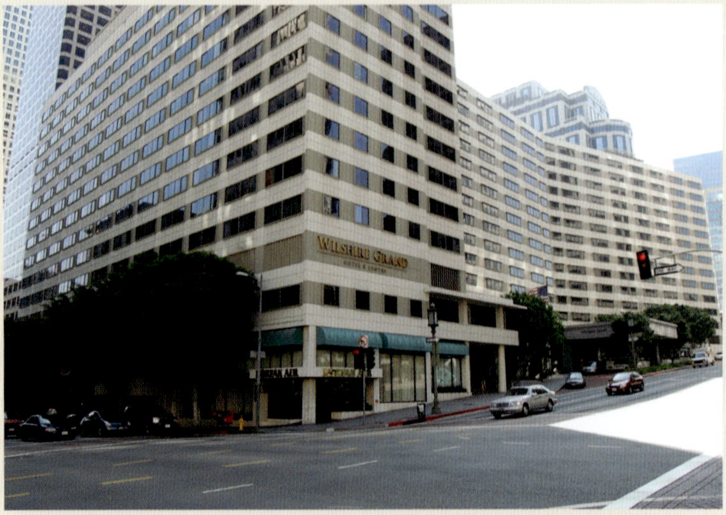

Hotel Statler was located at 930 Wilshire Boulevard. The building remains, though it is no longer houses the Hotel Statler; at the time of this writing, it was vacant and scheduled for demolition.

Set for execution, this hotel building holds its head up with dignity. It has served the downtown area since the early 1950s. (Note: If current demolition plans are carried out, the building will no longer be standing at the time of this book's publication date.)

THEN

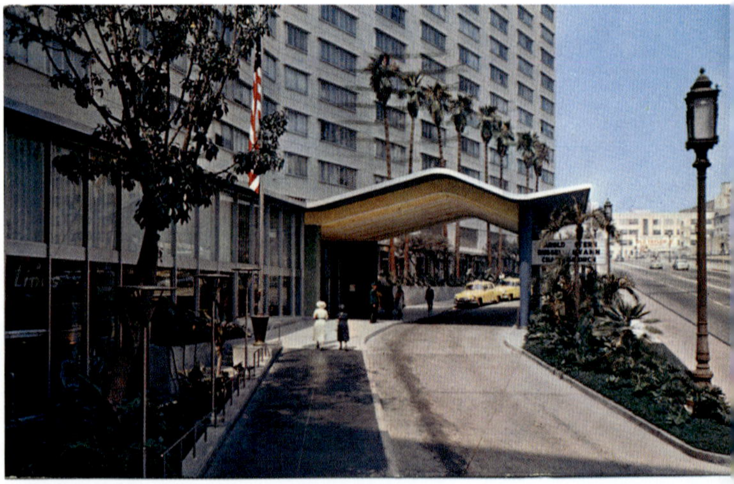

Hotel Statler.

NOW

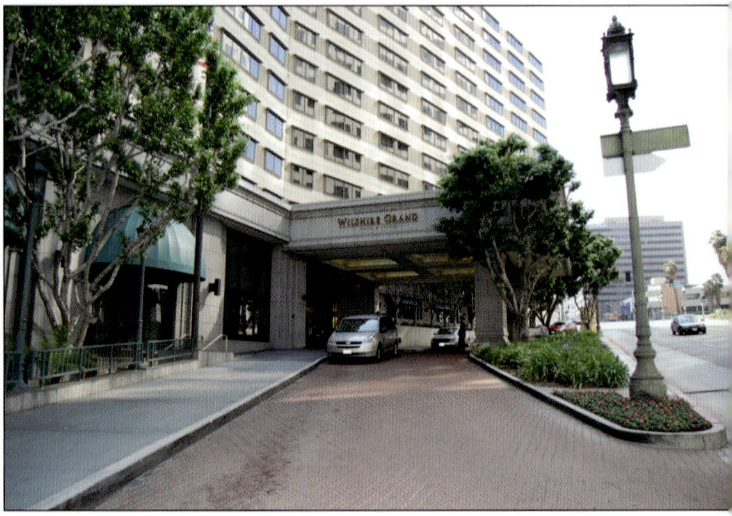

Hotel Statler, looking west on Wilshire Boulevard. The building no longer houses the hotel.

The hotel complex, last called the Wilshire Grand Hotel, closed in December 2011. A new office towers is planned after the hotel grounds are leveled.

THEN

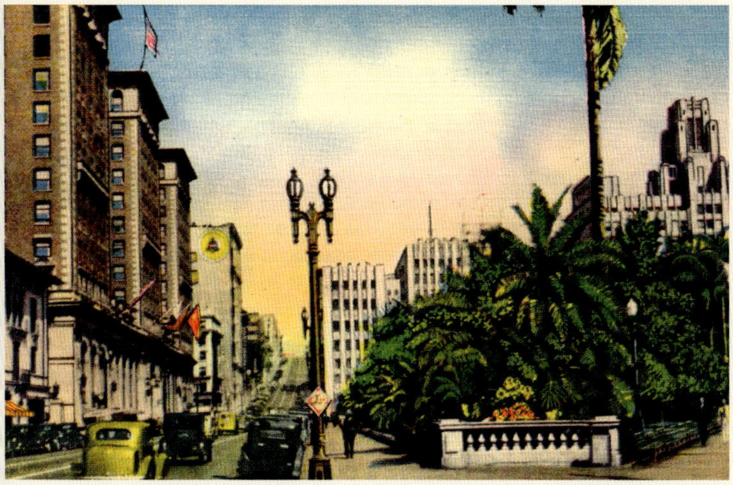

Biltmore Hotel (left) and New Auditorium Building (center) with Pershing Square (right, foreground).

NOW

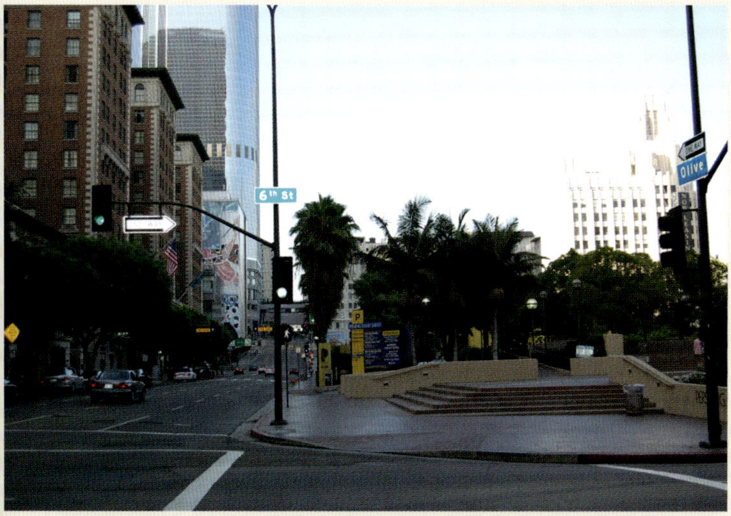

Biltmore Hotel is on the left, as shown from this view looking north on Olive Street from 6th Street. Pershing Square is on the immediate right. (Note: The Auditorium no longer stands.)

Pershing Square remains a center of busy atmosphere. Today, the square is excellent for people-, car-, and building-watching.

THEN

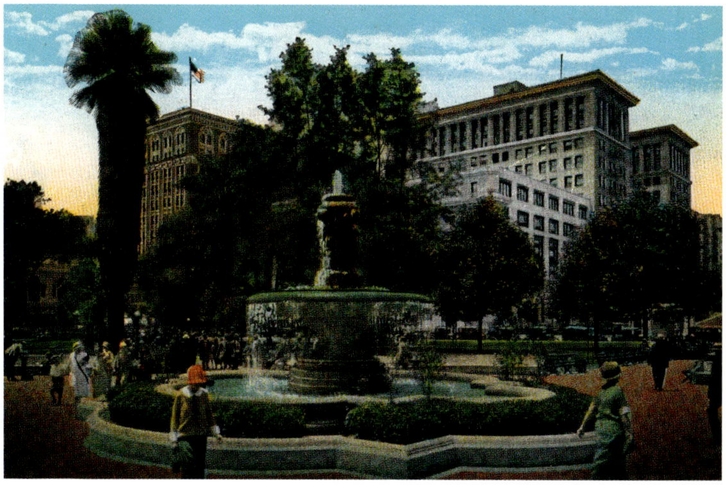

Fountain in Pershing Square. Pacific Finance and Pacific Mutual buildings in background.

NOW

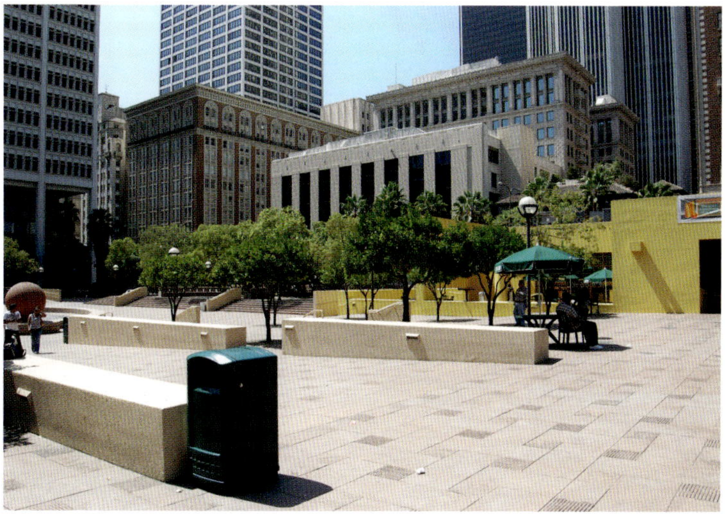

The fountain in Pershing Square was located here. The main background buildings in the postcard view remain with new structures towering around them. The Pacific Mutual Building is the smaller building and is centered in the background.

There is more concrete than greenery in the Pershing Square of today when compared to when it had a fountain at its center.

THEN

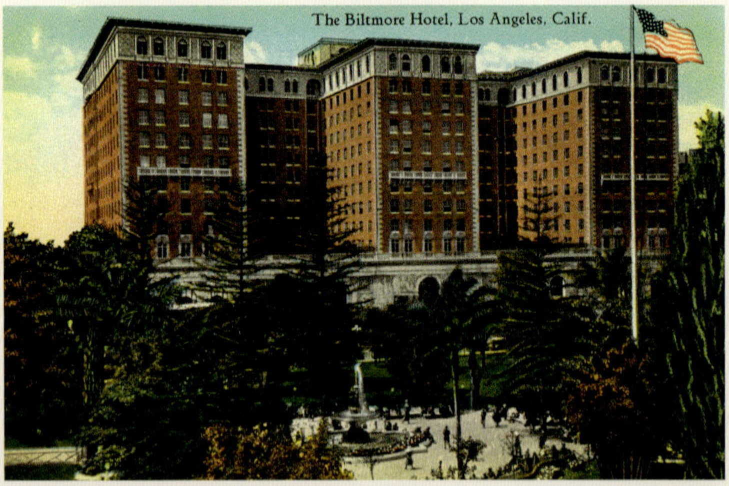

The Biltmore Hotel.

NOW

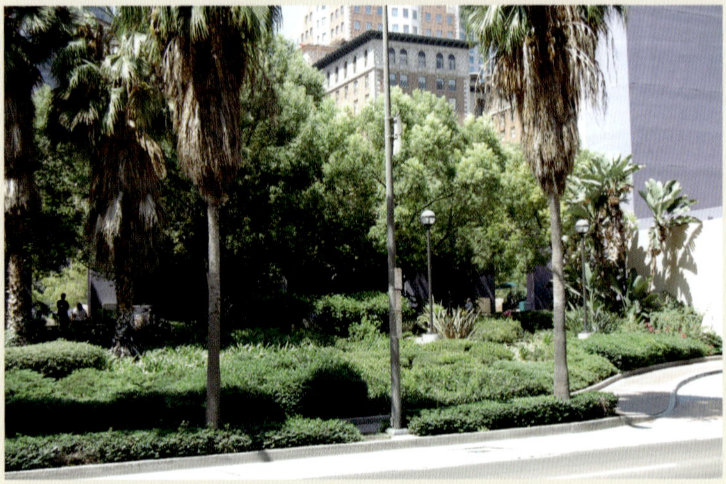

The Biltmore Hotel.
(Foliage blocks a clear view of the hotel.)

NOW

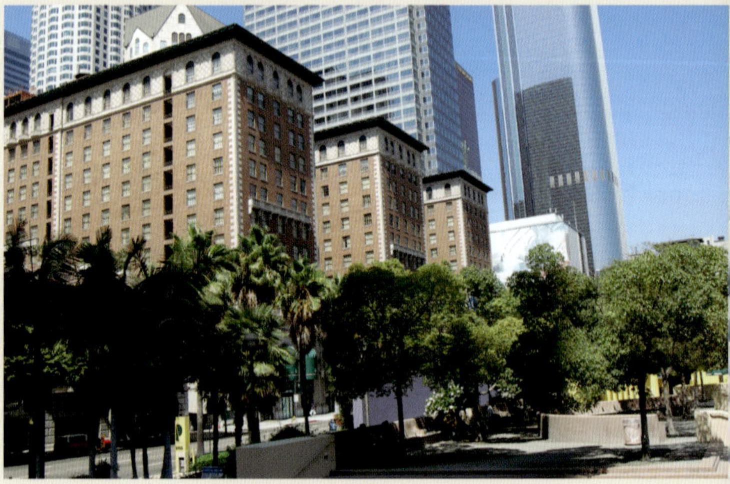

The Biltmore Hotel is located at 506 South Grand Avenue. (The hotel from another angle than the postcard view.)

Since its opening in 1923, the Biltmore Hotel has stood watch over Pershing Square. The best way to experience historic hotels is to not only stand in front of them, but to also walk in.

THEN

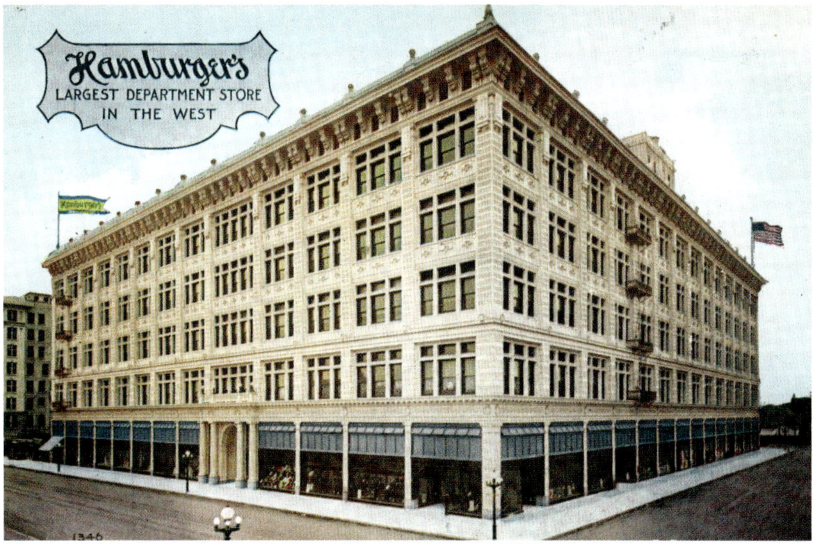

Hamburger's Department Store.

NOW

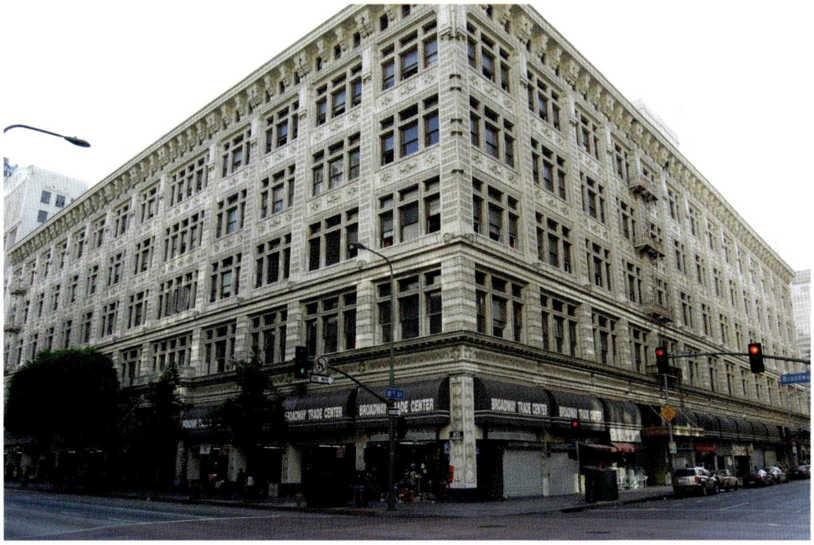

Hamburger's Department Store was located at the southwest corner of 8th Street and Broadway. The building remains, but the department store is no longer in business.

Despite its continued hustle and bustle, downtown can no longer support modern department stores. Downtown can only remember them via their former homes.

THEN

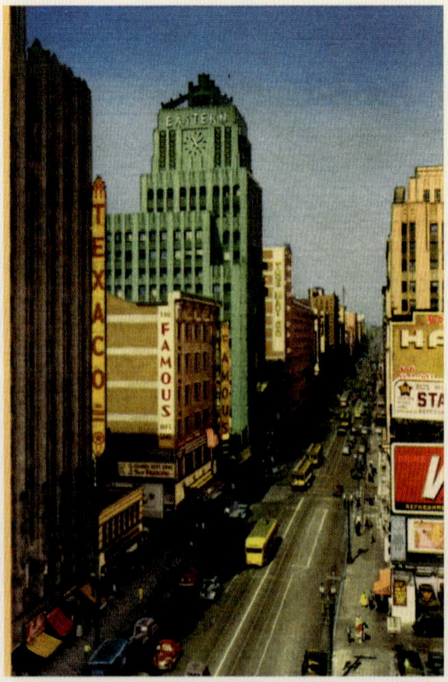

Broadway.

THEN

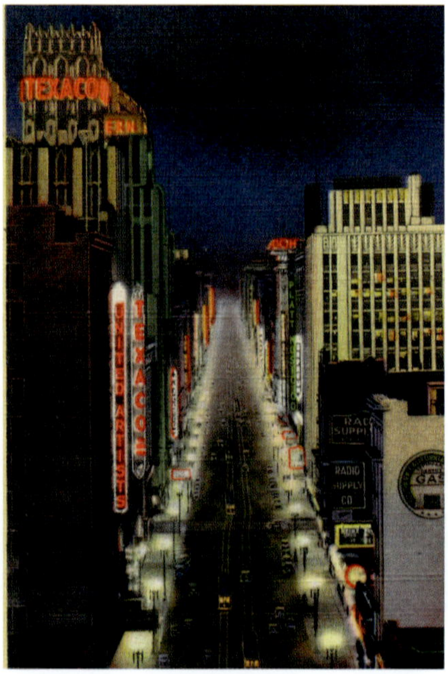

Broadway.

NOW

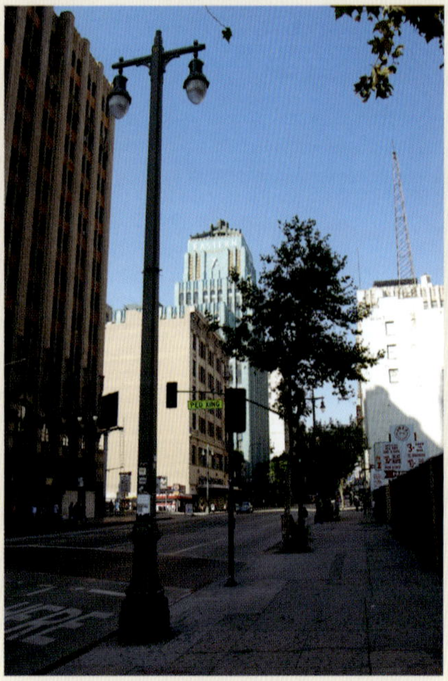

Broadway, looking north. The Eastern Columbia Building, with its clock tower, is prominently displayed here. It stands at 849 South Broadway.

When comparing the "then" and "now" views, be sure to take notice of everything. In this case, the designs of the street lamps have changed since the postcard view.

NOW

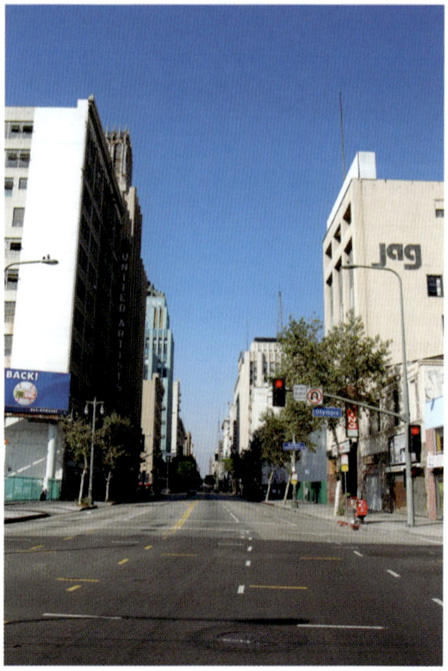

Broadway, looking north. This view is from the intersection of Olympic Boulevard and Broadway.

The nightlife of today's Broadway is certainly different than it was decades back. People used to come for department stores and entertainment venues.

THEN

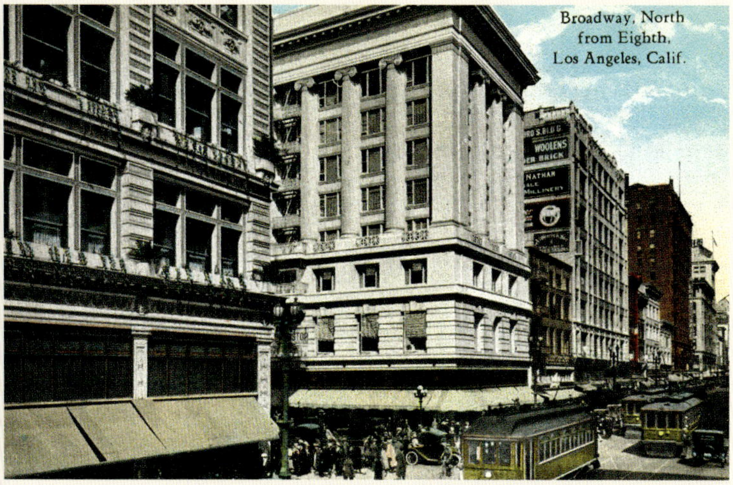

Broadway, north from 8th Street.

NOW

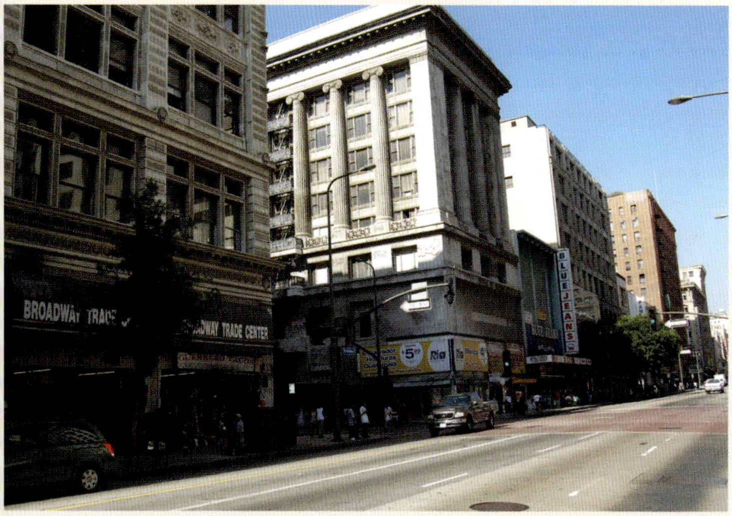

Broadway, looking north just before 8th Street.

Stand at Broadway and 8th Street and dream of street cars going past. It once happened.

THEN

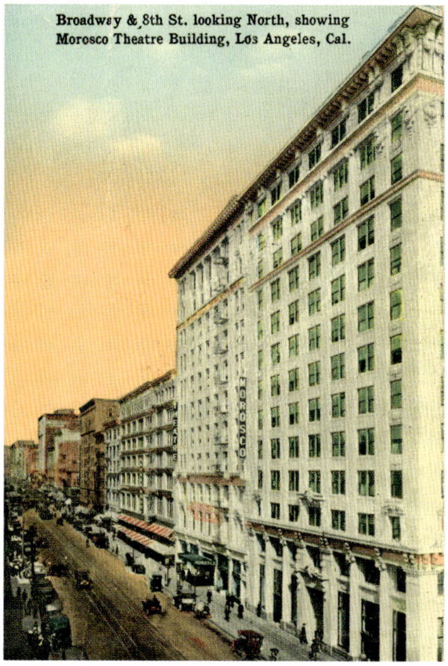

Broadway and 8th Street looking north. This view shows the Morosco Theatre building.

NOW

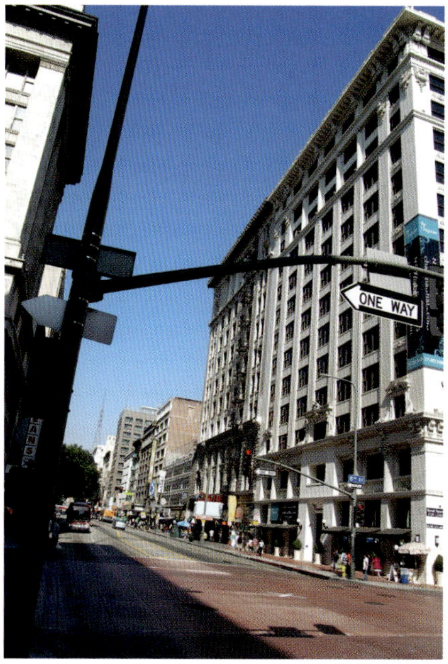

Broadway and 8th Street looking north. The building where the Morosco Theatre was located remains, but the theatre is no longer in operation.

The Broadway Historic Theatre District is still filled with the buildings that were once vibrant movie and vaudeville houses.

THEN

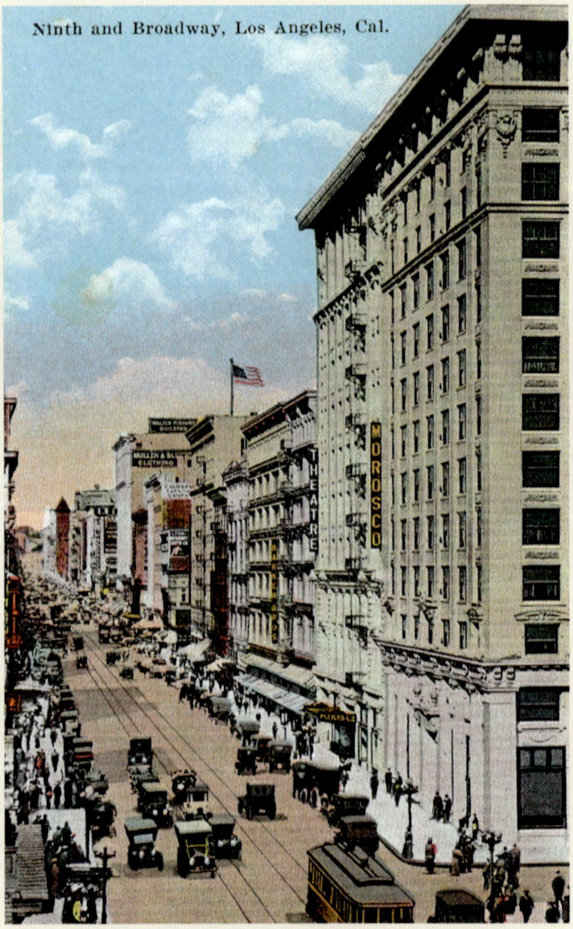

Eighth and Broadway. (Note: The card states "Ninth and Broadway," but the intersection in the foreground is 8th Street and Broadway.)

NOW

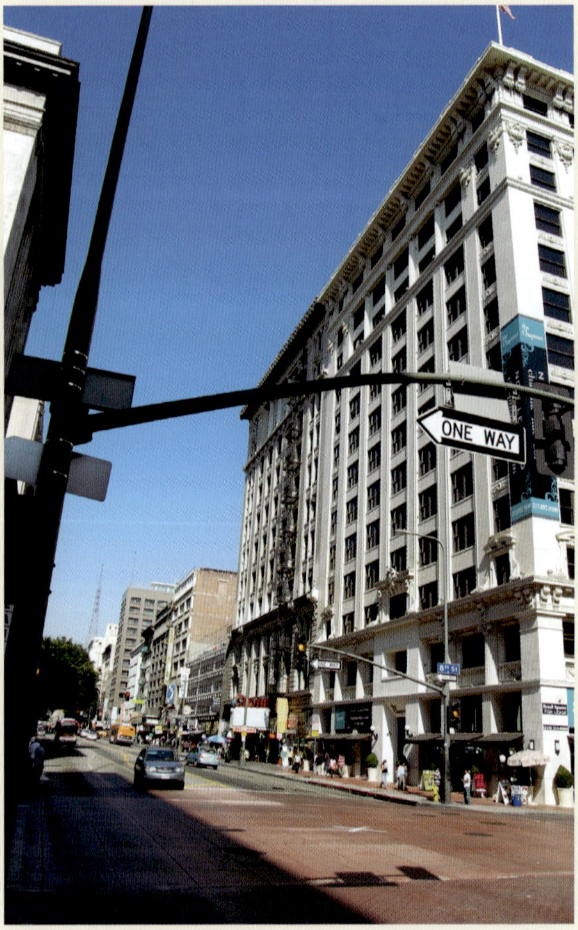

Eighth and Broadway, looking north on Broadway.

Change has indeed come to Broadway where residential loft buildings can now be found fronting it.

THEN

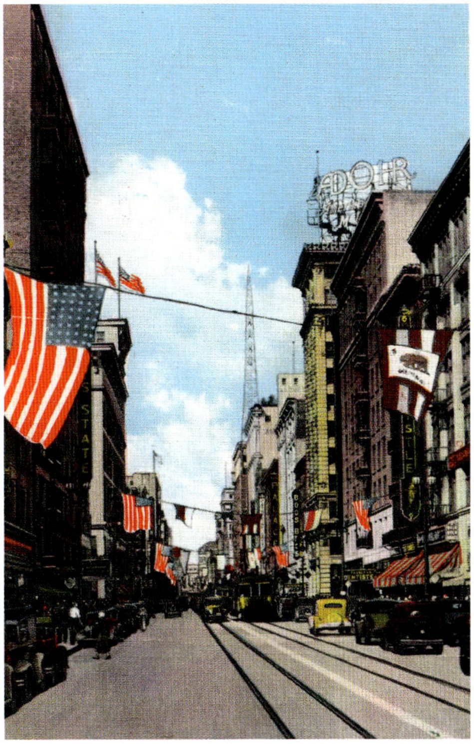

Broadway looking north.

NOW

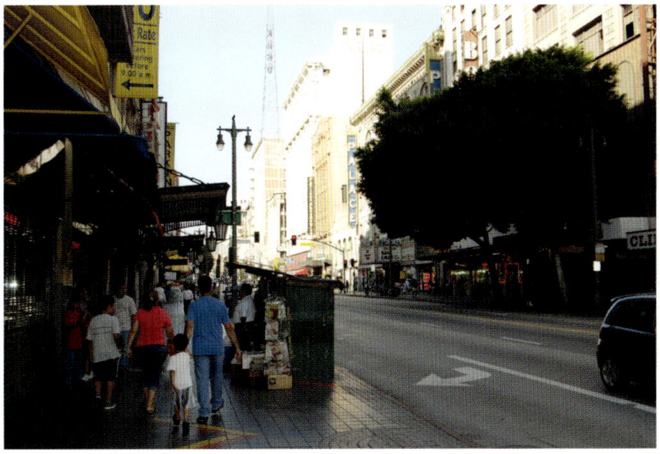

Broadway looking north. This rectangular view looks north towards intersection of 6th Street and Broadway.

Today, daily bargain hunters stroll the sidewalks of Broadway with music often blaring out from the retail shops trying to tempt them inside.

THEN

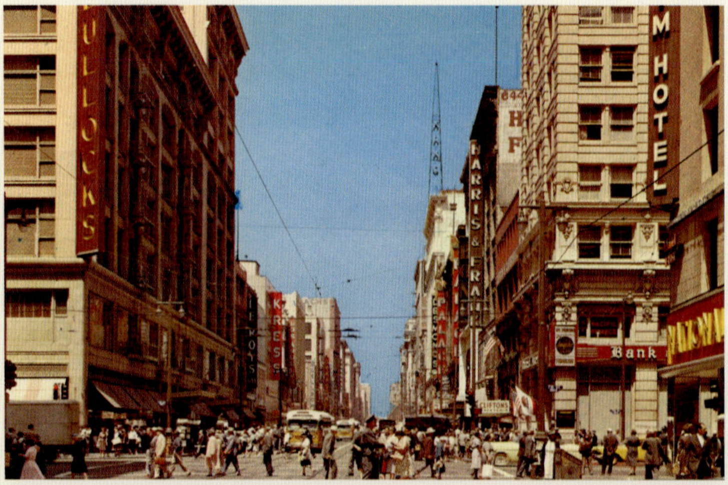

Broadway street scene.

THEN

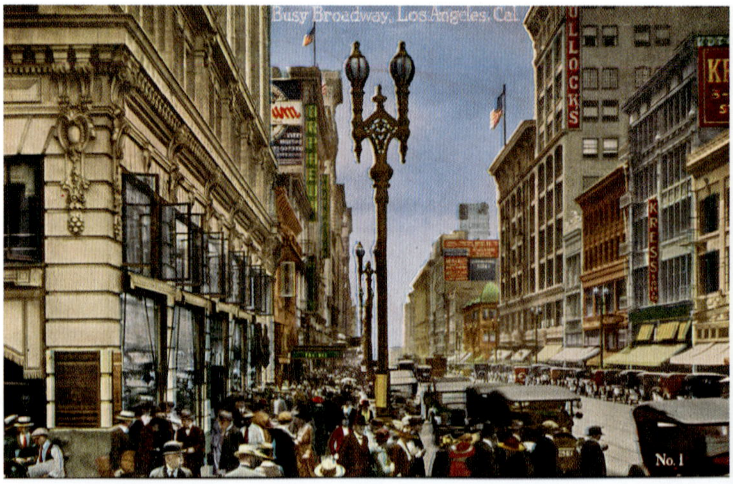

A busy Broadway.

NOW

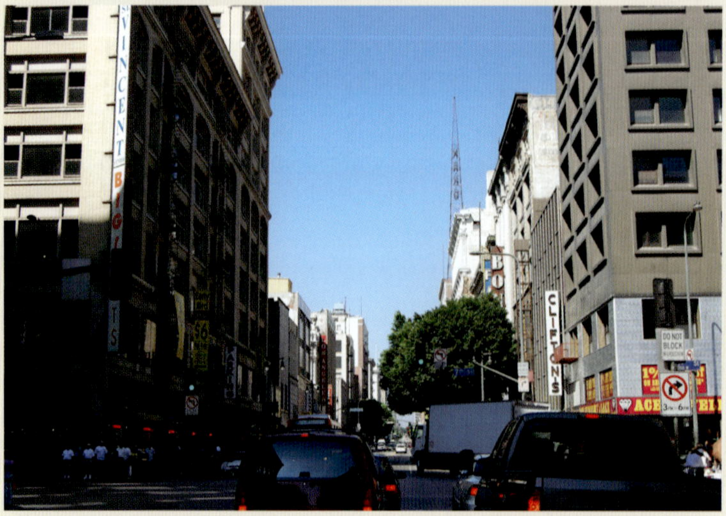

Broadway street scene looking north from the intersection of 7th Street and Broadway.

NOW

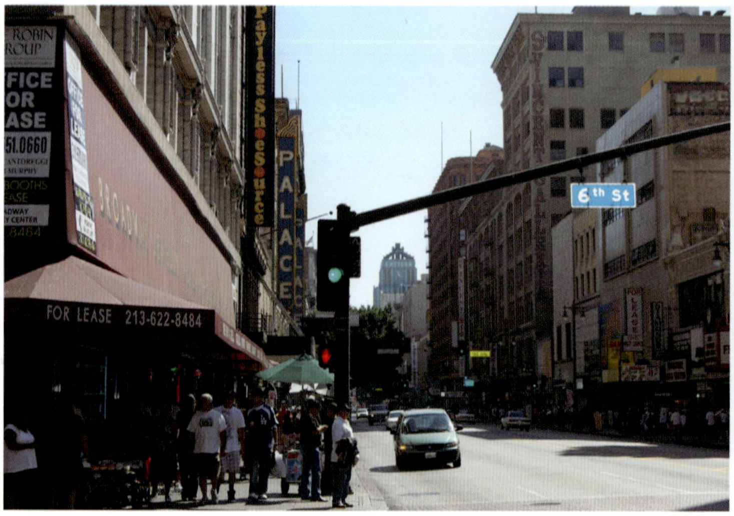

A busy Broadway, looking south from the intersection of 6th Street and Broadway.

Clifton's Cafeteria (on the right of both views) has provided a calming presence of permanency among Broadway's sea of changes.

People once got dressed up to do business or pleasure activities downtown. In vintage postcard views of Los Angeles, it is difficult to find someone casually dressed.

THEN

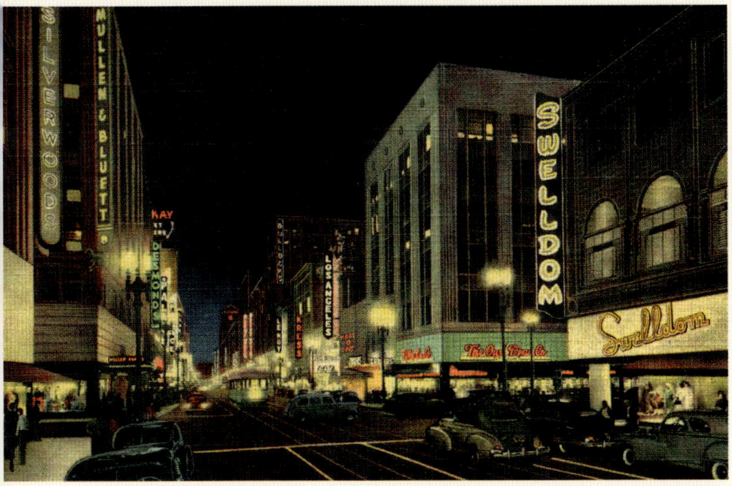

Broadway south from 6th Street.

THEN

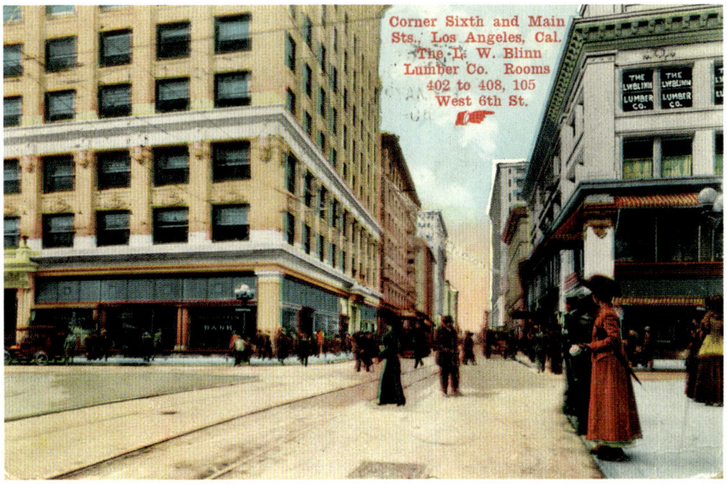

Corner 6th and Main streets...The L.W. Blinn Lumber Co.

NOW

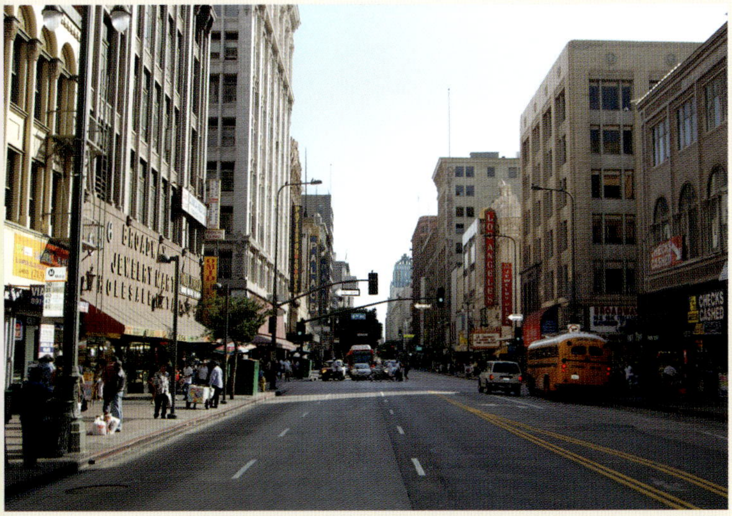

Broadway south from 6th Street.

NOW

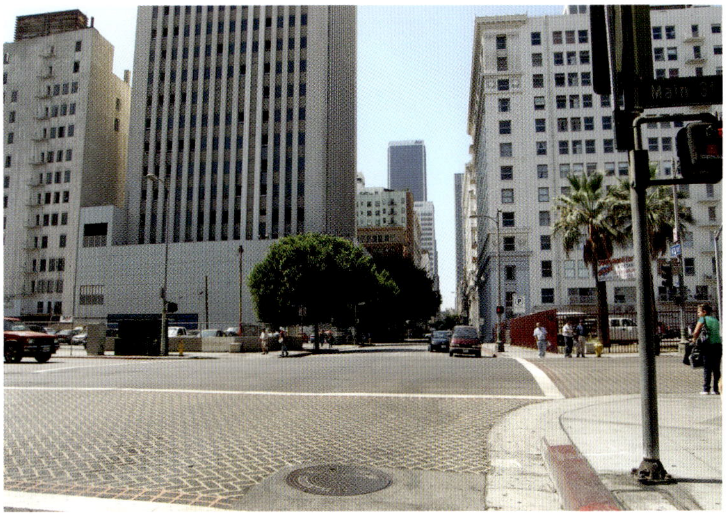

Corner of 6th and Main streets, looking east on 6th Street from Main Street. The building that housed the L.W. Blinn Lumber Co. no longer stands.

The brightly-lit shop windows of the Swelldom Department Store building in the postcard view are now filled with a number of small shops dealing in various trades.

Downtown Los Angeles holds much in the way of mystery and lore. Lost underground tunnels and ghost-filled buildings are among the stories that have generated around downtown.

THEN

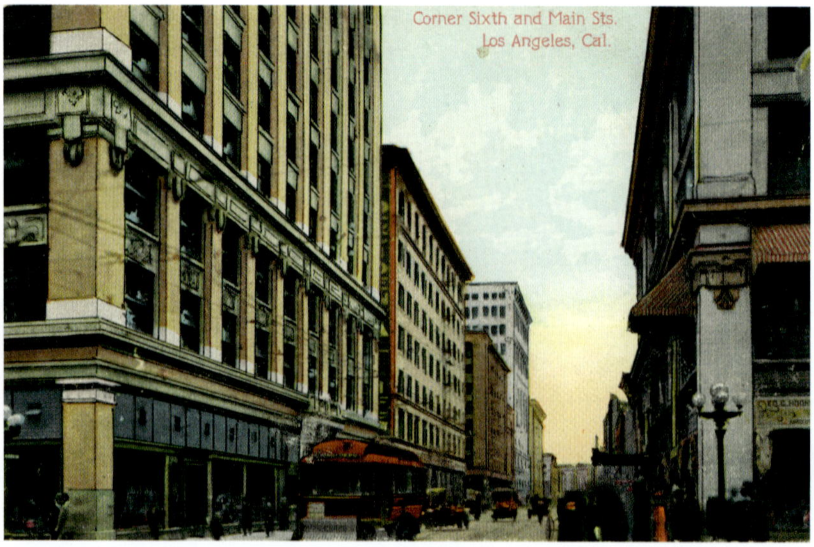

Corner of 6th and Main streets.

NOW

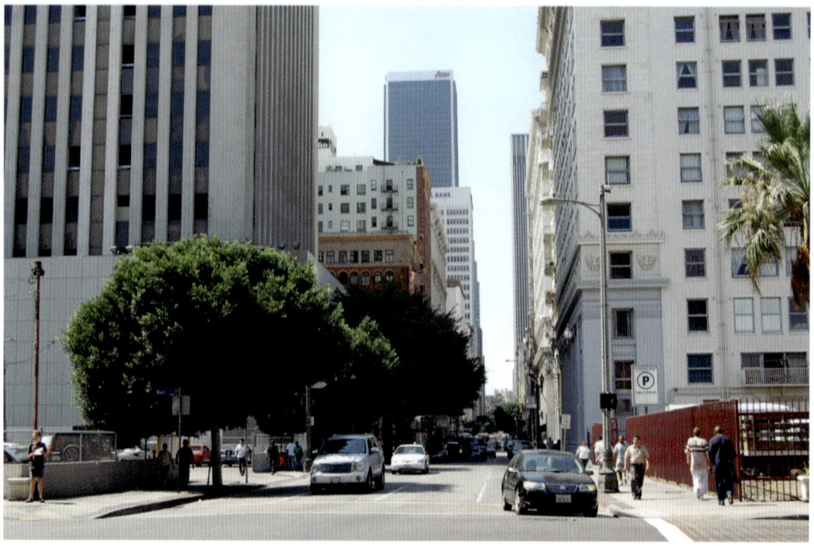

Corner 6th and Main streets, looking east on 6th Street from Main Street.

Business growth in the downtown area took off between the 1910s and early 1930s.

THEN

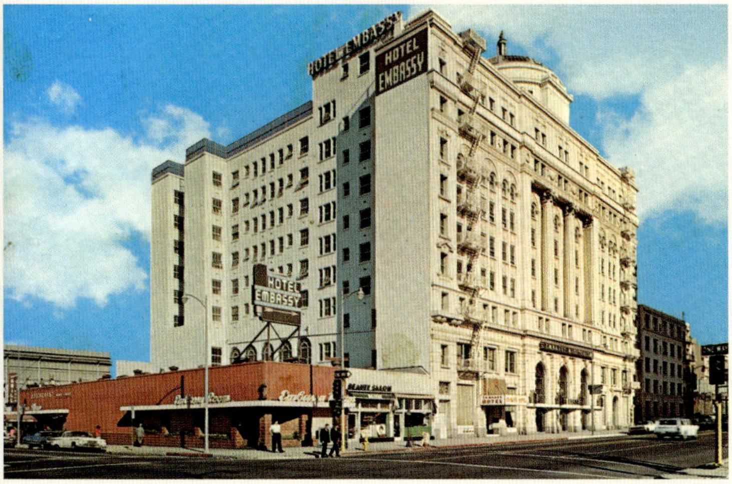

THEN

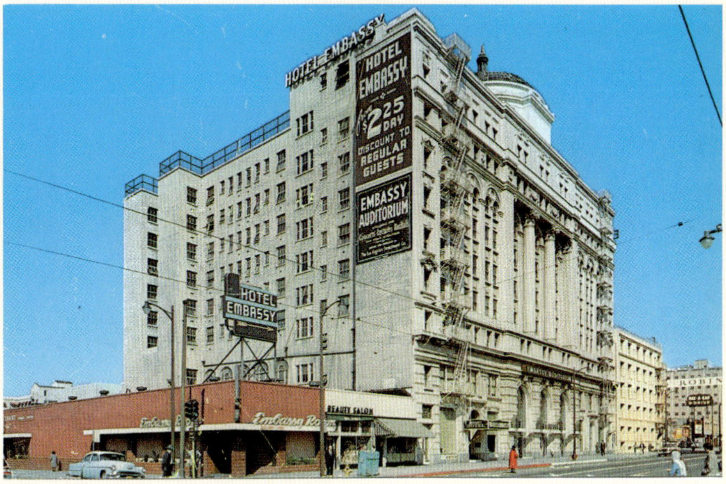

Hotel Embassy.

NOW

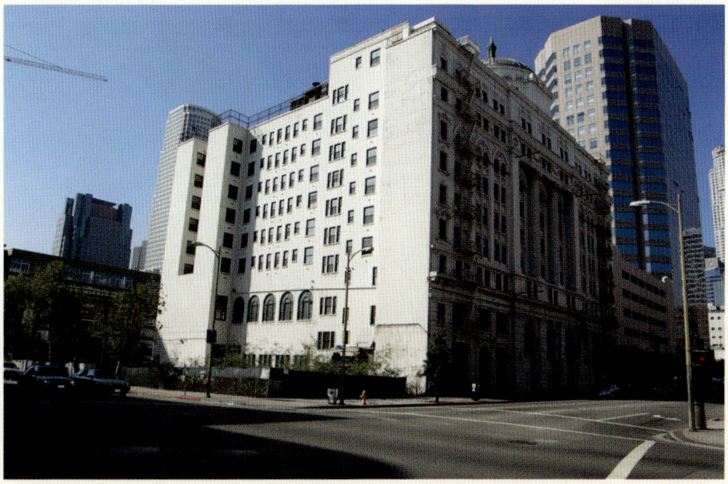

Hotel Embassy was located on the northwest corner of 9th Street and Grand Avenue. The building remains, but no longer houses the Hotel Embassy.

Hotel Embassy was housed in what once was the Trinity Auditorium, which was, at one time, a church, entertainment house, and hotel all-in-one.

THEN

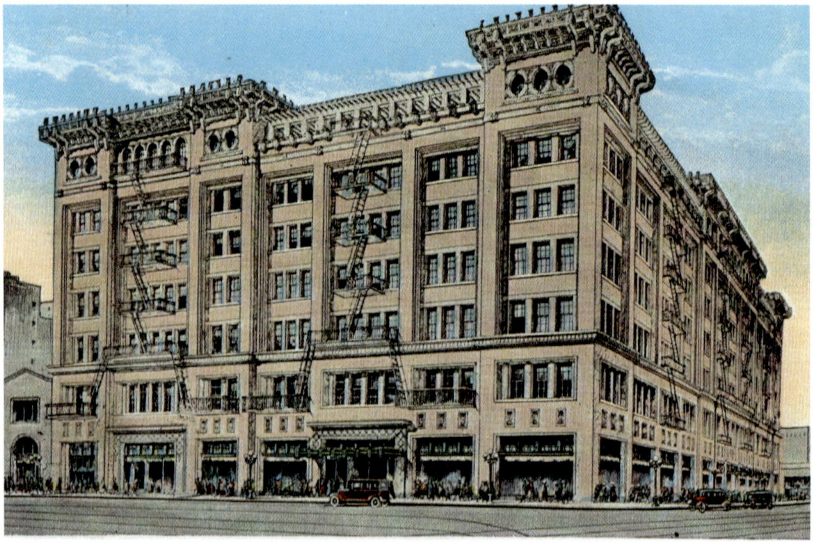

J. W. Robinson Company store building.

NOW

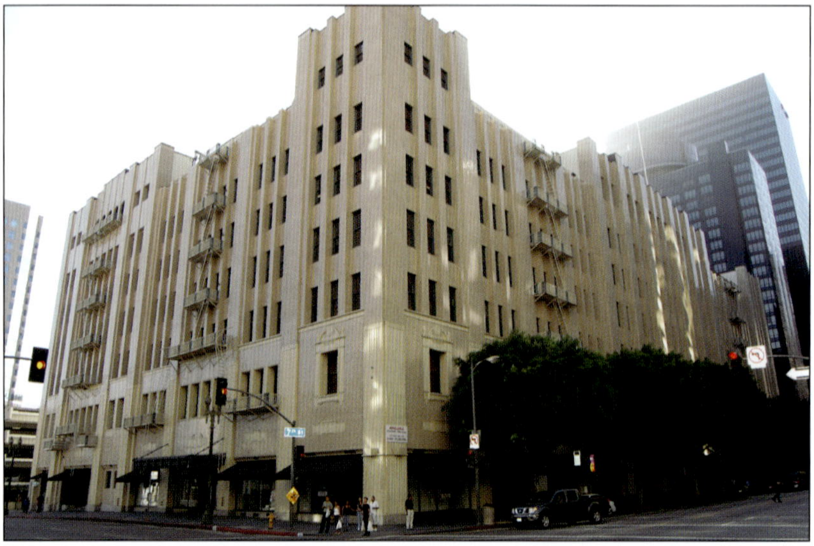

The J. W. Robinson Company store building was located on the southwest corner of 7th Street and Grand Avenue. The building remains, but no longer houses the store.

For decades, people would get dressed up and head downtown to shop. A typical excursion might be a mother, wearing gloves and high heels, her excited teenage daughter in tow. After a stop at Clifton's Cafeteria for lunch, it was off to buy outside of their budgets.

THEN

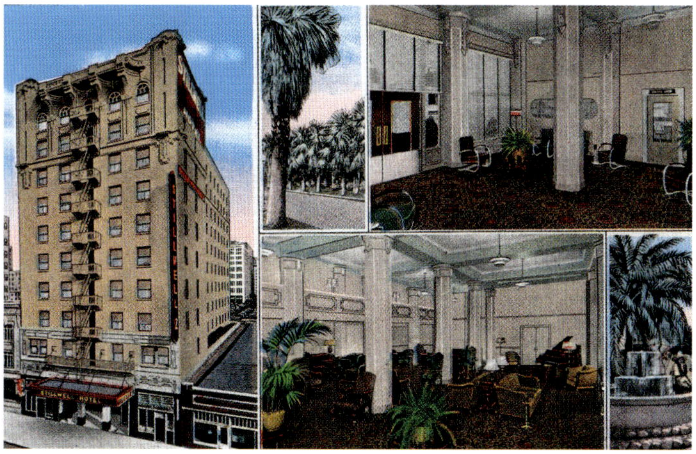

Stillwell Hotel.

NOW

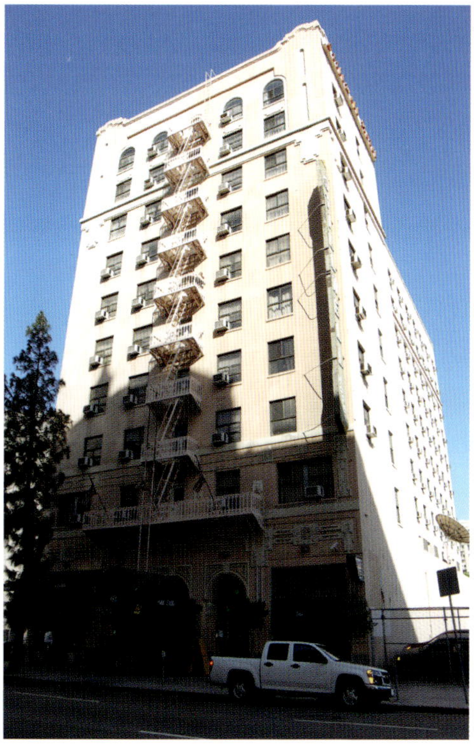

Stillwell Hotel remains in business at 838 South Grand Avenue.

The Stillwell Hotel was built in 1913. It was designed by Kysor and Noonan.

THEN

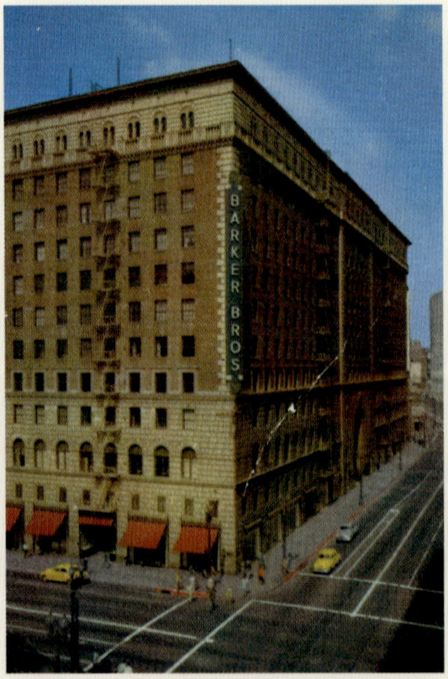

Barker Bros.

THEN

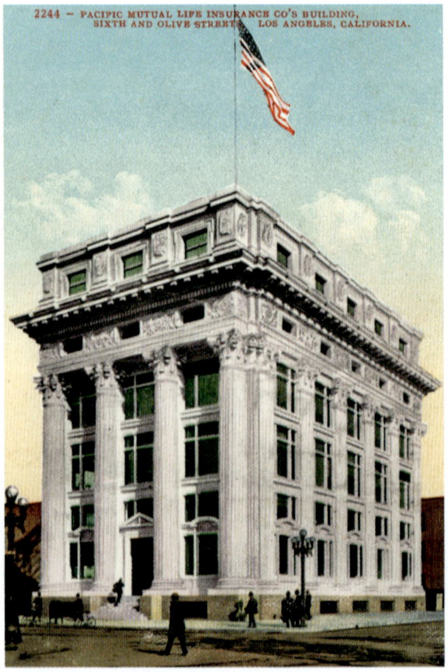

Pacific Mutual Life Insurance Company Building.

NOW

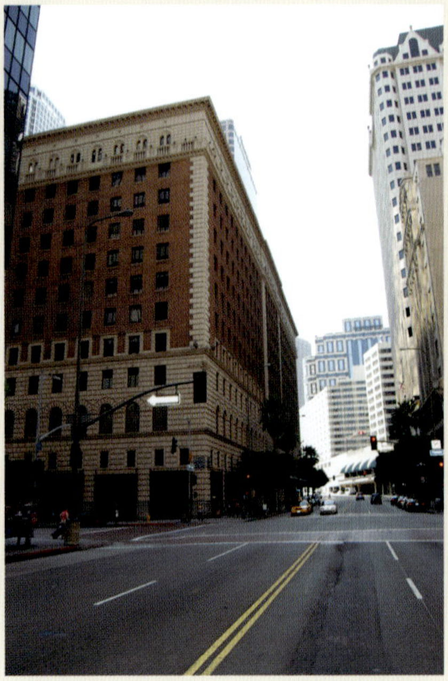

Barker Bros. was located on West 7th Street. The business has closed, but the building remains standing on the southwest corner of 7th and Flower streets.

Barker Bros. furniture stores date back to 1880. Besides downtown Los Angeles, it had locations in such places as Hollywood, Santa Monica, and Westwood. Barker Bros. closed in the early 1990s.

NOW

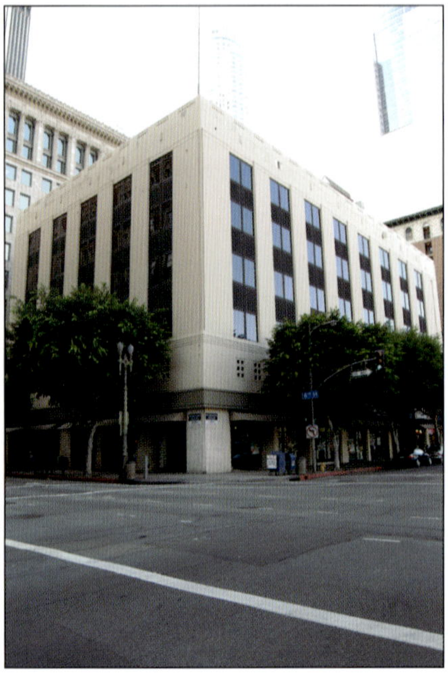

The Pacific Mutual Life Insurance Company building, aka Pacific Mutual Building, remains on the northwest corner of 6th and Olive streets. The building has changed hands, and names, over the years.

The Pacific Mutual Building has been altered so much over the years it seems like nearly another building today.

THEN

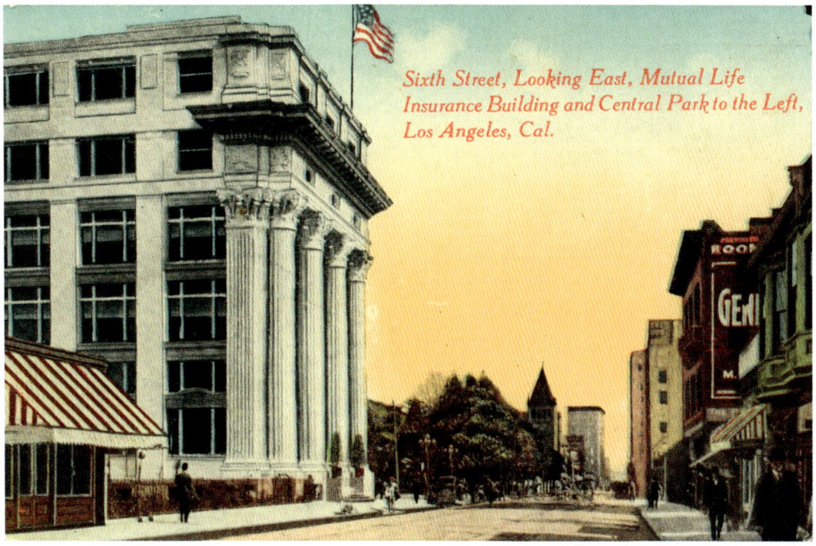

6th Street, looking east. The Mutual Life Insurance Building and Central Park are to the left.

NOW

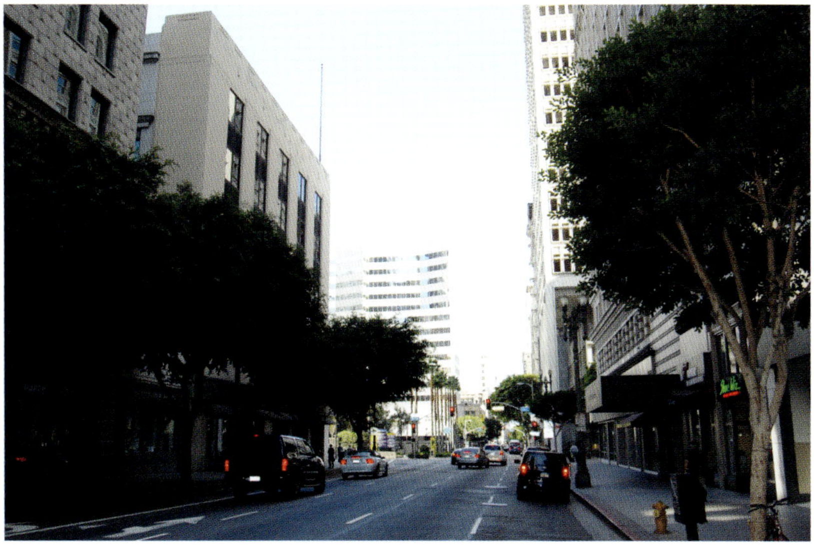

6th Street, looking east, a half block shy of Olive Street. While both the Pacific Mutual Life Insurance Building and Central Park remain, they have since been renamed.

The ownership of Central Park, now called Pershing Square, dates back to the late 1700s. It was then that Spain granted the acres that make up the park to Los Angeles.

THEN

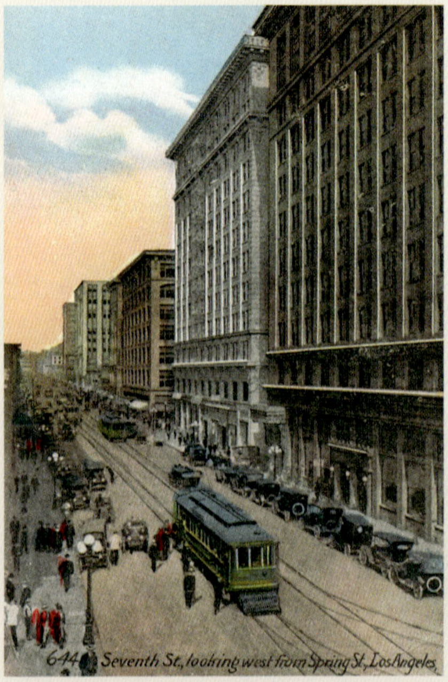

7th Street, looking west from Spring Street.

NOW

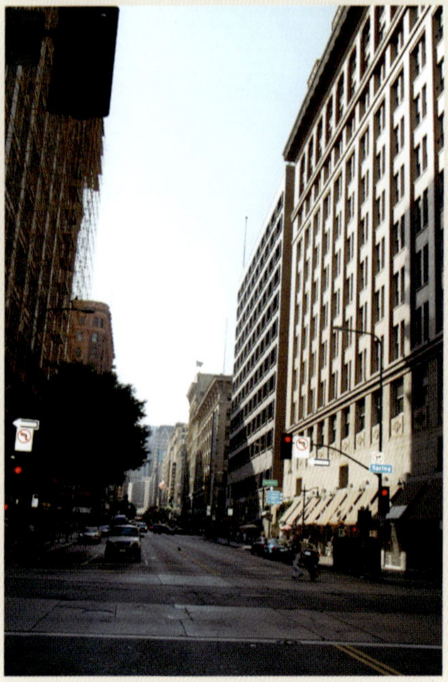

7th Street, looking west from Spring Street.

Many of the older buildings in central downtown are about the same height. This phenomenon was due to city-imposed height restrictions on buildings, which were lifted in the 1950s.

THEN

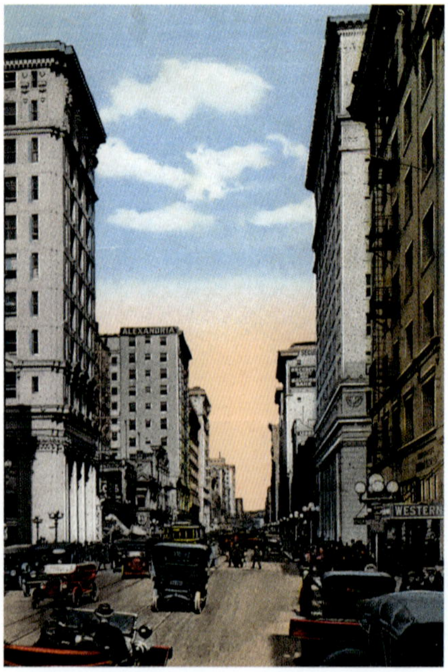

Spring Street, looking north from 7th Street.

NOW

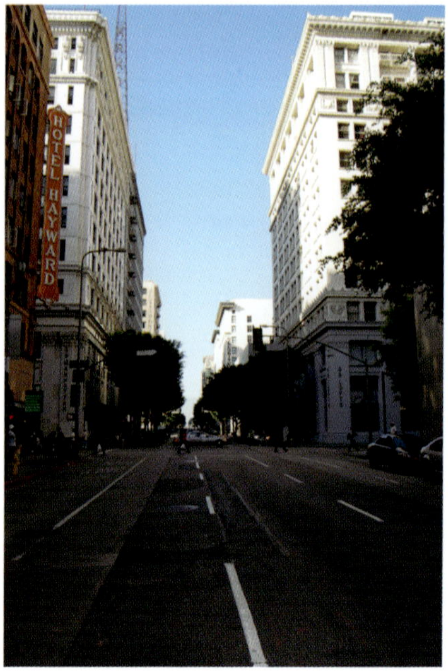

Spring Street, looking north from 7th Street. This view shows 6th Street a quarter block ahead.

Fire-escape stairways are ever-present in both postcard and now views of downtown.

THEN

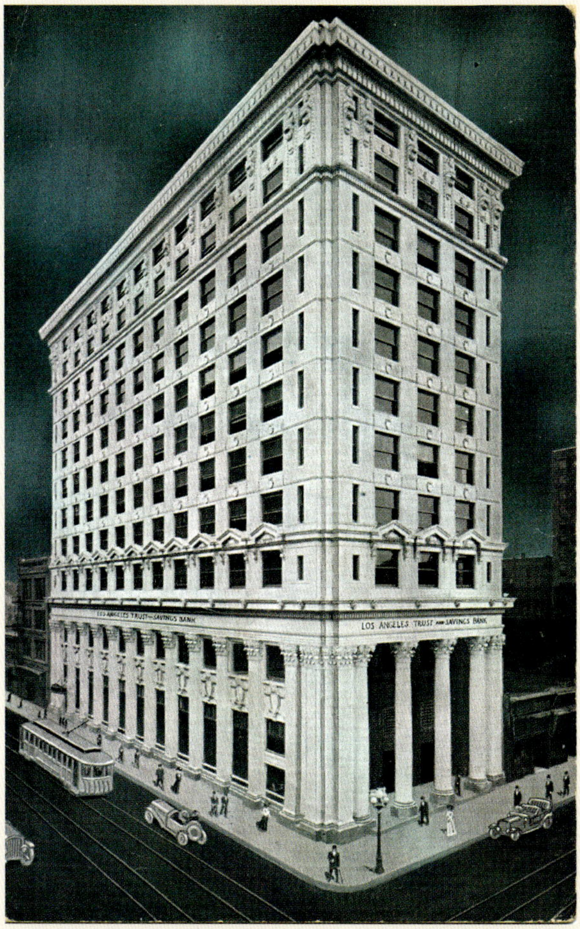

The Los Angeles Trust & Savings Bank. On the back of the postcard, the bank touts its "massive armor plate safe deposit vault."

NOW

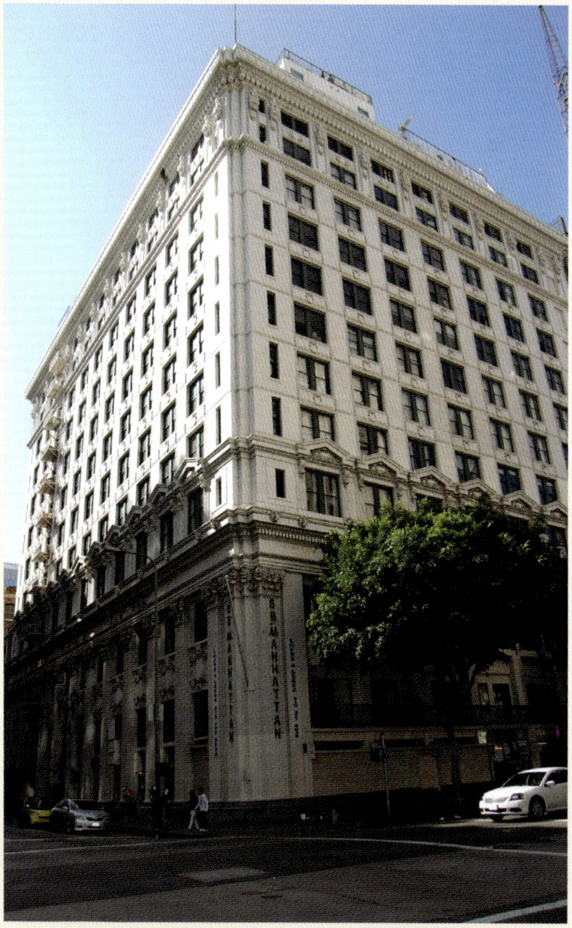

The Los Angeles Trust & Savings Bank was located on the northwest corner of 6th and Spring streets. The building remains, but it has gone through a physical expansion since the postcard was printed, along with name changes.

THEN

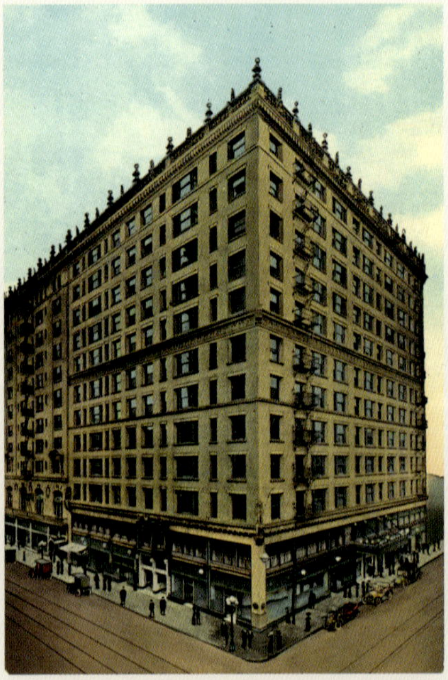

THEN

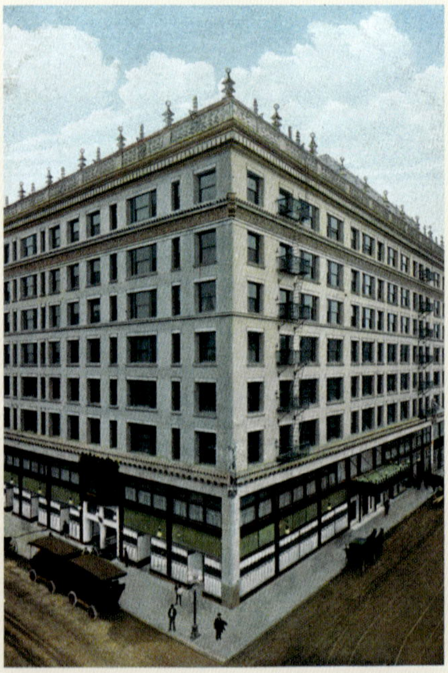

Alexandria Hotel.

NOW

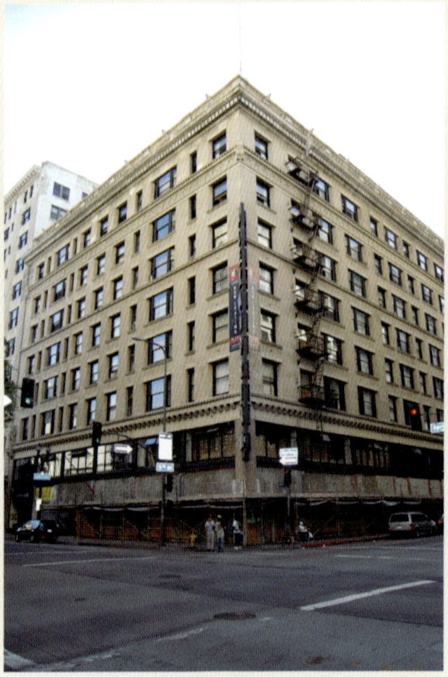

Alexandria Hotel was located at the southwest corner of 5th and Spring streets. The building remains, but the hotel is long gone.

Silent-film legend Rudolph Valentino called the Alexandria Hotel home before he hit it big on the silver screen.

THEN

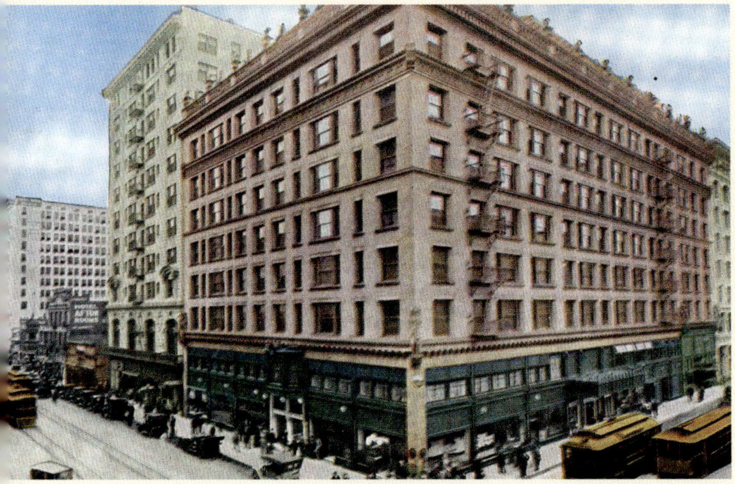

Alexandria Hotel.

NOW

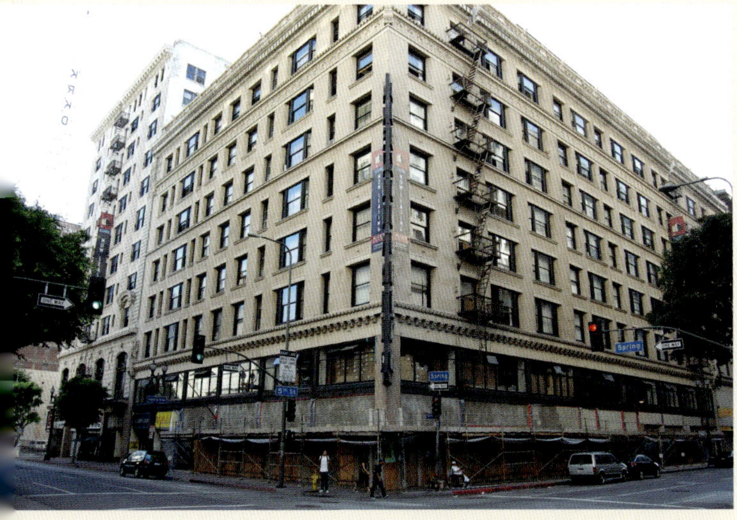

Alexandria Hotel had entrances on both 5th and Spring streets.

In 1919, Gloria Swanson was married inside a private parlor of the hotel. Comic actor Charles Chaplin once duked it out with movie producer Louis B. Mayer in the lobby in 1920.

THEN

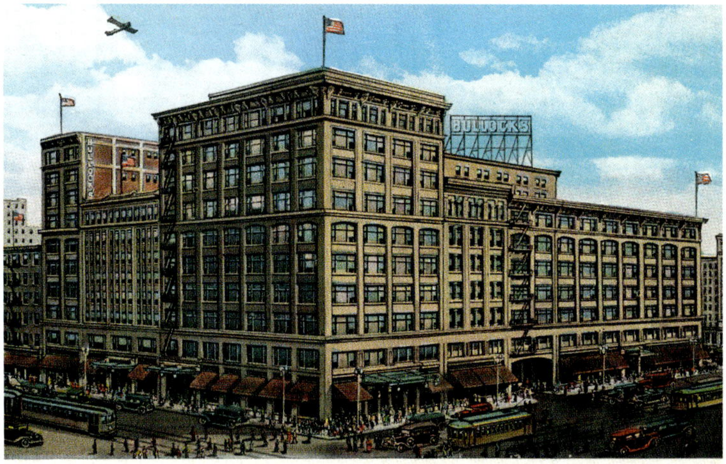

Bullock's Broadway, Hill and 7th Street.

NOW

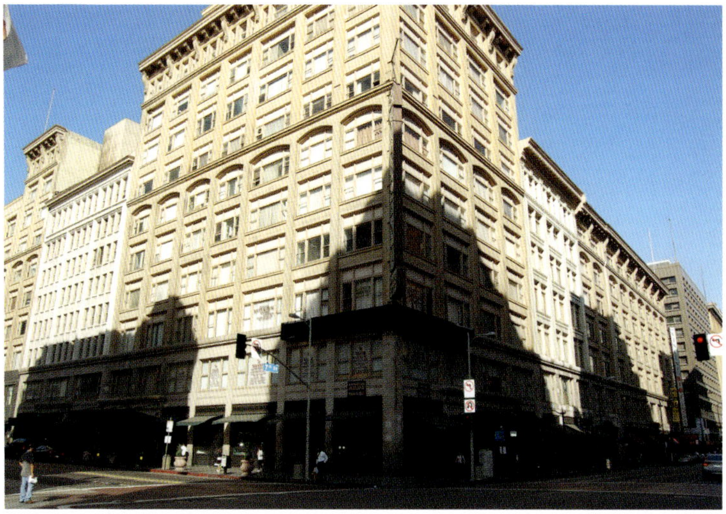

Bullock's Broadway is shown here at the northeast corner of 7th and Hill streets. The building remains, but Bullock's is defunct.

Bullocks opened downtown in 1907. It physically expanded as the store grew in popularity.

THEN

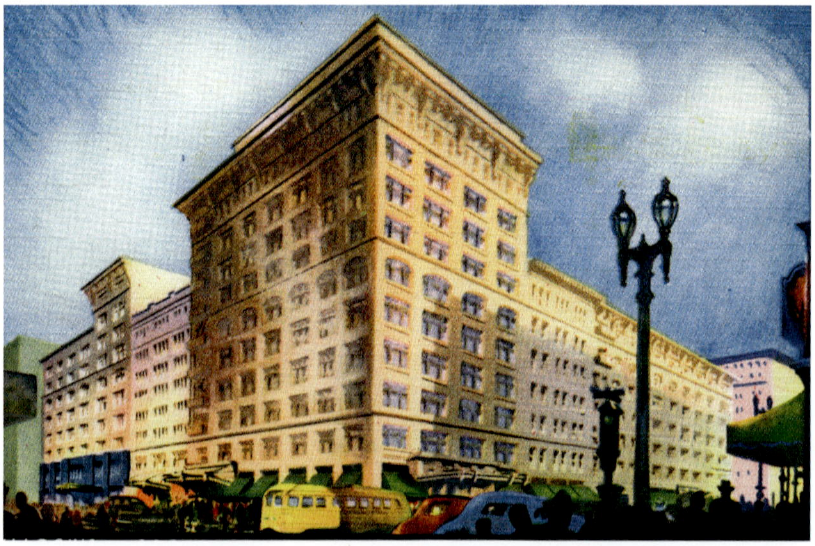

Bullock's...Broadway, Hill, and 7th.

NOW

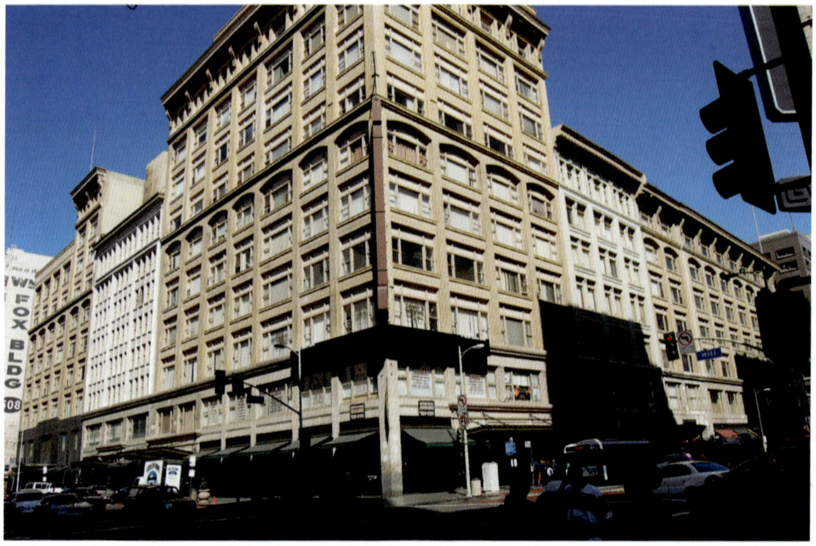

Bullock's Broadway was located here.
View is from the intersection of 7th and Hill streets.

At one time, the Bullock's Broadway offered puppet shows and bridge lessons during the holiday season.

THEN

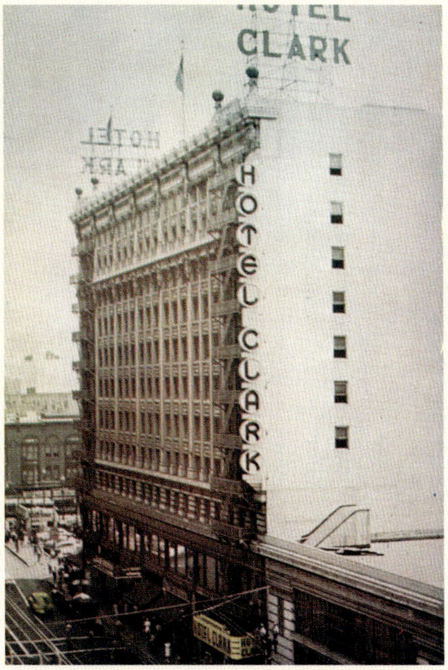

Hotel Clark.

NOW

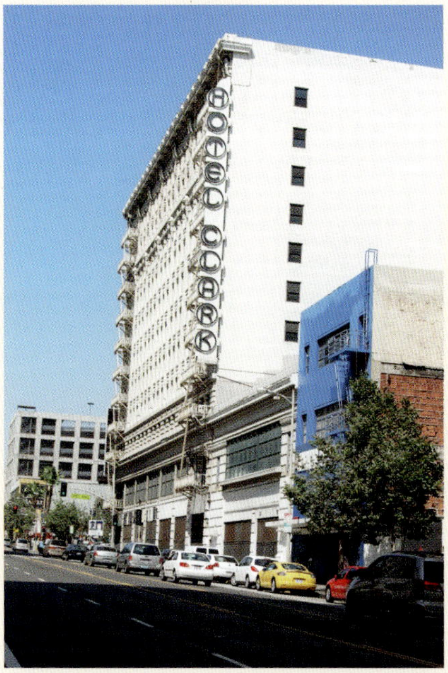

Looking north on South Hill Street, Hotel Clark was located near the southeast corner of 4th and Hill streets. The building remains, though it has been vacant for years; new plans have recently been proposed to fill it.

Vintage buildings should be thought of as "alive" and updatable to reflect a new era.

THEN

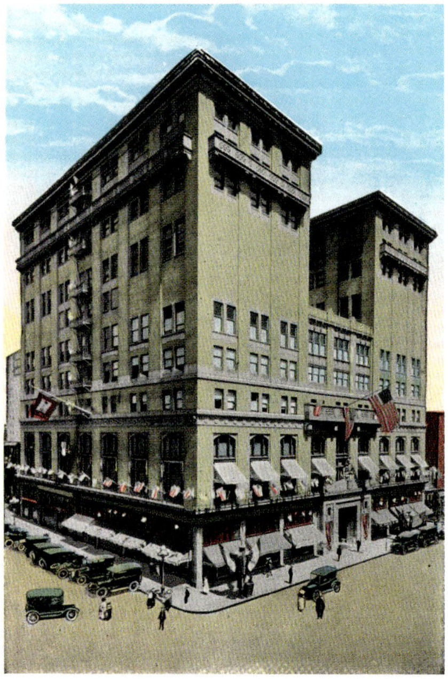

Los Angeles Athletic Club.

NOW

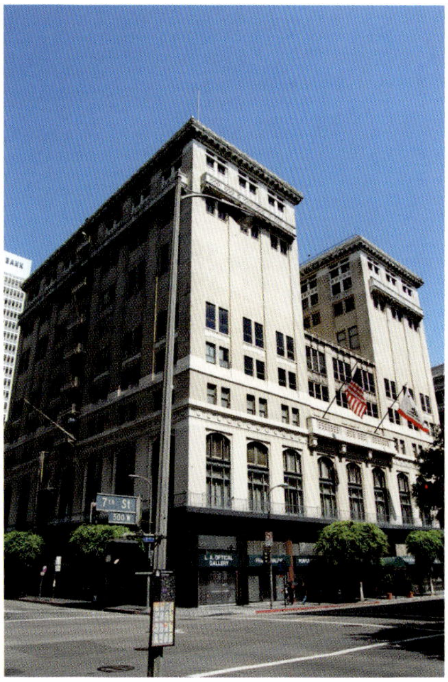

The Los Angeles Athletic Club remains on the northeast corner of 7th and Olive streets.

Early in his silent film career, actor Richard Barthelmess called the Los Angeles Athletic Club home.

THEN

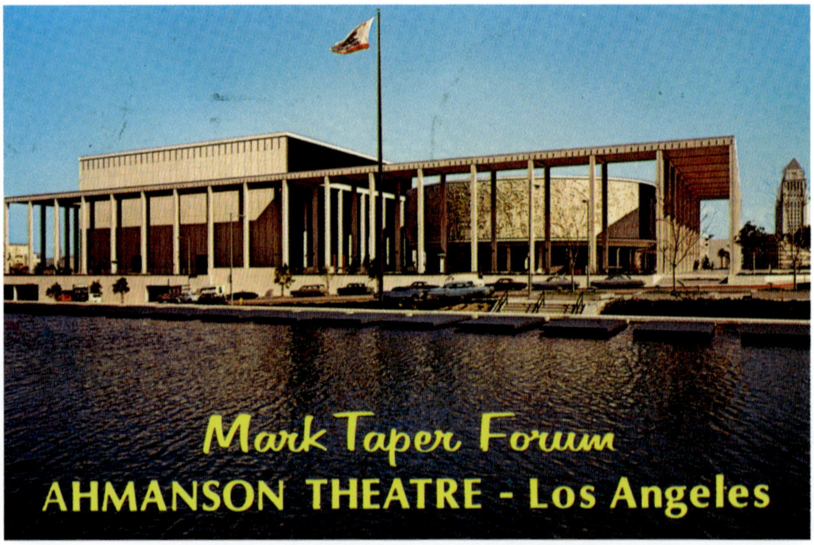

*Mark Taper Forum. Ahmanson Theatre.
Both were designed by Welton Becket and Assciates.*

NOW

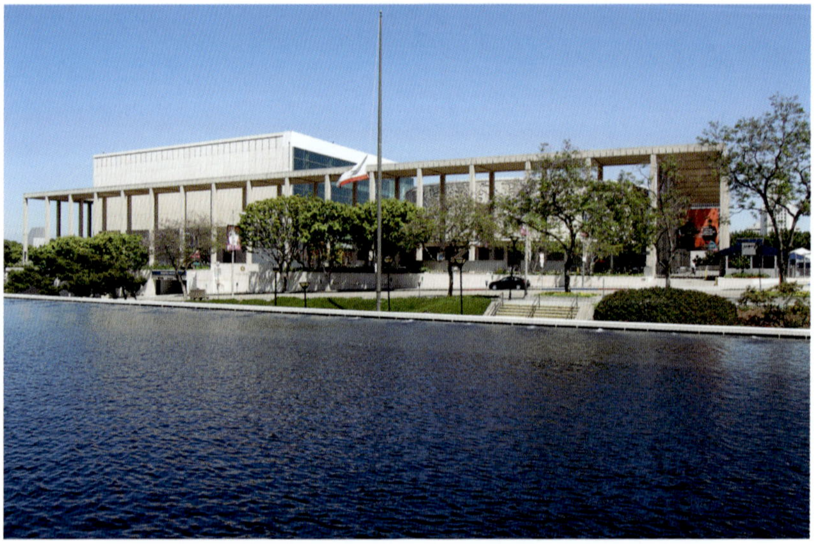

Mark Taper Forum is the circular structure on the right. Ahmanson Theatre is the taller structure on the left. The view is from the John Ferraro Building that sits across from the Mark Taper Forum at 111 North Hope Street.

THEN

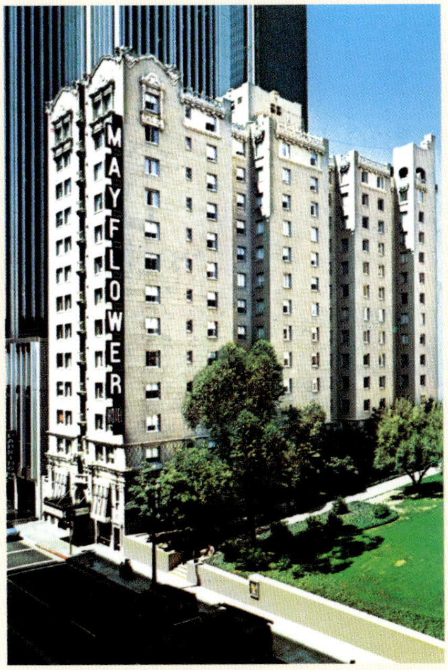

THEN

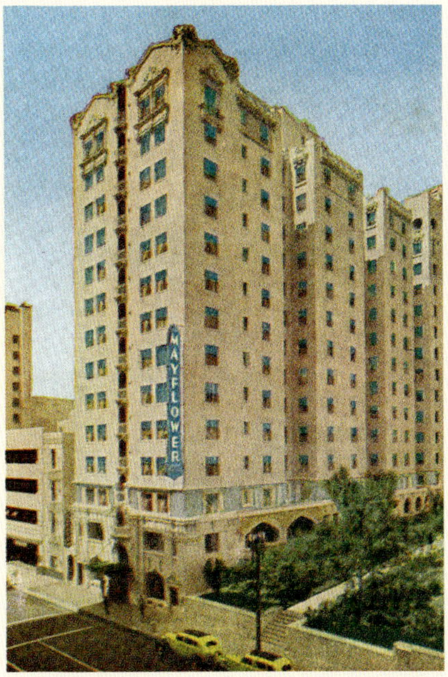

The Mayflower Hotel advertised "two guests—one price."

NOW

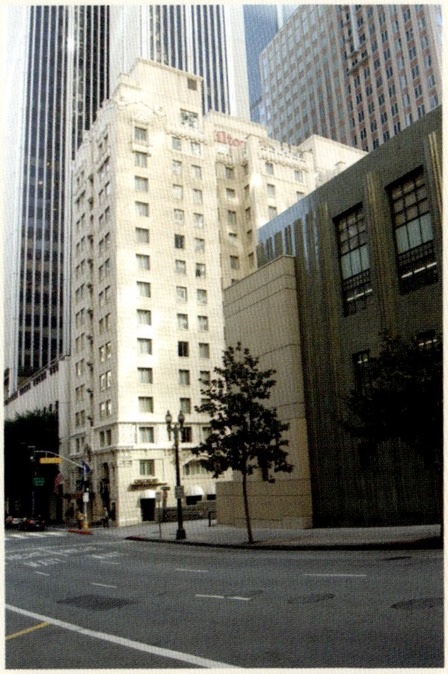

Looking south on South Grand Avenue, the Mayflower Hotel once operated here at 535 South Grand.

The Mayflower Hotel opened its doors in 1927. The Spanish-style building remains a hotel, but it no longer carries the Mayflower name.

THEN

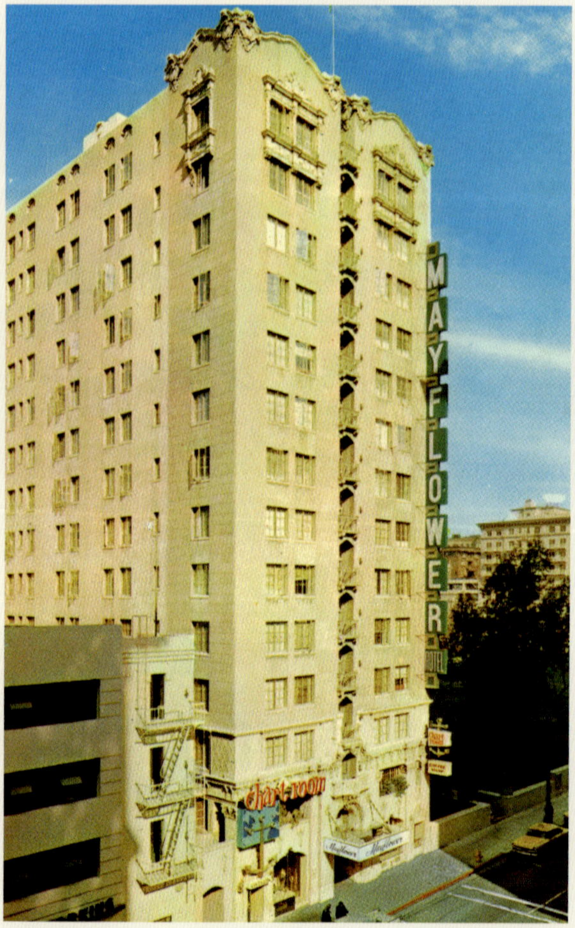

Mayflower Hotel.

NOW

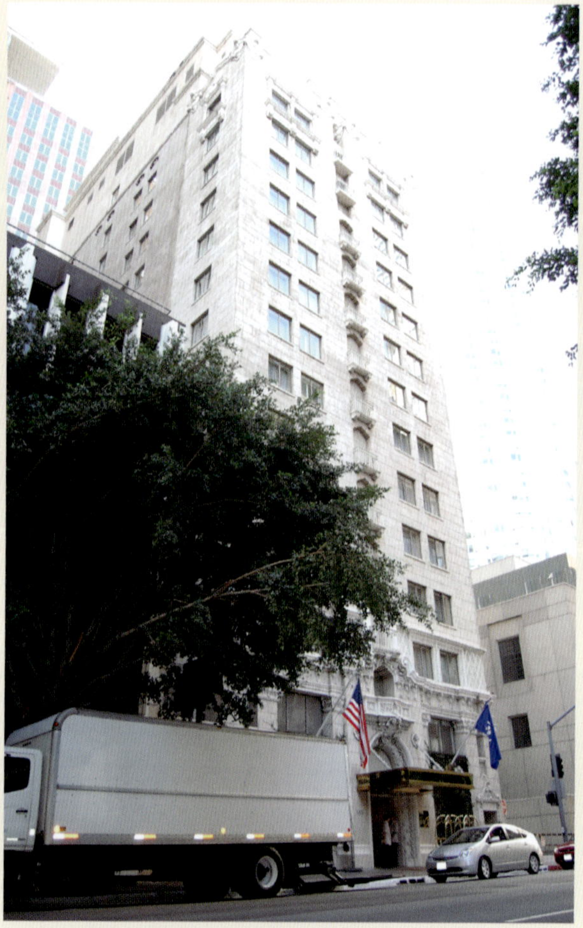

Looking north on South Grand Avenue, the Mayflower Hotel was located on South Grand, between 5th and 6th streets.

The grass and trees to the north of the hotel property (right in postcard view) have been replaced with a building.

THEN

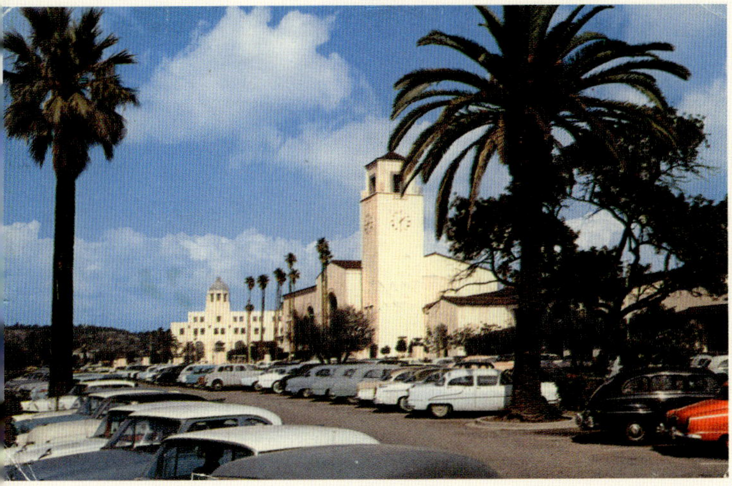

Union Station.

NOW

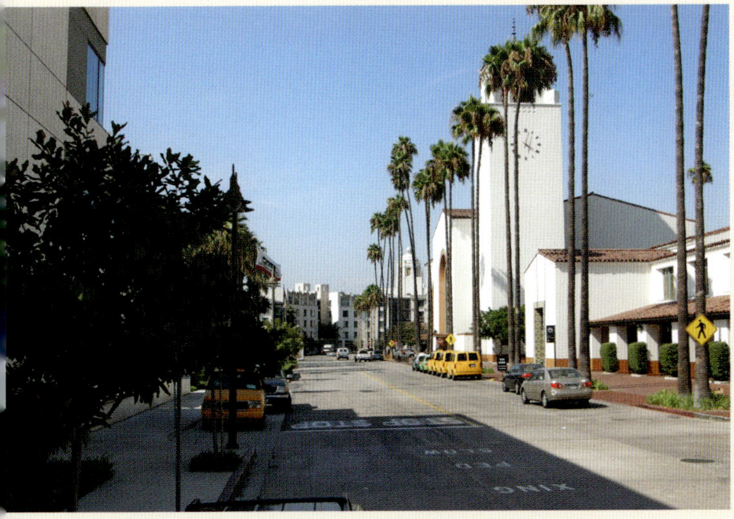

The train terminal Union Station remains in operation at 800 North Alameda Street.

Union Station was built in 1939 on the site of Old Chinatown.

THEN

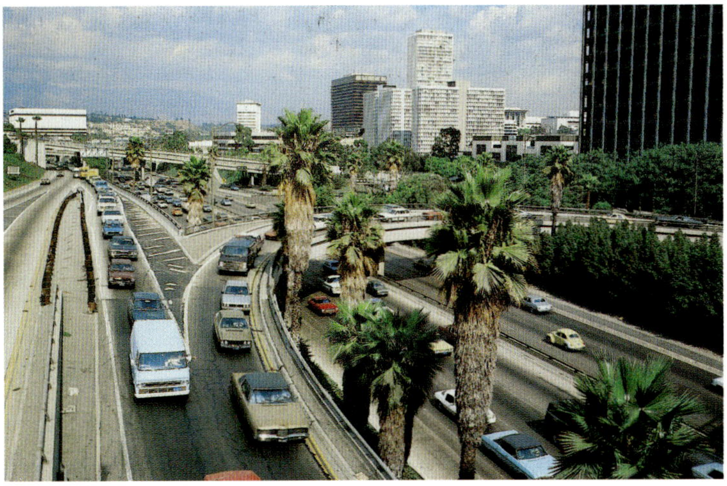

Harbor Freeway.

NOW

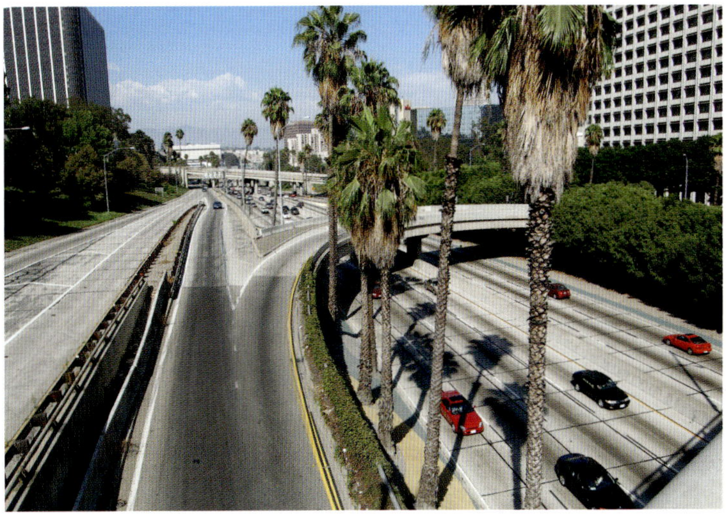

Harbor Freeway, looking over the freeway from the West 5th Street overpass.

Los Angeles is famous for its maze of freeways. Harbor, Hollywood, and Santa Monica freeways are just a few of them.

THEN

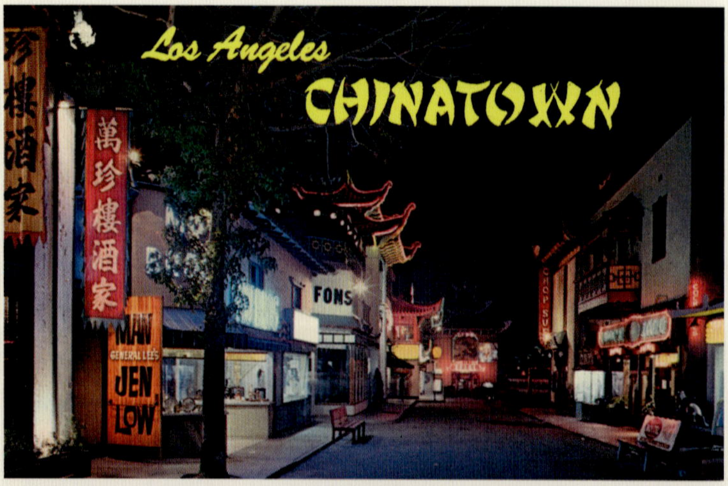

Chinatown.

NOW

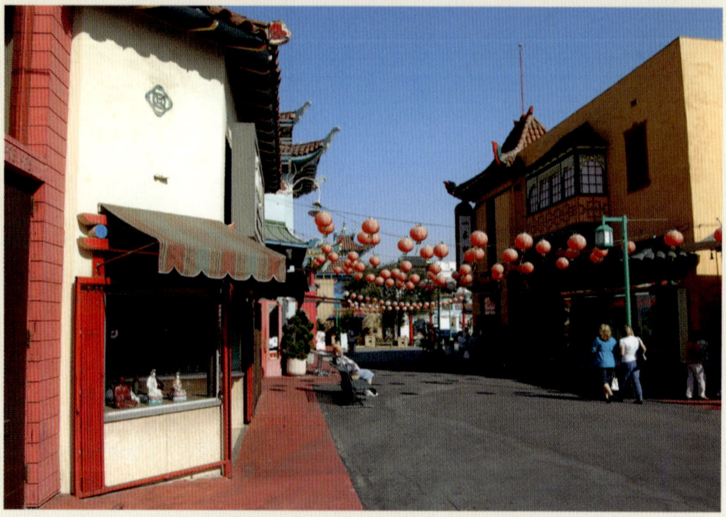

Chinatown, looking east on Gin Ling Way, in the direction of North Broadway.

The Chinatown of today began in 1938, after relocating from its former location at Union Station.

THEN

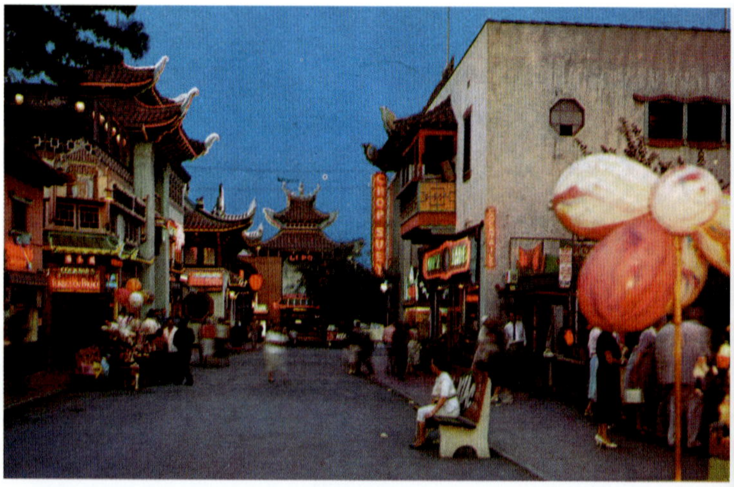

Chinatown.

NOW

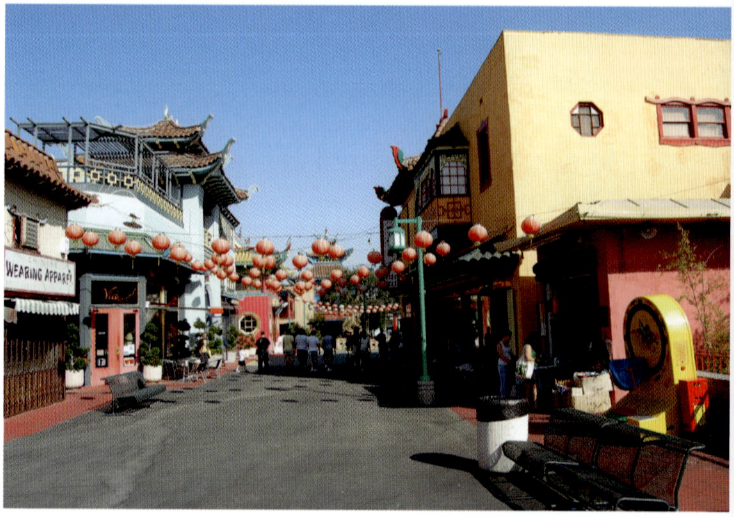

Chinatown, looking east on Gin Ling Way, in the direction of North Broadway.

Per the back of the postcard: "The fantastic towers and pagodas along Gin Ling Way are just part of this enchanting settlement of shops crowded with art treasures of the Orient and Chinese restaurants serving delicately flavored foods."

THEN

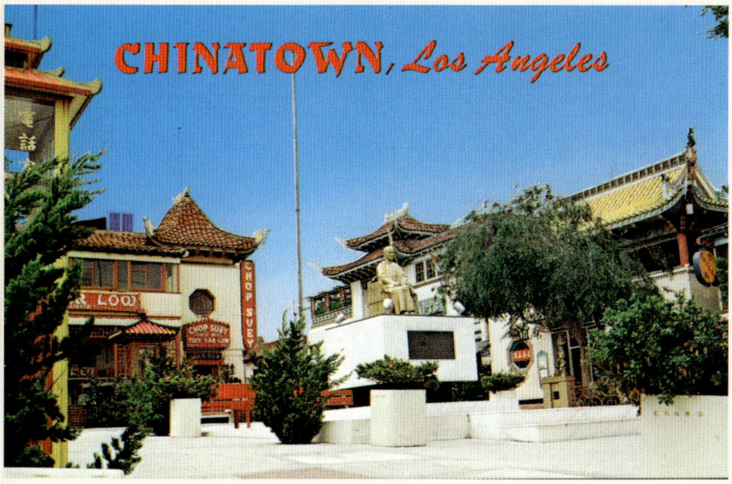

Chinatown, showing the Dr. Sun Yat-sen statue in the foreground.

NOW

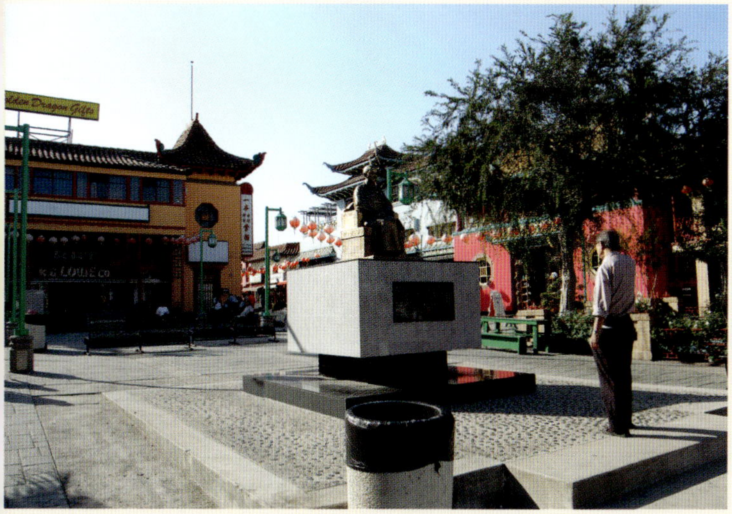

Chinatown. The Dr. Sun Yat-sen statue is in the foreground. The statue faces in the direction of North Broadway. This view is a few feet from where Gin Ling Way meets North Broadway.

Dr. Sun Yat-sen is the founder of the Republic of China.

THEN

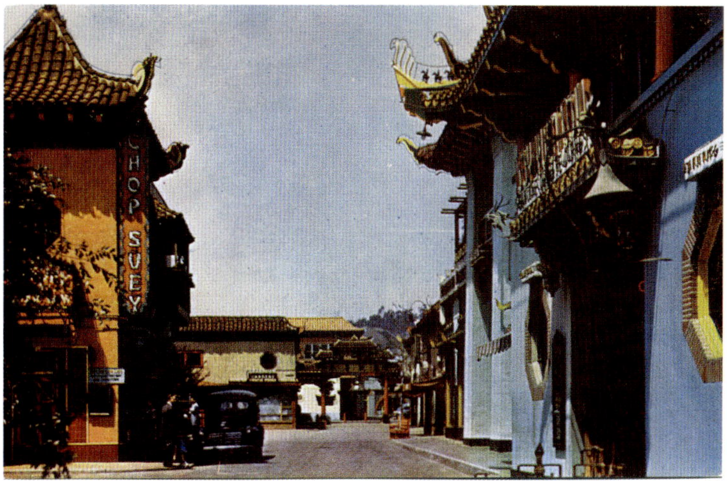

Chinatown.

NOW

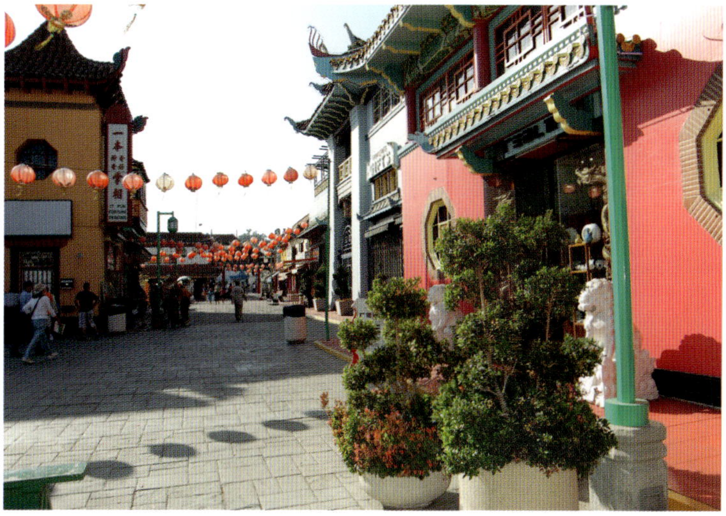

Chinatown, looking west on Gin Ling Way, in the direction of North Hill Street.

Central Plaza, shown here in both views, is all awash in colors.

THEN

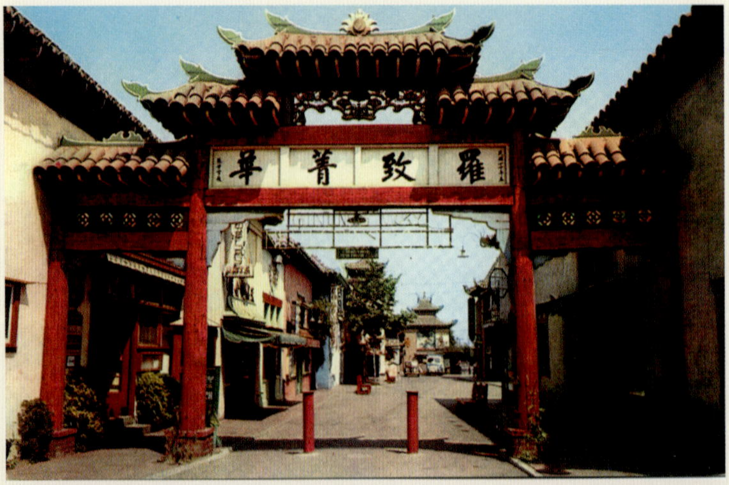

Chinatown.

NOW

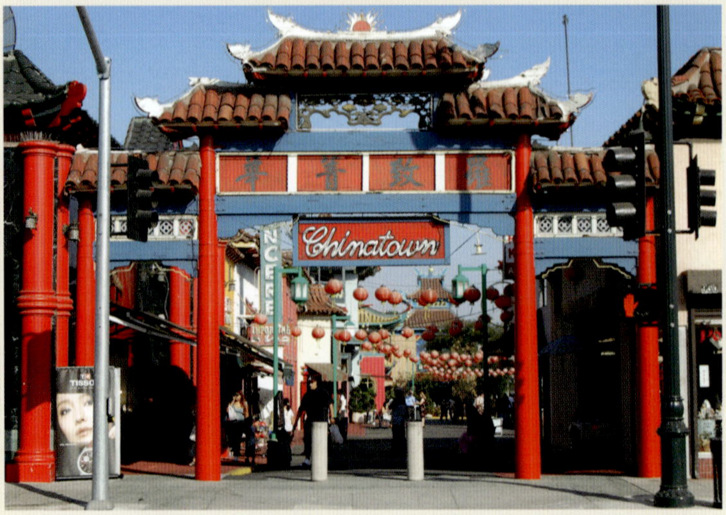

Chinatown, looking east onto Gin Ling Way from North Hill Street.

THEN

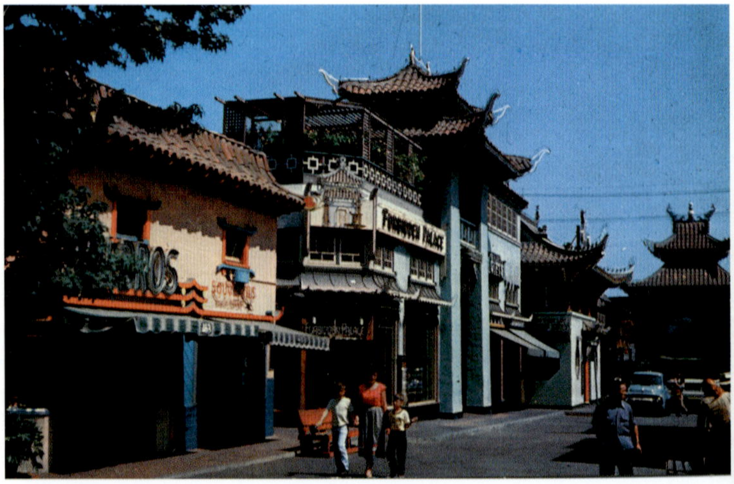

Chinatown.

NOW

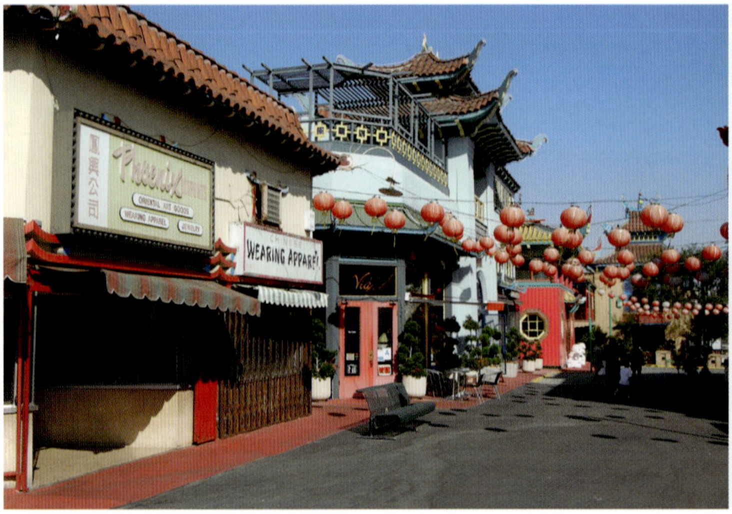

Chinatown, looking east on Gin Ling Way, in the direction of North Broadway.

Gin Ling Way connects the two gates of the Central Plaza in Chinatown. The west gate welcomes visitors from Hill Street while the east gate welcomes them from Broadway.

Hollywood directors have capitalized on the look of Chinatown. A piece of the 1974 film called *Chinatown* was shot in the area.

THEN

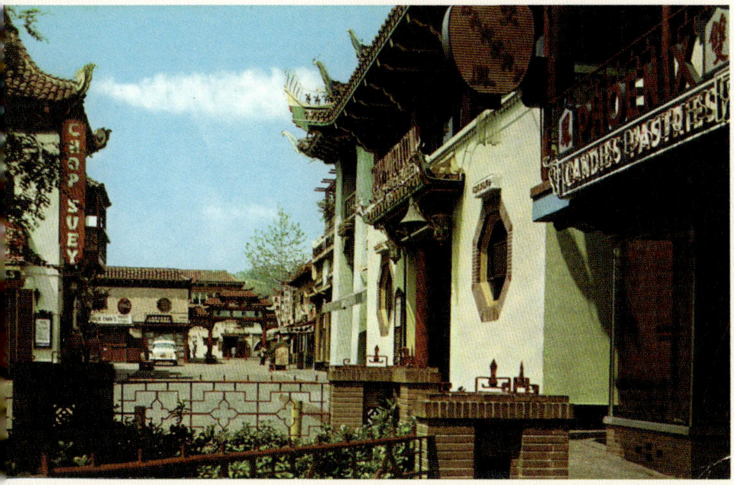

Chinatown.

NOW

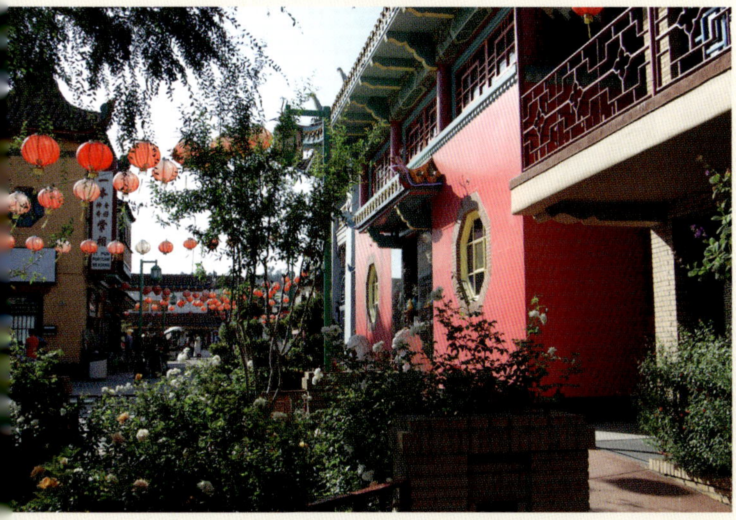

Chinatown, looking west on Gin Ling Way, in the direction of North Hill Street.

In the now view, colored lanterns hang over the strollers on Gin Ling Way.

THEN

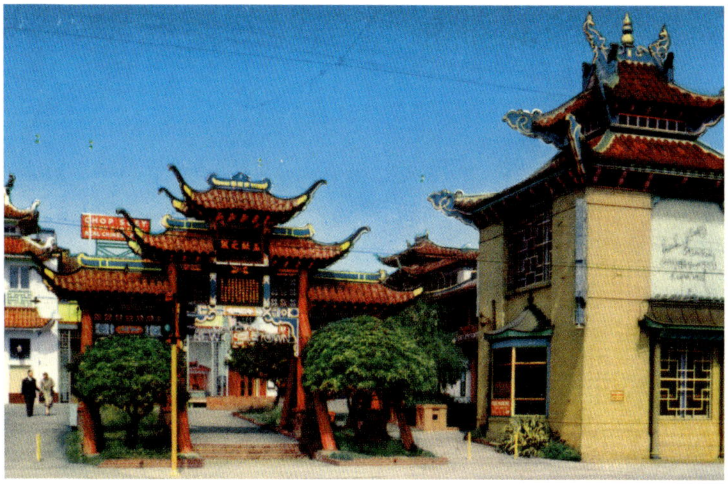

Chinatown.

NOW

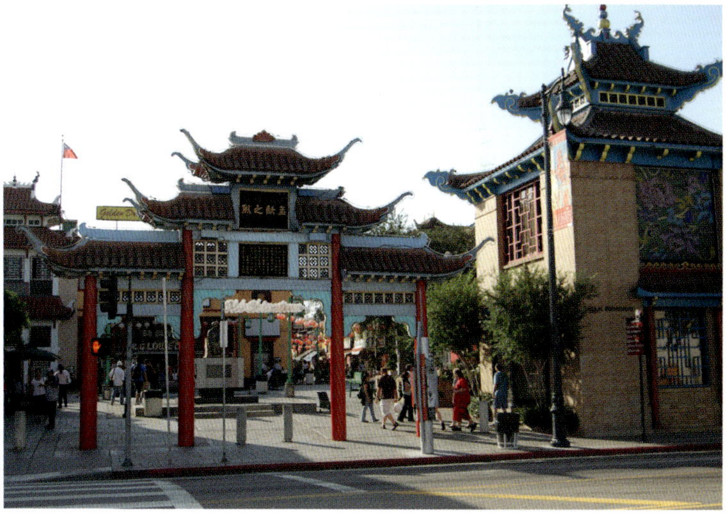

Chinatown, looking west onto Gin Ling Way from North Broadway.

Chinatown has been searching for a new identity of sorts over the last several decades. In a 2010 *Los Angeles Times* article, former Los Angeles City Council member Michael Woo states, "Chinatown is in a state of evolution and is no longer the Chinatown of past years."

THEN

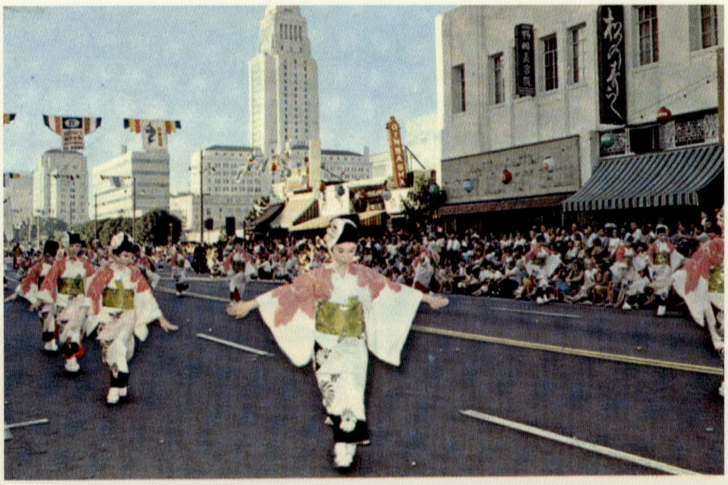

Greetings from Li'l (Little) Tokyo.

NOW

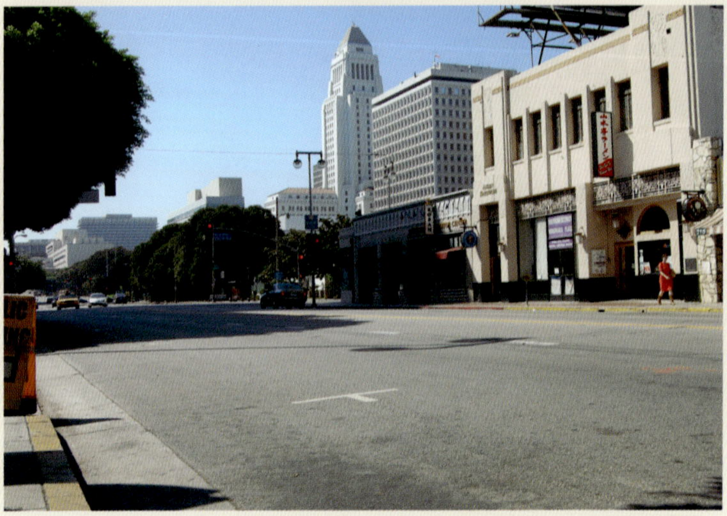

Little Tokyo, looking west on East 1st Street, just shy of where it splits San Pedro and Judge John Aiso streets.

Little Tokyo is roughly bounded by Los Angeles Street (west end), Alameda Street (east end), 1st Street (north end), and 3rd Street (south end).

THEN

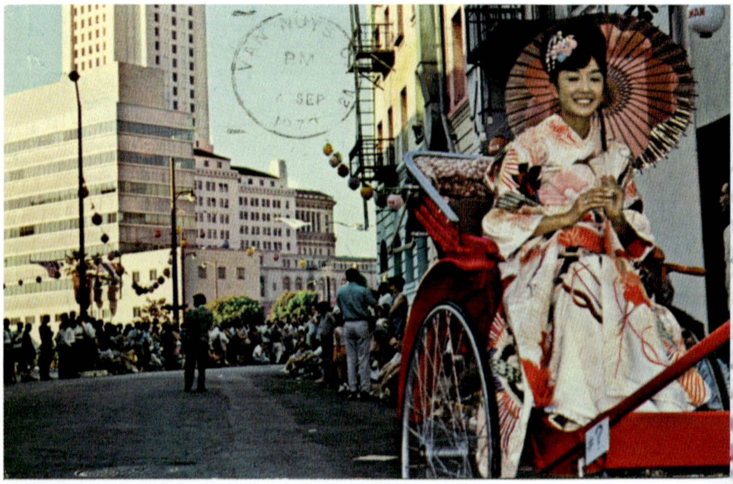

Little Tokyo.

NOW

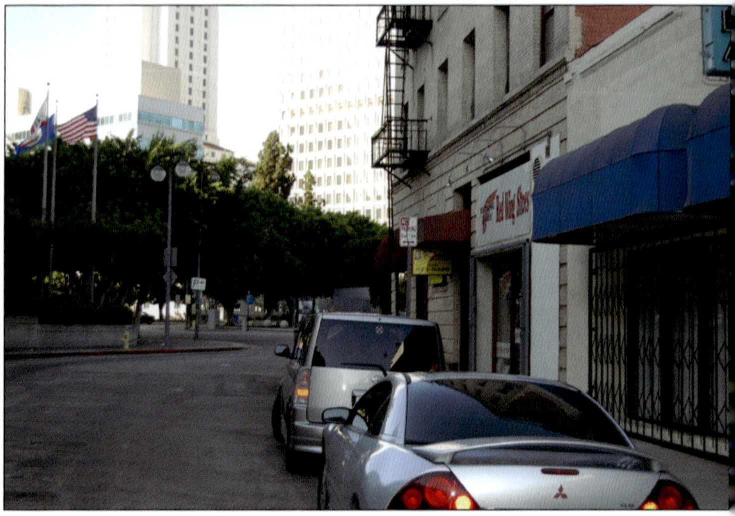

Little Tokyo, looking toward East 1st Street from Astronaut E S Onizuka Street.

In 2012, Little Tokyo celebrated the 72nd Annual Nisei Week Japanese Festival. Nisei Week is a cultural festival. It is a celebration of the way the Japanese culture has merged with the American culture.

THEN

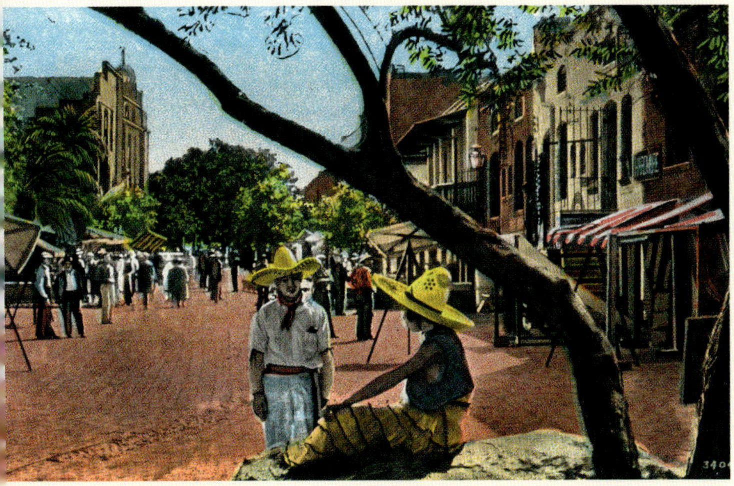

El Paseo de Los Angeles (Olvera Street).

NOW

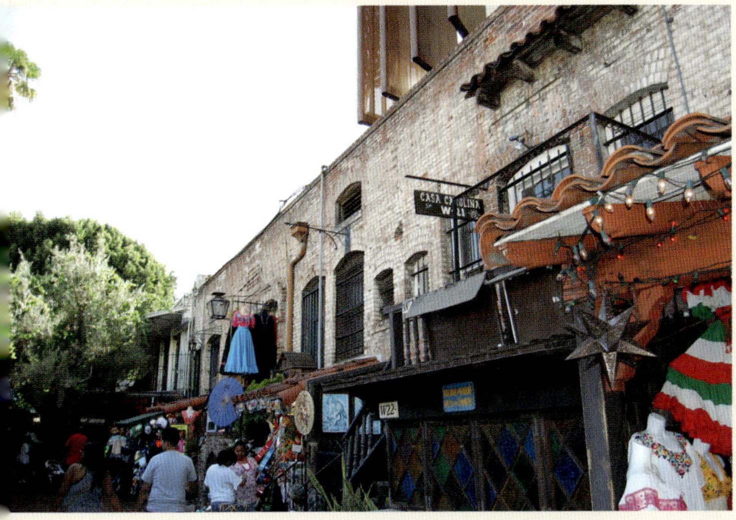

El Paseo de Los Angeles (Olvera Street), looking south on Olvera Street.

Olvera Street is all about enjoying Mexican culture in the way of food, shopping, and music-filling air.

THEN

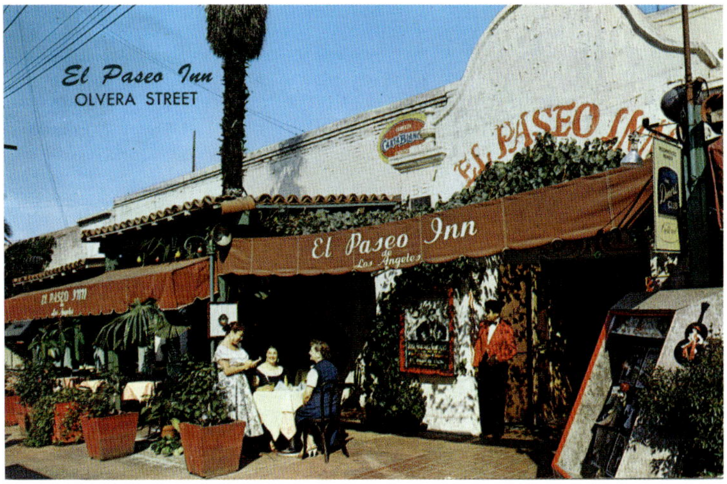

El Paseo Inn (Olvera Street).

NOW

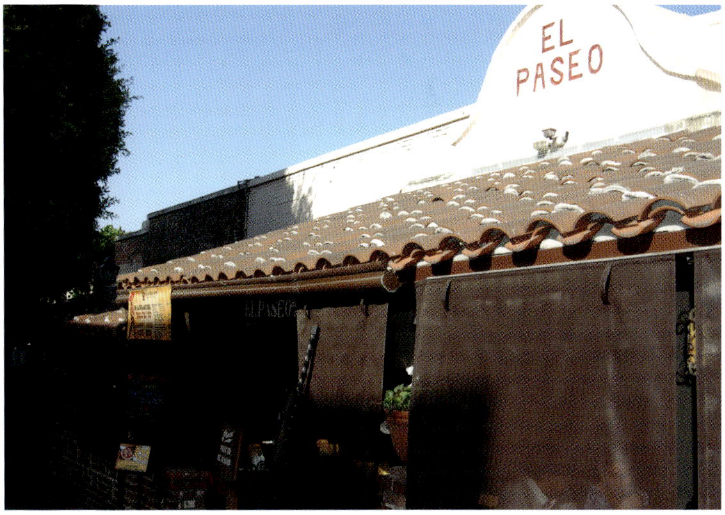

El Paseo Inn Restaurant remains in business at 11 East Olvera Street.

The El Paseo Inn Restaurant dates back to the 1930s. In 1953, it moved to its current location.

CHAPTER 4
DOWNTOWN: THEN & NOW GONE

THEN

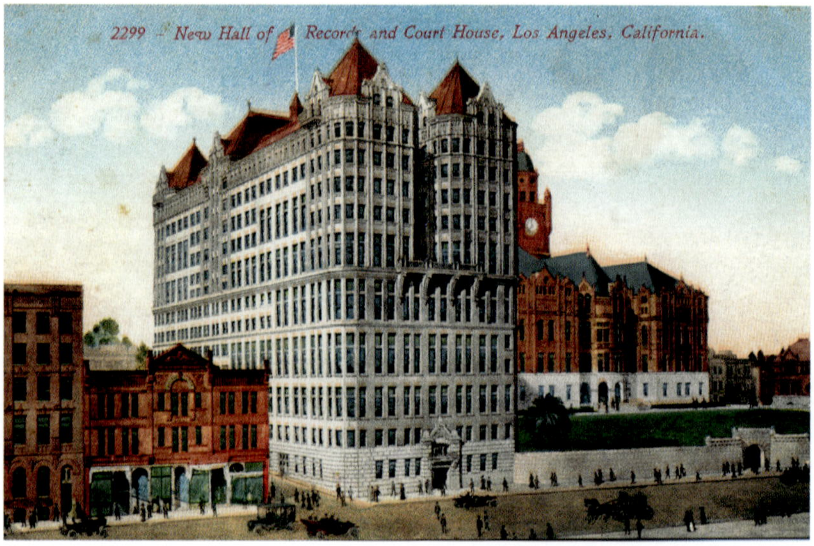

Hall of Records (center) and Court House (right).

NOW

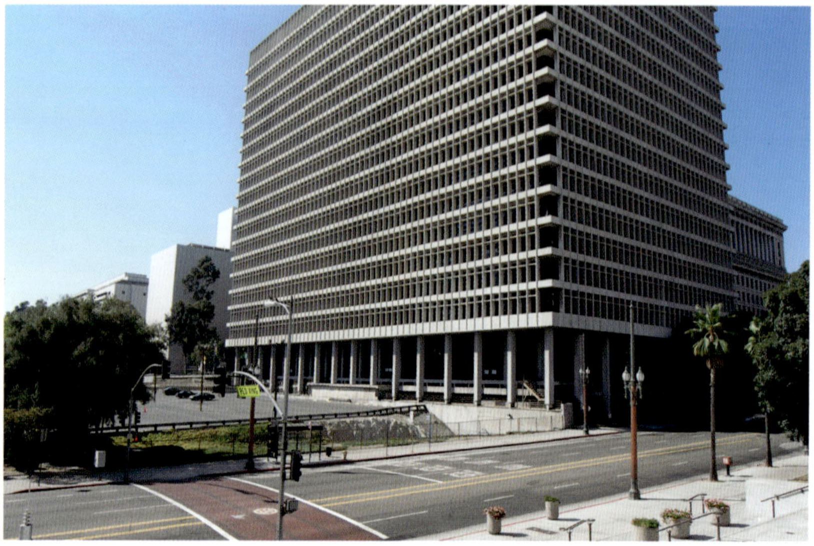

The Hall of Records and Court House were located on Spring Street. The Court House sat on southwest corner of Temple and Spring streets, where the building shown here sits. The Hall of Records was located about where the parking lot is located in this view, to the left of the building. Both the Hall of Records and the Court House stretched to Broadway. (Note: The parking lot is now part of Grand Park.)

The "then" was the Court House and Hall of Records that a visitor could justify eyeing for hours, enjoying their details. (Note: In 2012, a section of Grand Park opened where the parking lot is seen in the "now" view.)

NOW

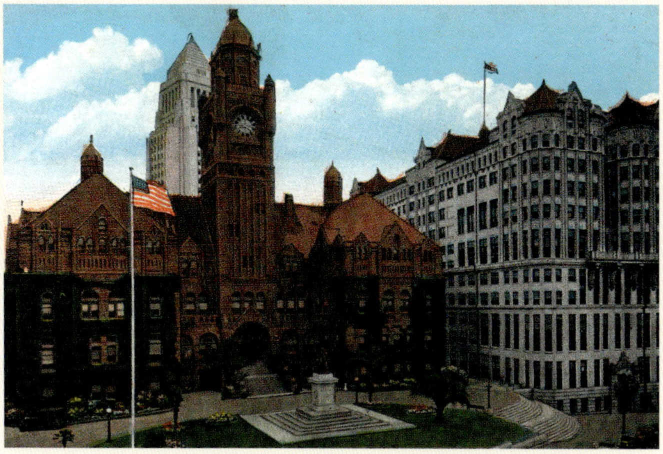

Hall of Records (right) and Court House (left)

THEN

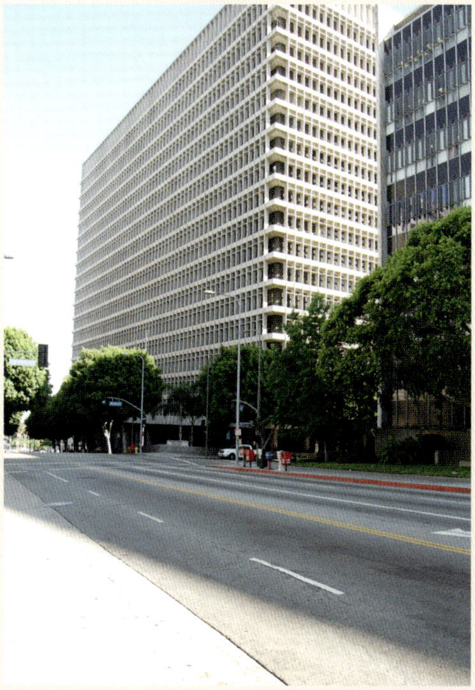

Hall of Records and Court House, looking east on Temple Street. The Court House sat on the southeast corner of Temple Street and Broadway, where the prominent building shown here sits, while the Hall of Records was to the right of said prominent building (the area where it sat is blocked from view). Both the Hall of Records and the Court House stretched to Spring Street.

The red sandstone Romanesque Court House building took possession of its corner lot on Temple Street and Broadway in 1891, but lost its "lease" in 1936 when it was demolished. The Hall of Records stood its ground for over six decades before taking its final bow in 1973.

THEN

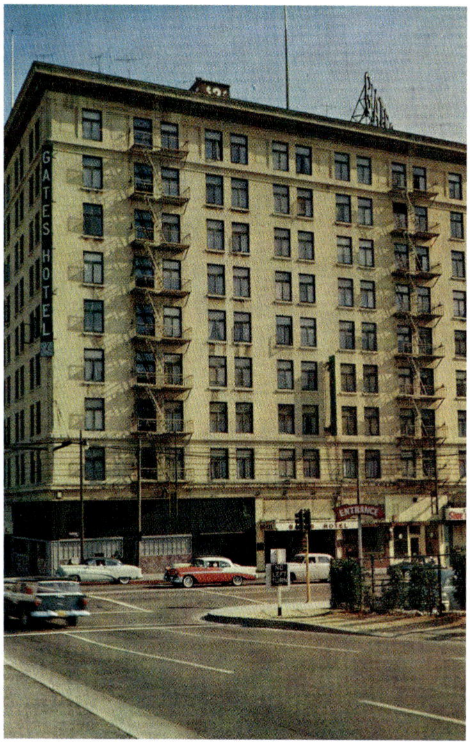

Gates Hotel.

NOW

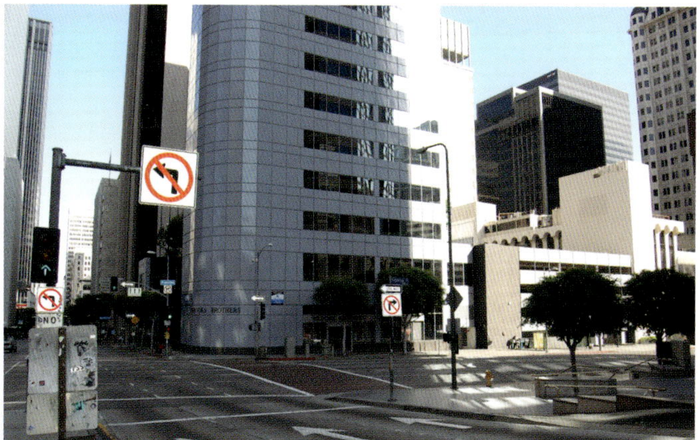

The Gates Hotel building stood at the southeast corner of Figueroa and 6th streets. The building no longer stands.

Buildings seen in decades'-old postcard views are mourned by preservationists. The cars seen in them are often overlooked in the grieving process, for they, too, are long gone.

THEN

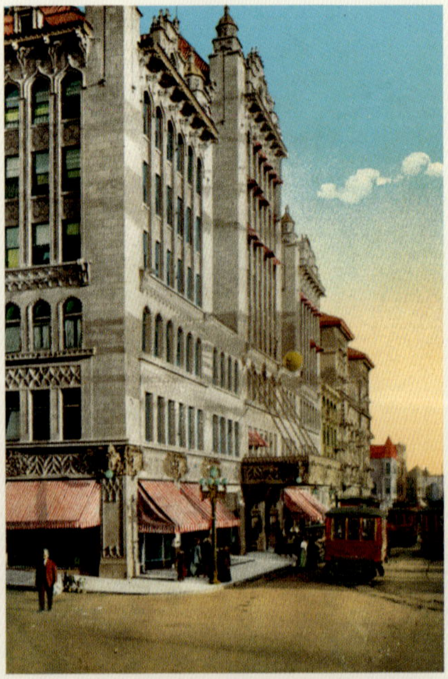

Auditorium Building.

NOW

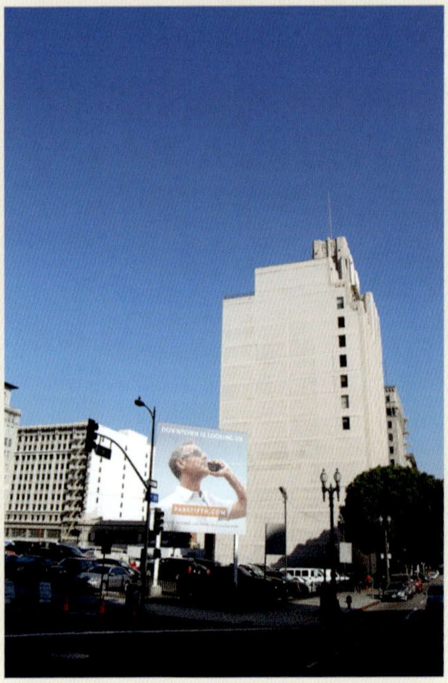

The Auditorium no longer stands. It was located on the northeast corner of Olive and 5th streets. Over its history, it had changed names.

Erected in 1906, the Auditorium building was demolished in the mid-1980s.

THEN

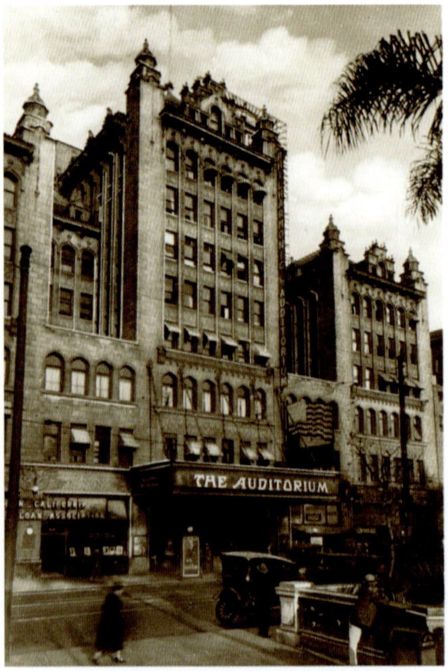

The Auditorium.

NOW

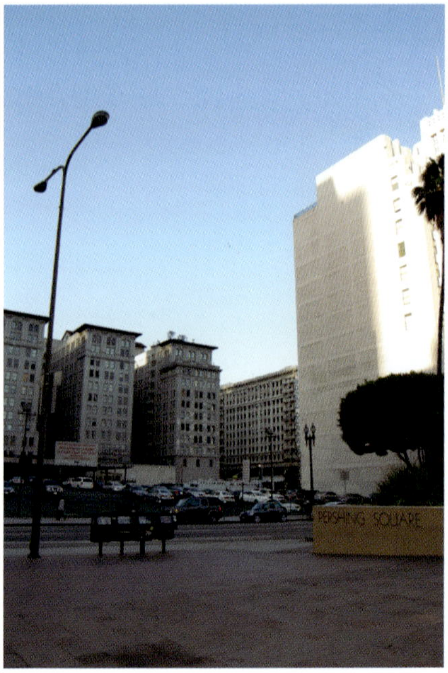

The Auditorium faced West 5th Street when it stood.

Where the music of the Los Angeles Philharmonic once could be heard, the sounds of parking cars play.

THEN

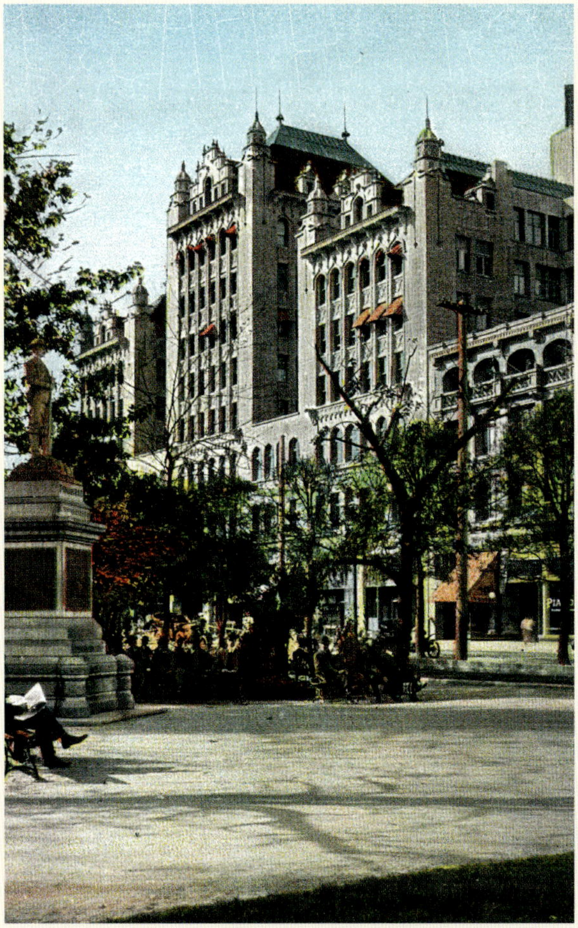

The nine-story, Gothic-style Auditorium was originally called Temple Auditorium.

NOW

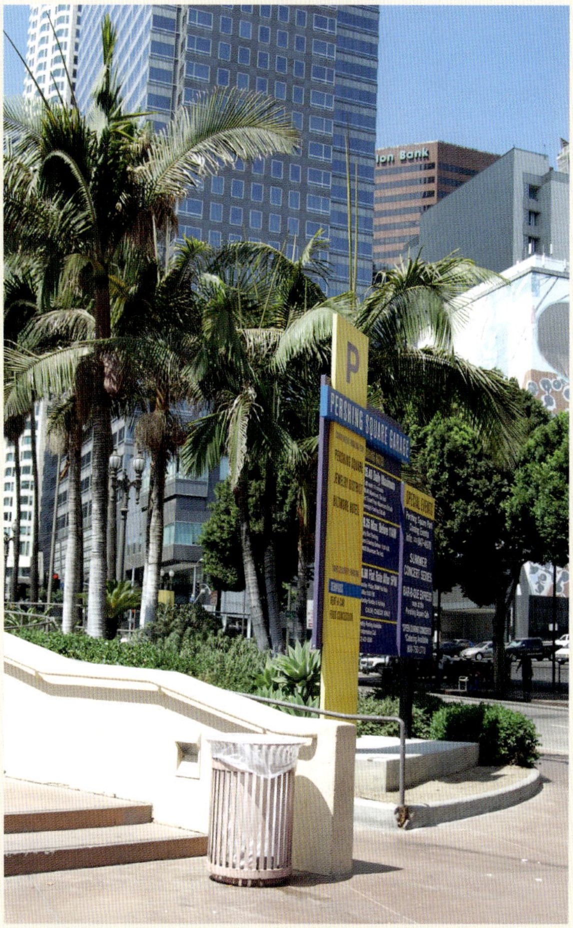

The Auditorium building, when it stood faced what is now Pershing Square. This view is from the southwest corner of 5th and Hill streets.

THEN

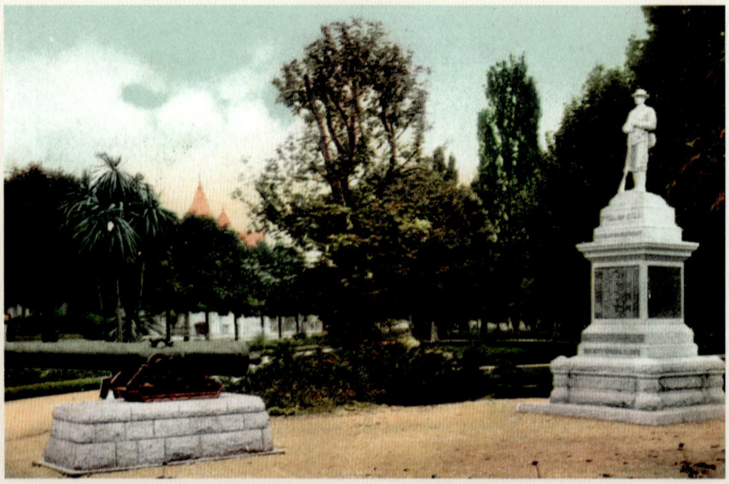

Soldiers' Monument, Central Park.

NOW

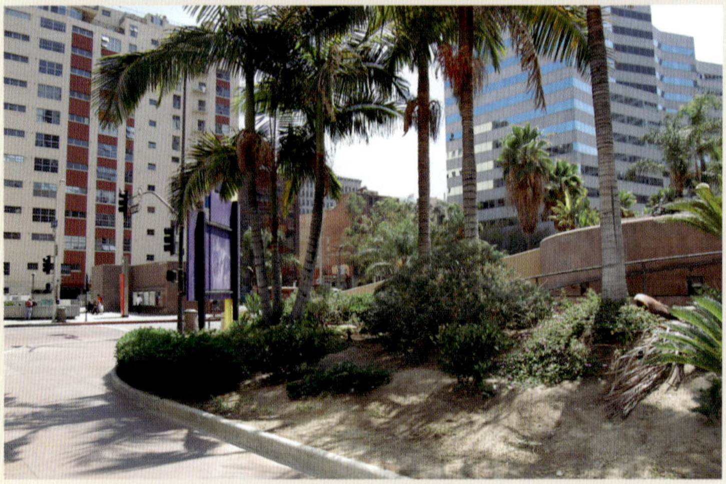

Soldiers' Monument in Pershing Square (formerly Central Park) was located on the southwest corner of 5th and Hill streets. It has since been moved away from the corner, but still rests in Pershing Square.

NOW

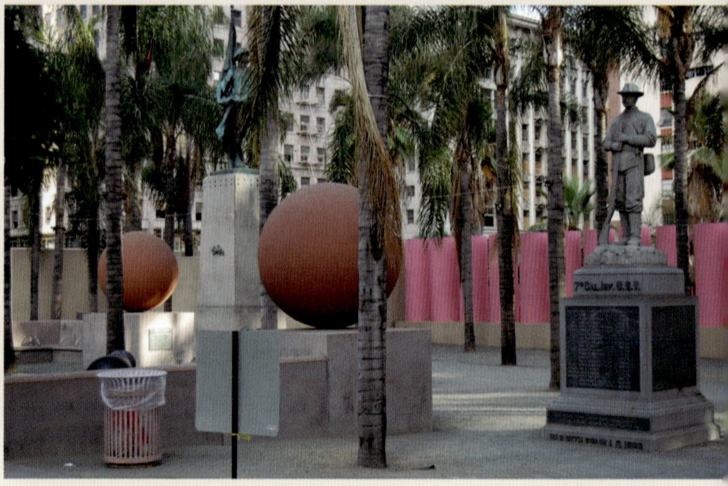

On the right, the Soldiers' Monument is shown resting at its current location inside Pershing Square.

Soldiers' Monument was created to honor the fighters of the Spanish-American War of 1898. One of the readings at the base of the monument reads: "Our Dead. They Lie In Scattered Graves, These Silent Heroes of Our Battalions."

THEN

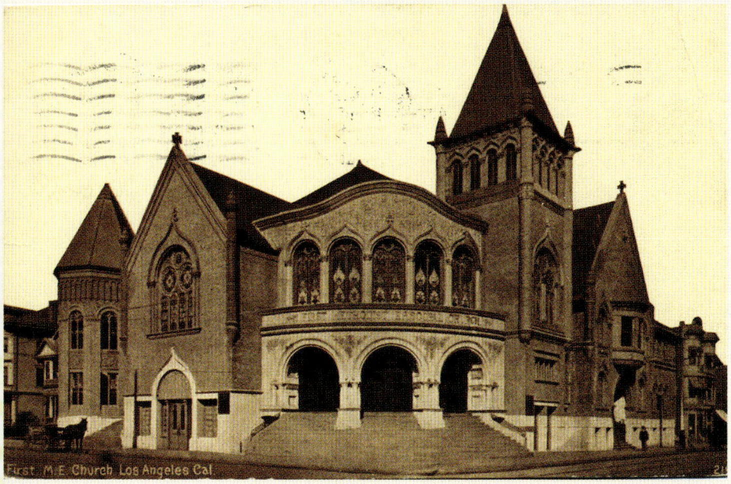

First Methodist Episcopal Church.

NOW

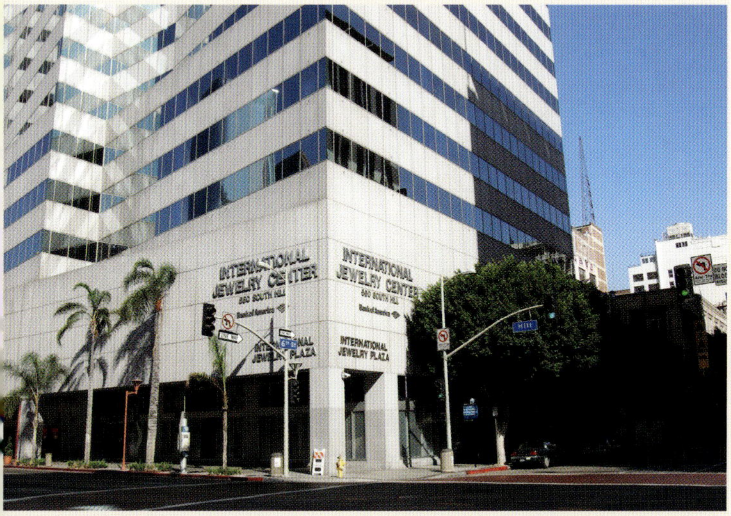

First Methodist Episcopal Church was located on the northeast corner of 6th and Hill streets. The church no longer stands.

The arched entranceways and stained glass windows of the First Methodist Episcopal Church were taken down, along with the building, in 1920.

THEN

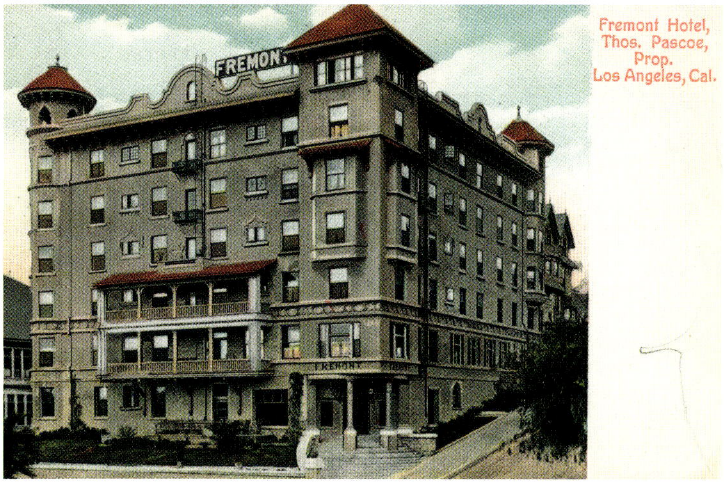

Fremont Hotel.

NOW

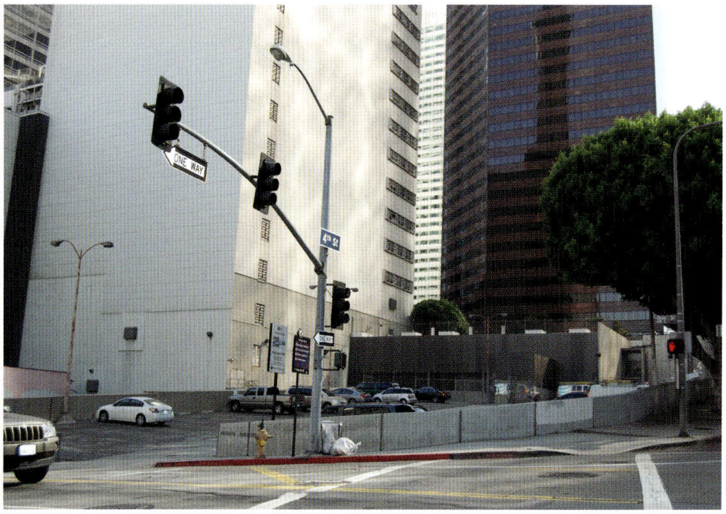

Fremont Hotel was located at the southwest corner of 4th and Olive streets when it stood.

The Fremont Hotel stood decades after its opening in 1902. A parking lot now greets visitors to the corner where the hotel once stood.

THEN

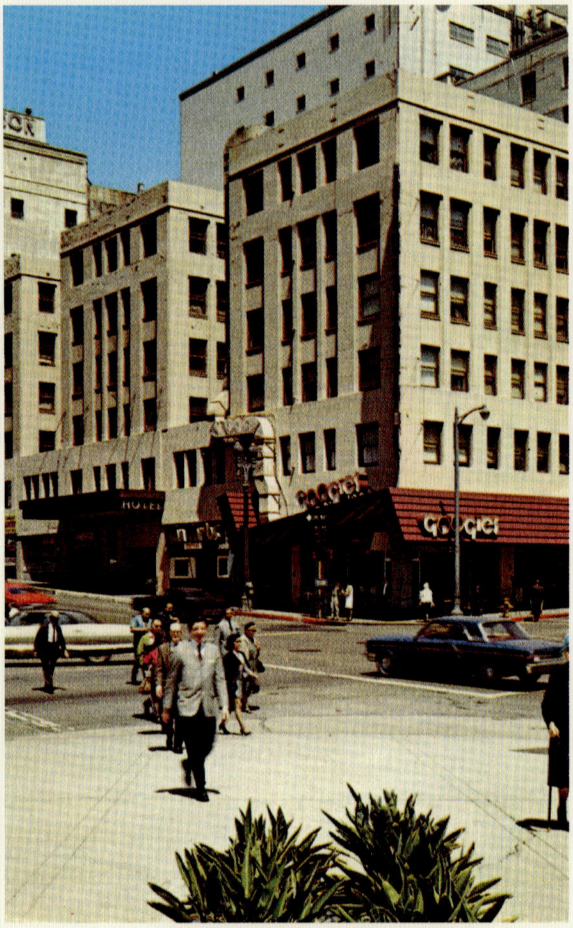

San Carlos Hotel.

NOW

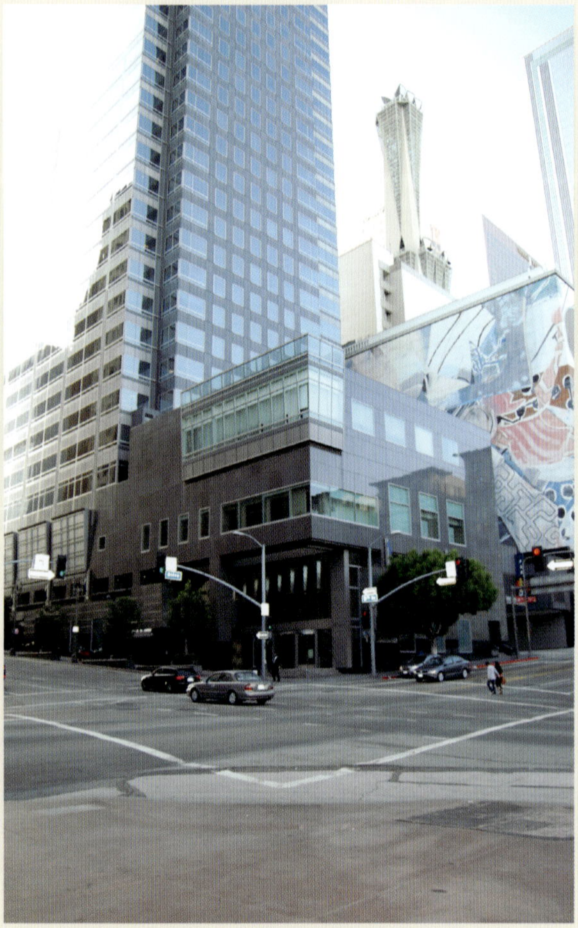

San Carlos Hotel was located at the northwest corner of 5th and Olive streets. It no longer stands.

A modern building replaces the San Carlos Hotel and Googies coffee shop (far center corner in postcard) with its Space Age architectural style.

THEN

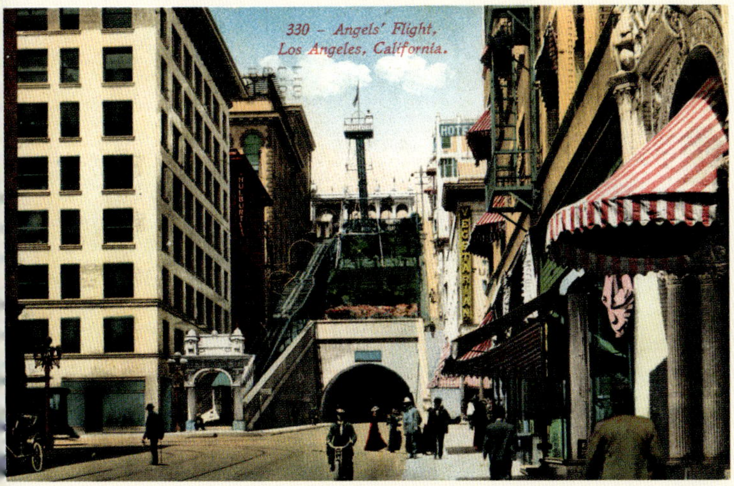

THEN

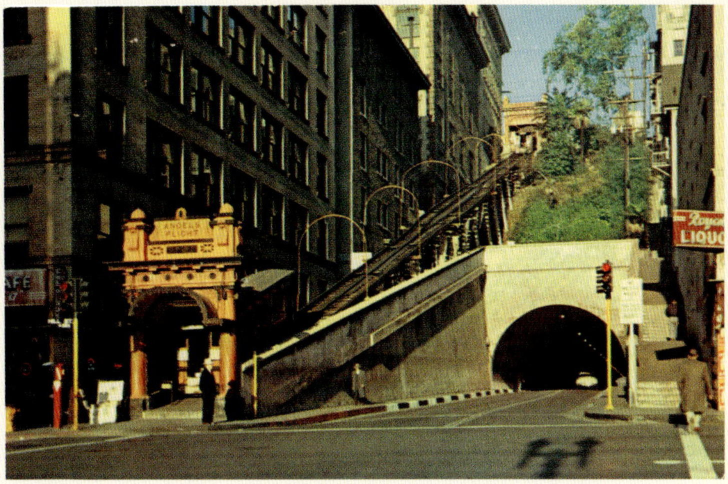

Angels Flight.

NOW

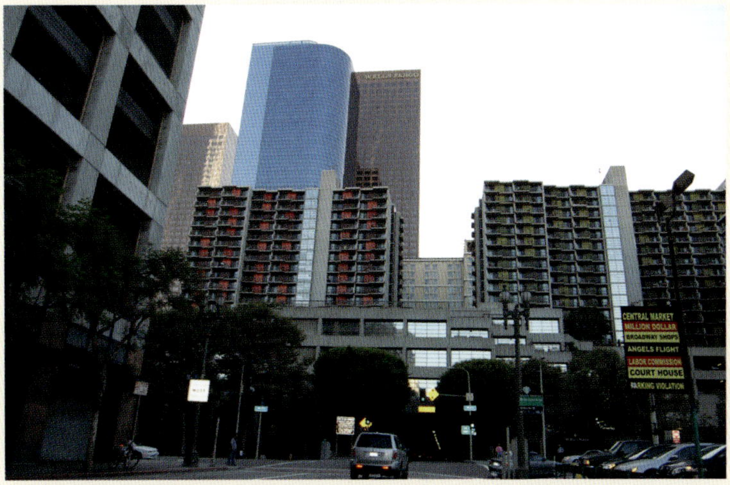

Angels Flight was located on the west end of the intersection of Hill and 3rd streets. This view is looking west on West 3rd Street.

The Angels Flight at 3rd and Hill streets was taken down in 1969. Angels Flight is now located a short distance south of the intersection on Hill Street.

THEN

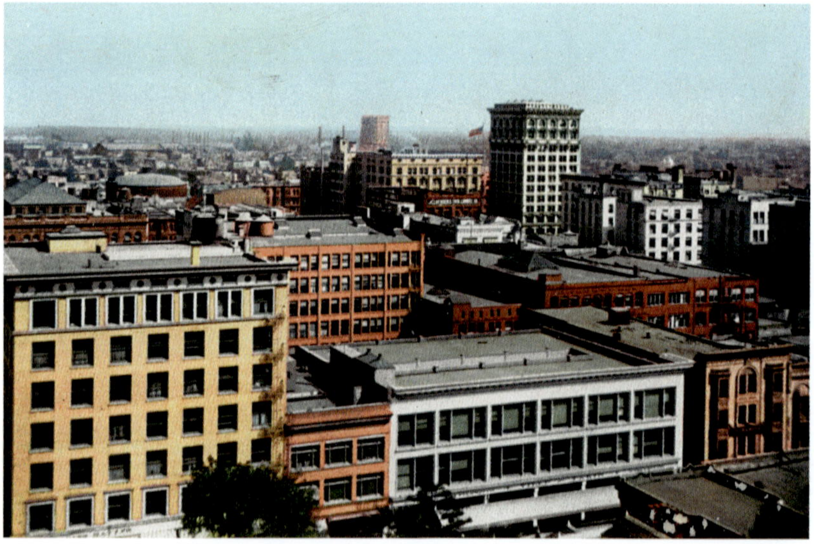

Los Angeles from Angels Flight.

NOW

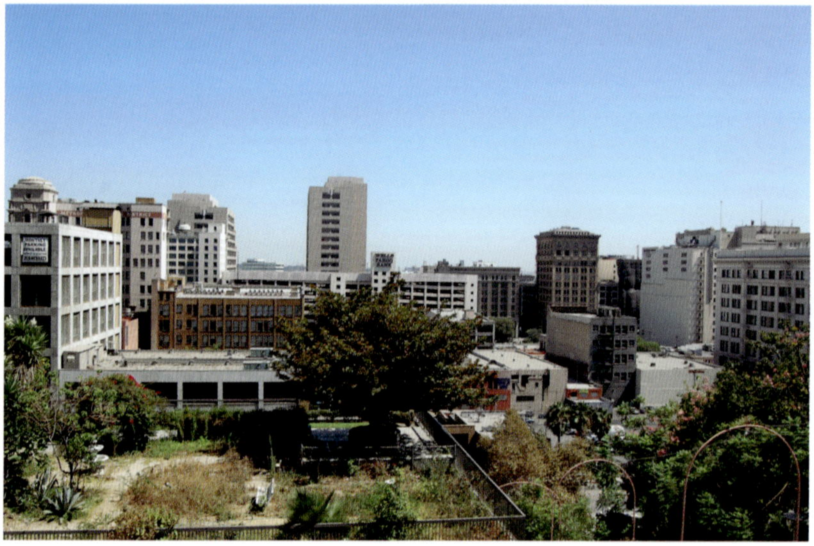

Los Angeles from the top of the Angels Flight of today. The postcard shows a view from the top of the original Angels Flight, which is now demolished. Angels Flight is now located a half-block south of its original location. Still, a few distinct buildings shown in the postcard can be recognized in this current-day view, which is a half-block south from where the postcard picture was taken.

Today, Angels Flight begins its climb at 351 South Hill Street and brings you to the California Plaza Watercourt at 350 South Grand Avenue.

CHAPTER 5
HOLLYWOOD

THEN

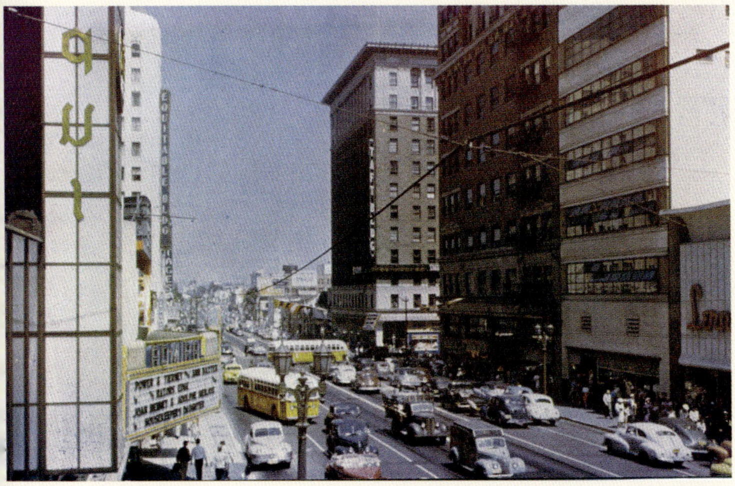

Hollywood Boulevard near where it intersects with Vine Street.

NOW

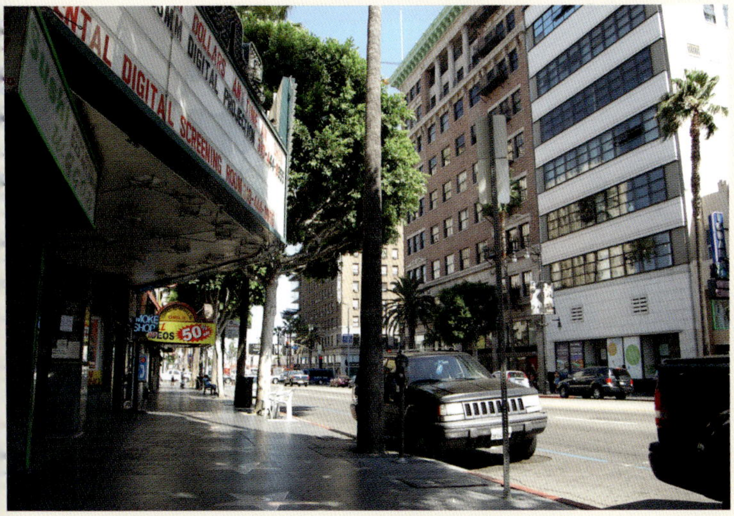

Hollywood Boulevard near where it intersects with Vine Street. Looking east on Hollywood Boulevard with the intersection of Hollywood and Vine ahead.

Since the 1920s, Hollywood Boulevard has been one of the most famous thoroughfares in the world. Silent stars, such as Douglas Fairbanks (circa 1919) and Carole Lombard (circa 1934), once lived on the boulevard.

THEN

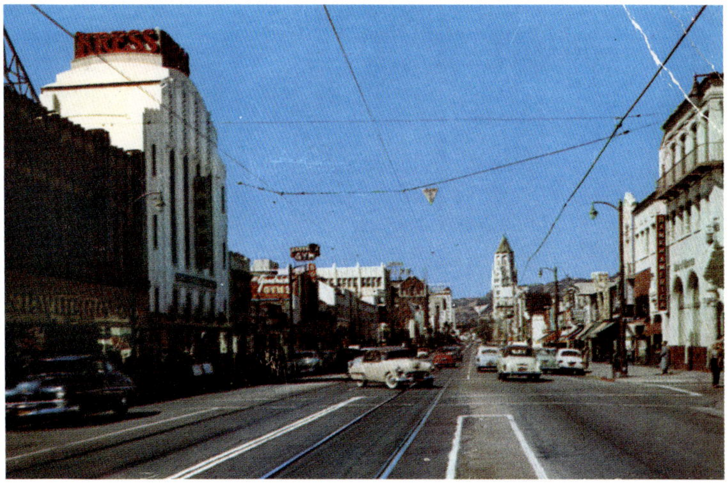

Hollywood Boulevard.

NOW

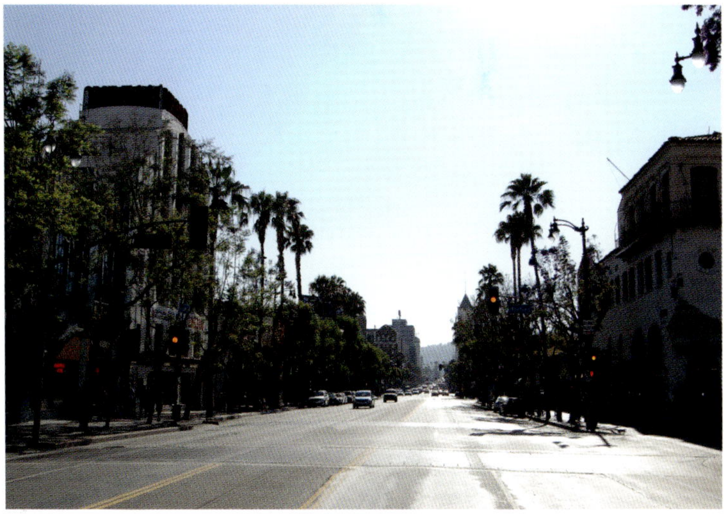

Hollywood Boulevard, looking west. The immediate signal ahead is where Whitley Avenue meets Hollywood Boulevard.

Hollywood Boulevard is guarded by numerous historic buildings. Annually, the Hollywood Christmas Parade runs along its path. The Hollywood Walk of Fame lines its sidewalks.

THEN

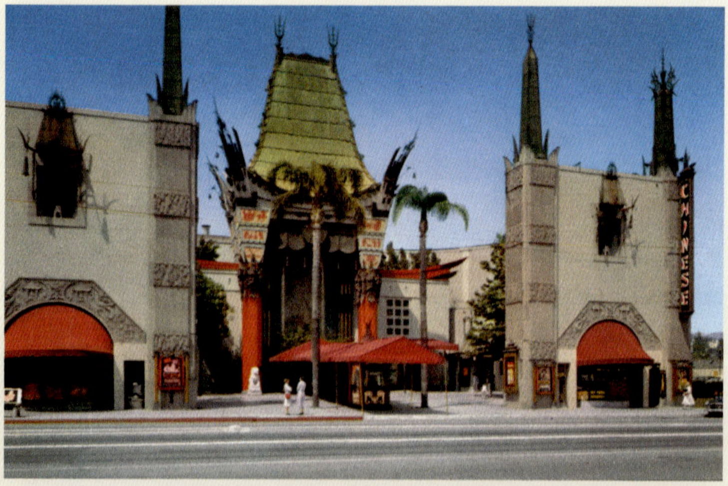

Grauman's Chinese Theatre.

NOW

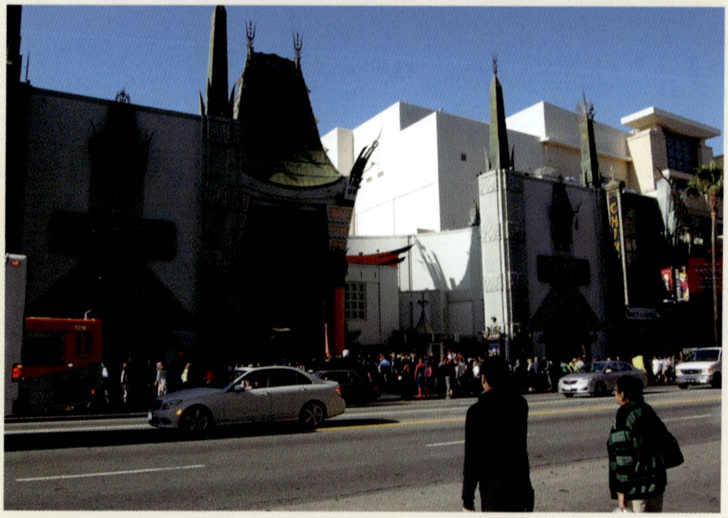

Grauman's Chinese Theatre remains in business at 6925 Hollywood Boulevard.

Sid Grauman opened Grauman's Chinese Theatre in 1927.

THEN

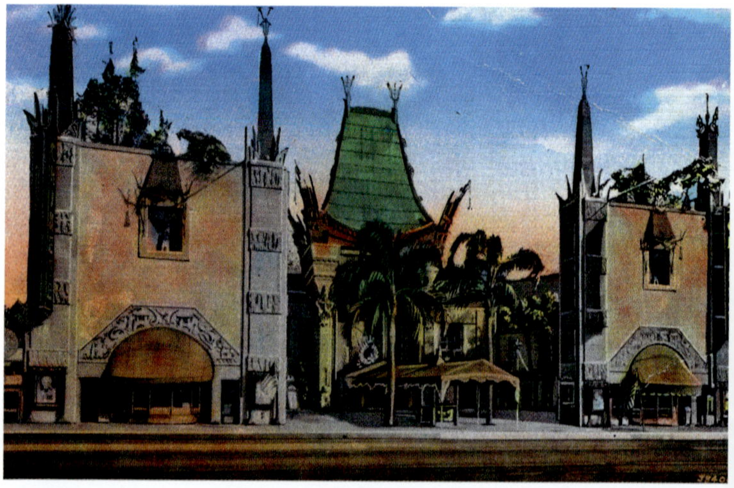

Grauman's Chinese Theatre.

NOW

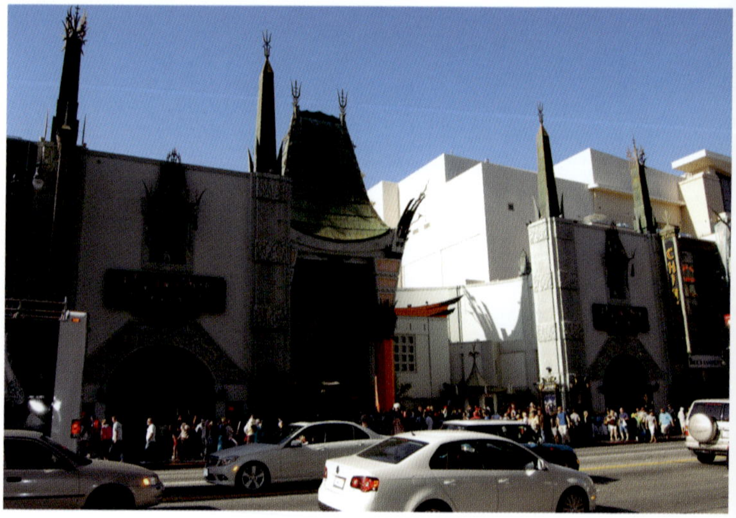

Grauman's Chinese Theatre stands on the north side of Hollywood Boulevard.

In the cement of the Grauman's Chinese Theatre forecourt, hand- and footprints of many movie stars can be found.

THEN

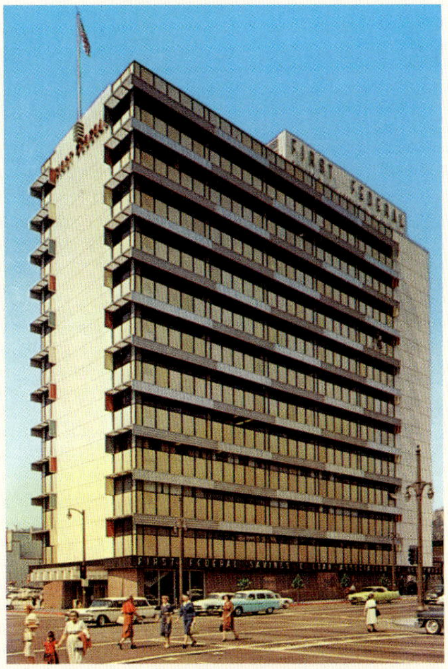

First Federal Savings & Loan Association of Hollywood.

THEN

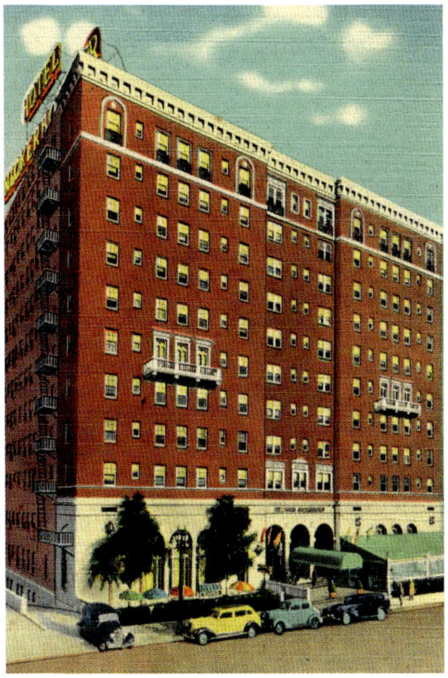

Hollywood Knickerbocker Hotel.

NOW

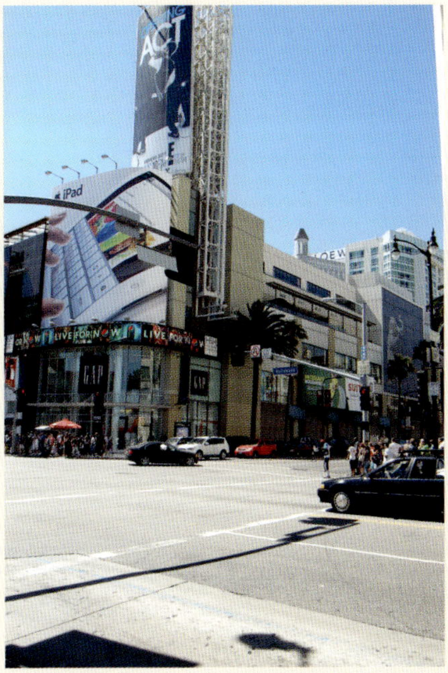

First Federal Savings & Loan Association of Hollywood stood at the northwest corner of Hollywood Boulevard and Highland Avenue. The building was torn down to build the Hollywood and Highland Center, a shopping and entertainment complex.

NOW

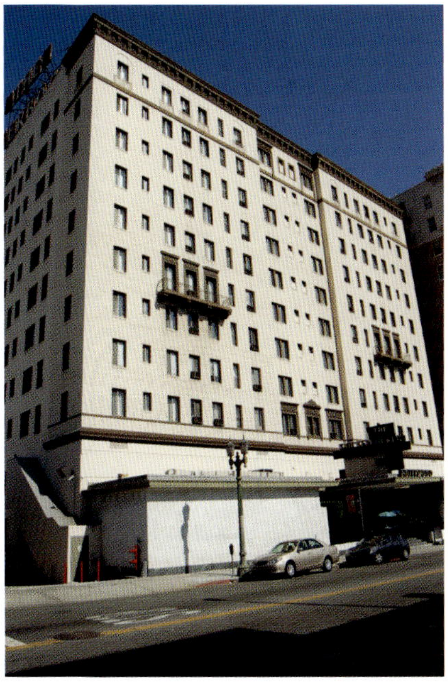

Hollywood Knickerbocker Hotel, designed by architect John M. Cooper, was located at 1714 Ivar Avenue, just north of Hollywood Boulevard. Though the building still stands, it is no longer a hotel.

THEN

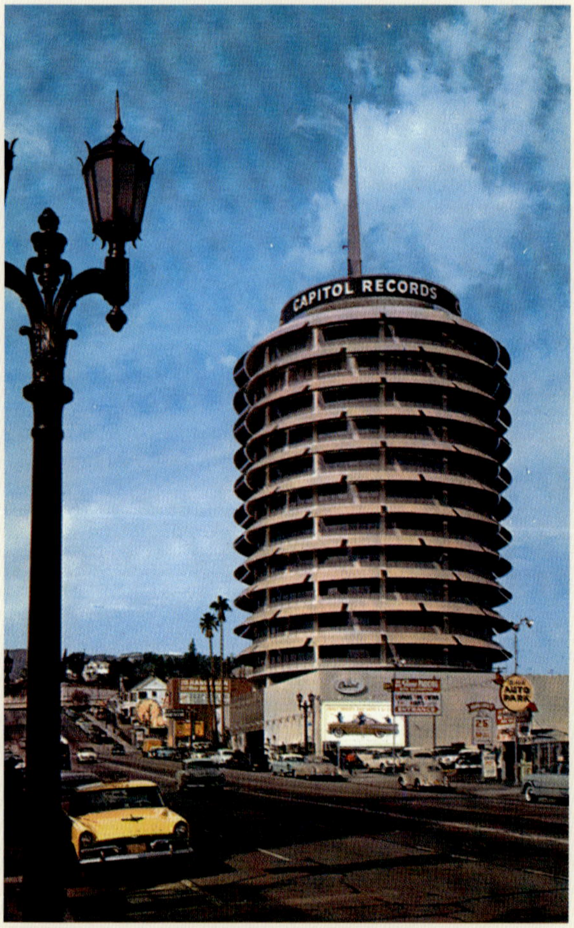

Capitol Records Tower.

NOW

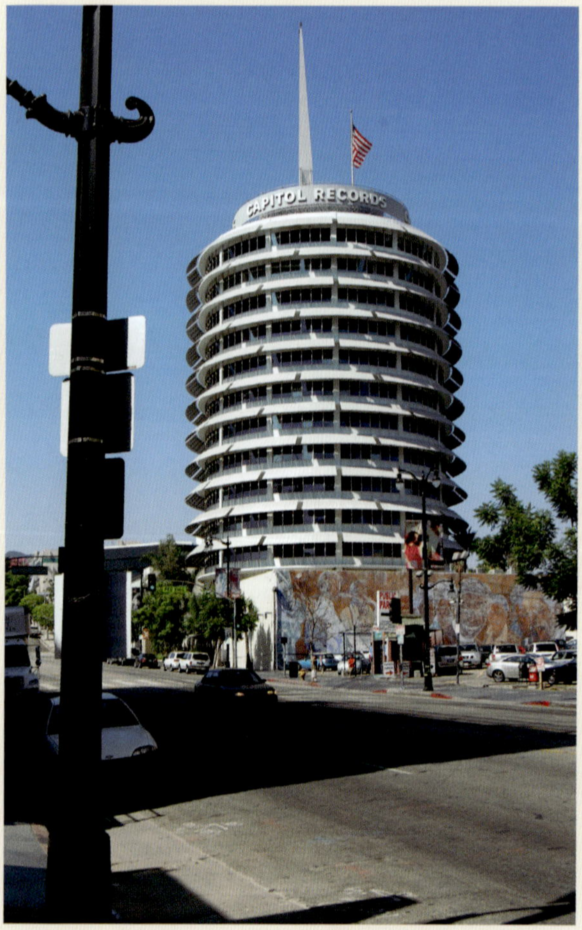

Capitol Records Tower remains standing at 1750 Vine Street.

The Capitol Records Tower has stood tall
on Vine Street since 1956.

THEN

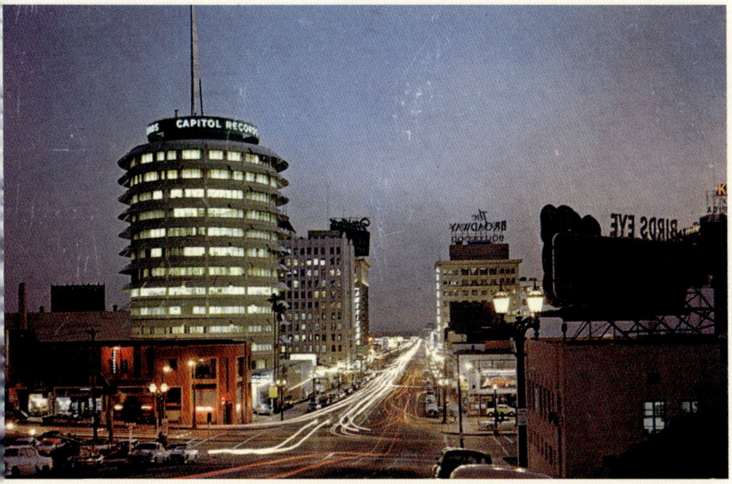

Vine Street.

NOW

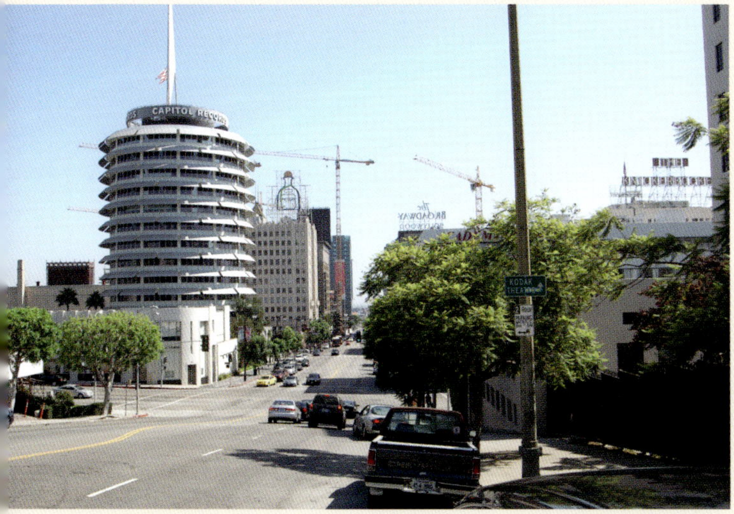

Looking south on Vine Street before it meets Yucca Street; the Capitol Records Tower, designed by Welton Becket, looms on the left.

THEN

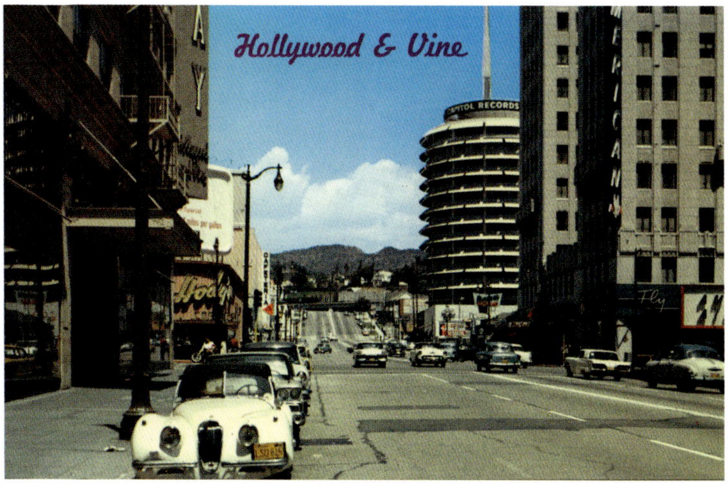

Hollywood & Vine.

NOW

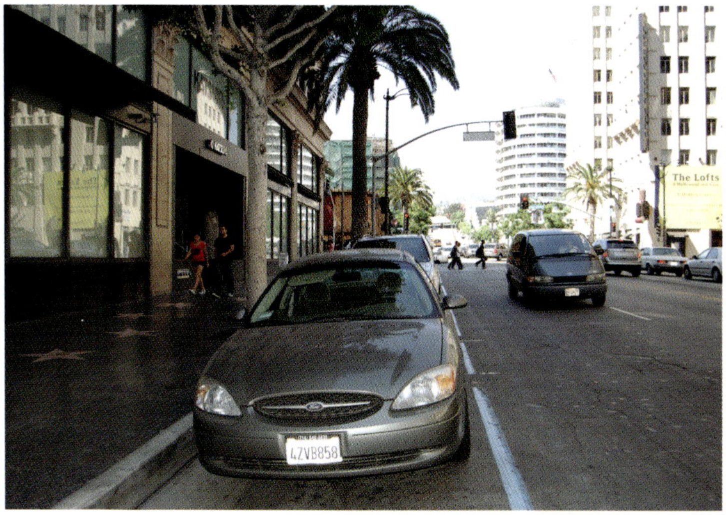

Hollywood & Vine, Hollywood's crown jewel intersection.

THEN

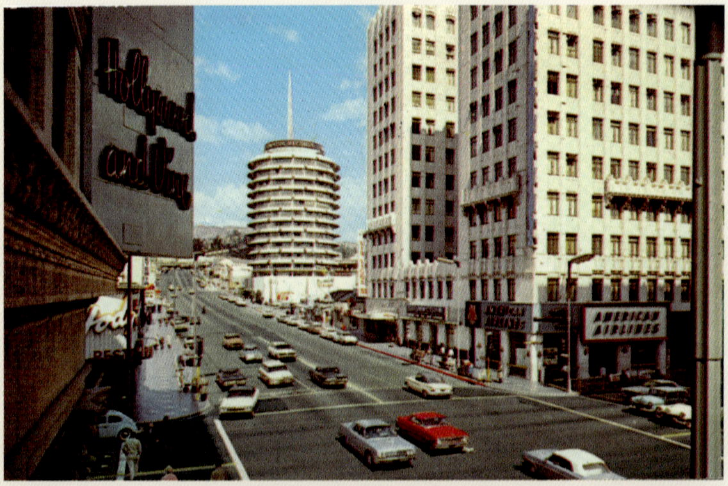

Hollywood & Vine.

NOW

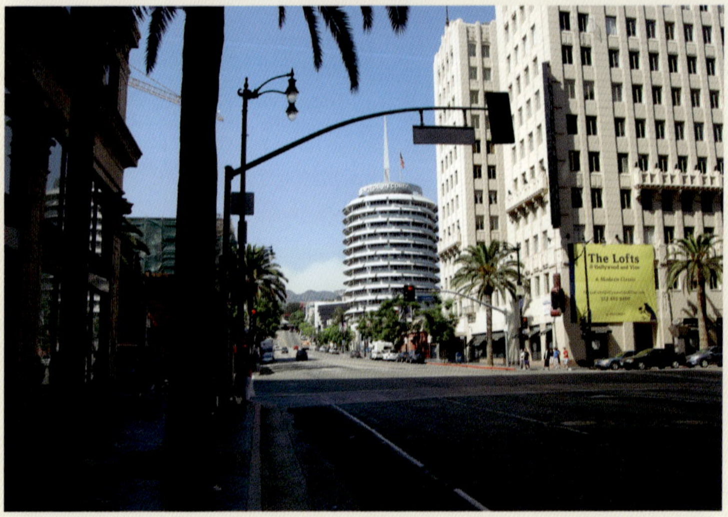

Hollywood & Vine, looking north on Vine Street before it intersects with Hollywood Boulevard.

Some historians trace the world-renowned recognition of the Hollywood and Vine intersection to the 1920s, when many media production companies were located around it.

THEN

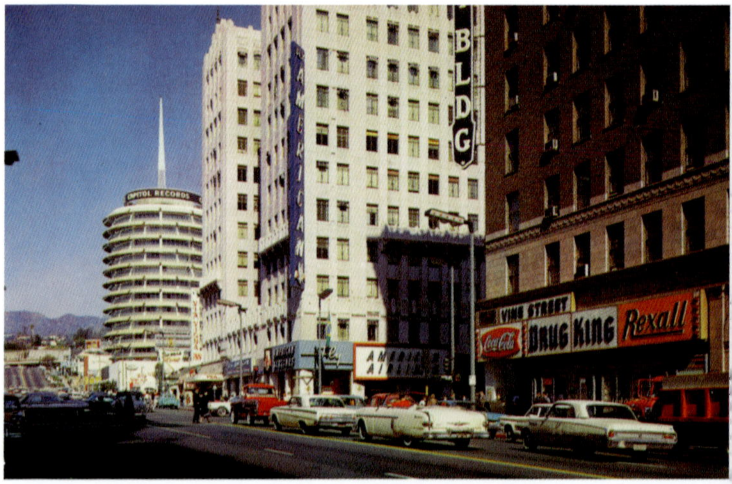

Hollywood & Vine.

NOW

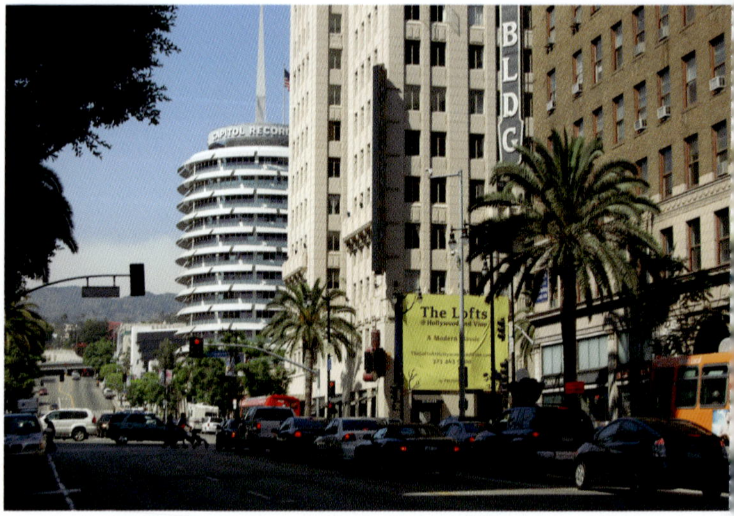

Hollywood & Vine, looking north on Vine Street, a short distance from where it meets Hollywood Boulevard.

In the 1930s, the Hollywood and Vine intersection hit its stride. This was when radio stations began bragging to their listeners that they were broadcasting, or were brought to you, "from Hollywood and Vine."

THEN

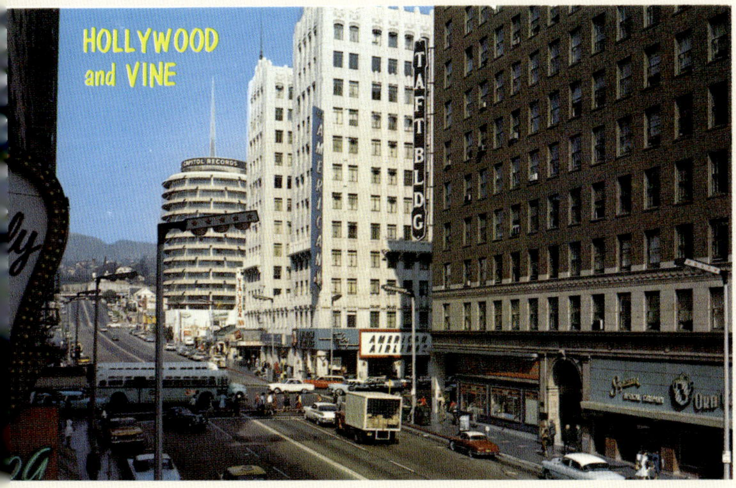

Hollywood & Vine.

NOW

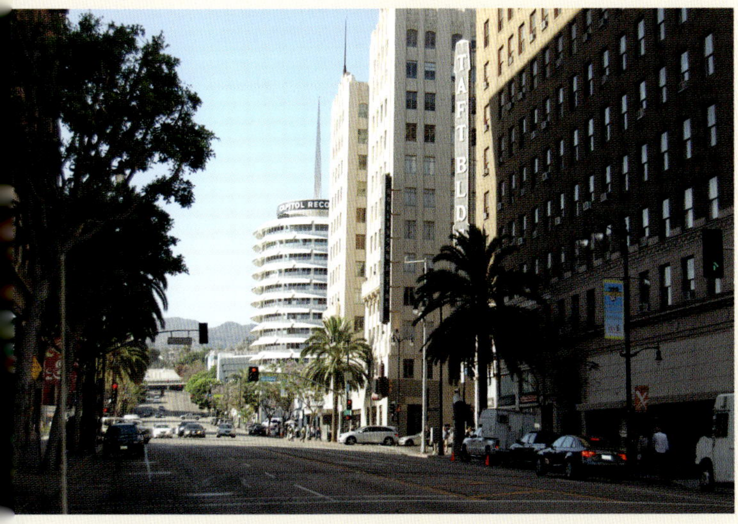

Hollywood & Vine, looking north on Vine Street, a quarter-block short of where it meets Hollywood Boulevard. The buildings on the right that dominate in the postcard view remain.

The Hollywood Memorial Church once stood on the southeast corner of Hollywood and Vine. Today, the Taft Building stands on the corner (building on right in the "then" and "now" views).

THEN

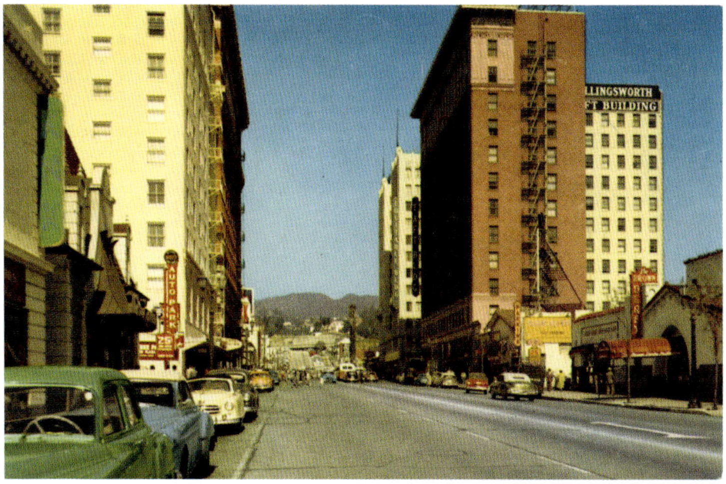

Vine Street, south of Hollywood Boulevard.

NOW

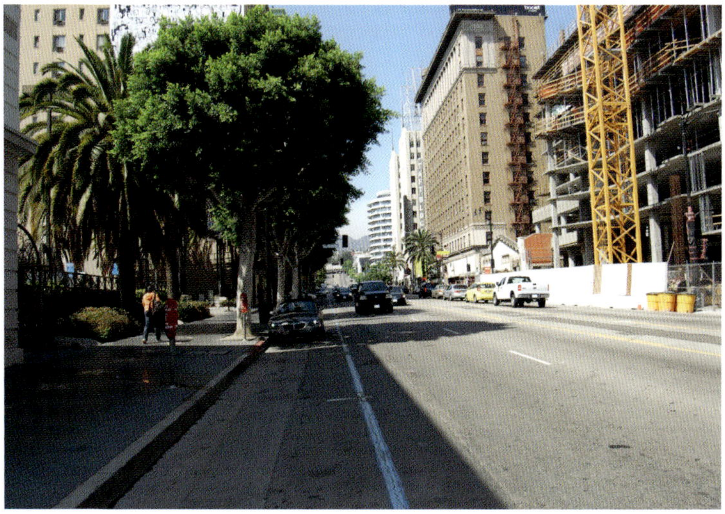

Vine Street south of Hollywood Boulevard, looking north on Vine, a half-block from where it meets Hollywood Boulevard. The Brown Derby Restaurant, on the immediate right in the postcard view, has been demolished, save for a small portion.

The Taft Building (first tall building on right in postcard view) is a twelve-story landmark of Hollywood. Built in the 1920s, it has survived the Hollywood changes over the years. At the time this photo was taken, there were plans underway for a restoration of the building.

THEN

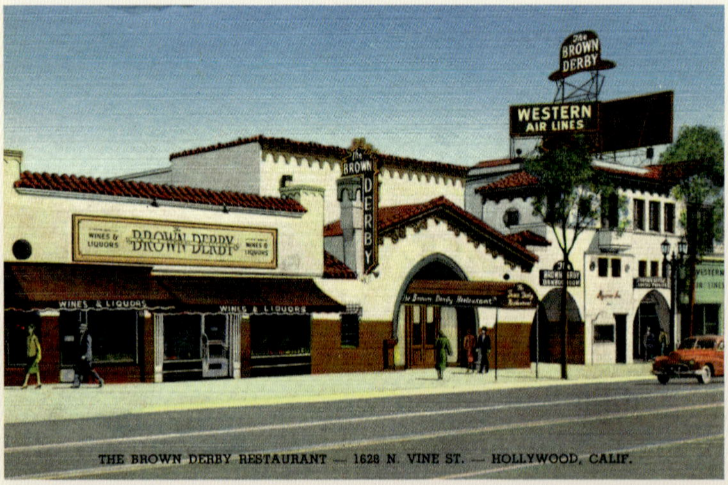

THEN

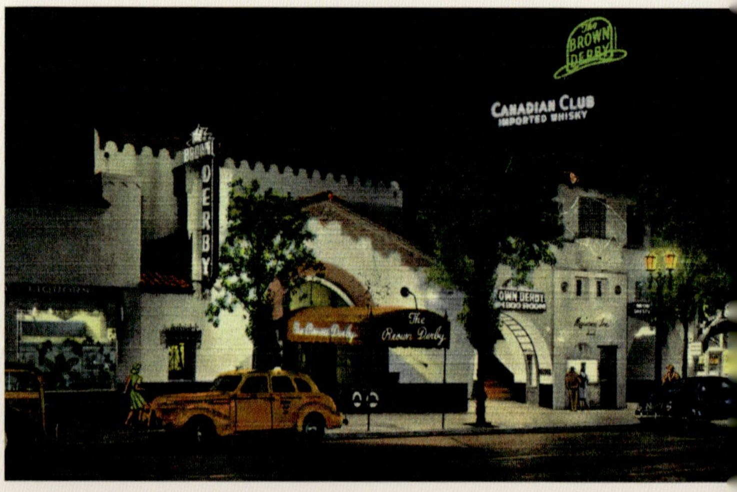

The Hollywood Brown Derby Restaurant opened on Vine Street in 1929.

NOW

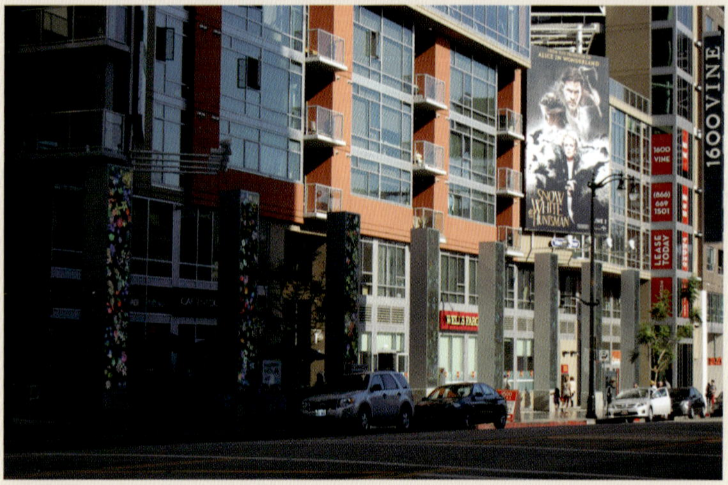

The Hollywood Brown Derby Restaurant was located at 1628 Vine Street.
It no longer stands, save for a small building on its north end.

THEN

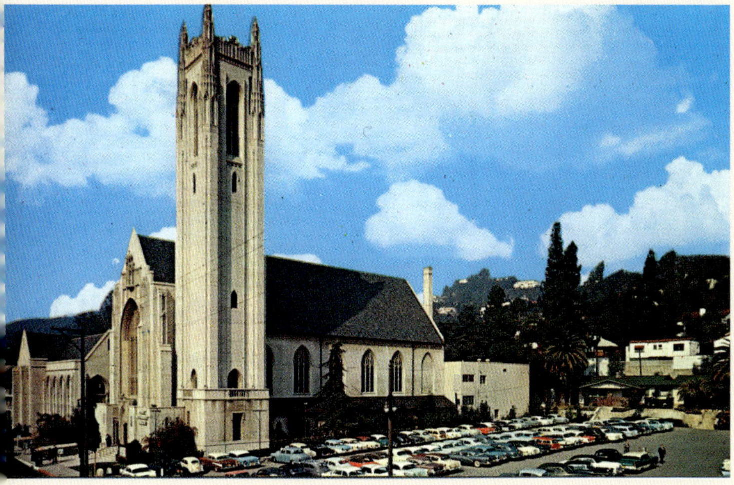

Hollywood First Methodist Church.

NOW

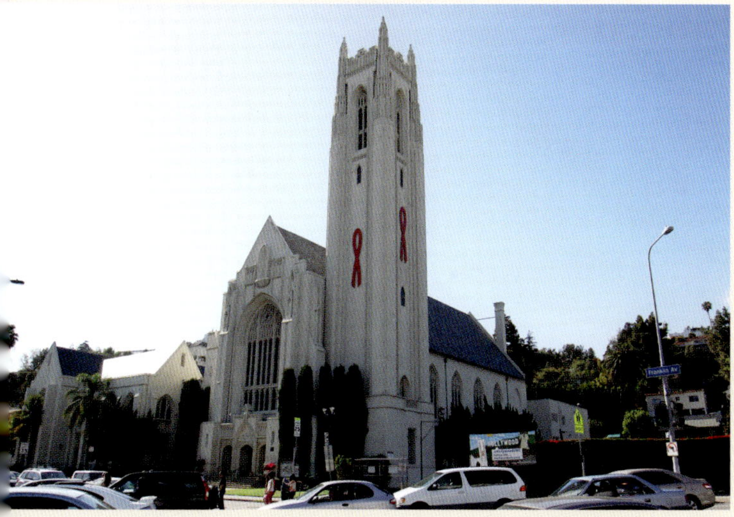

The Hollywood First Methodist Church building remains standing at 6817 Franklin Avenue and is still a Methodist church.

Construction began in 1927 on the Hollywood United Methodist Church (formerly Hollywood First Methodist Church). It was 1931 when the church was completed.

THEN

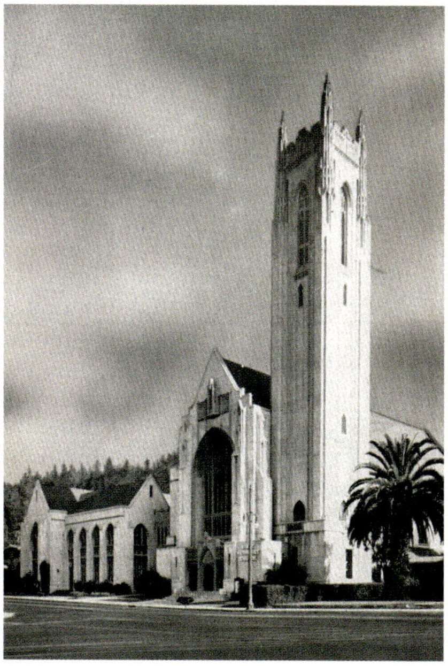

Hollywood First Methodist Church.

NOW

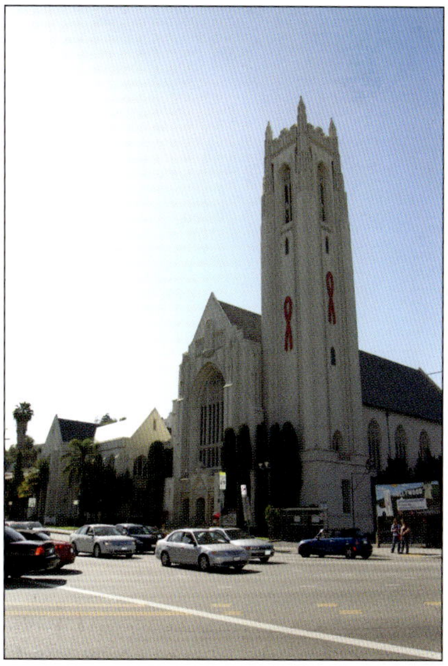

The Hollywood First Methodist Church building at the northwest corner of Franklin and Highland avenues.

The Hollywood United Methodist Church (formerly Hollywood First Methodist Church) was declared a Historical-Cultural Monument (#248) in 1981 by the City of Los Angeles.

THEN

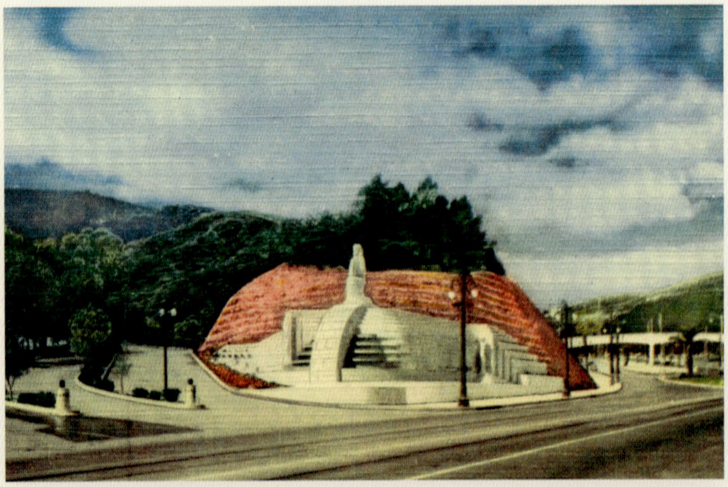

Hollywood Bowl entrance and Cahuenga Pass Freeway.

NOW

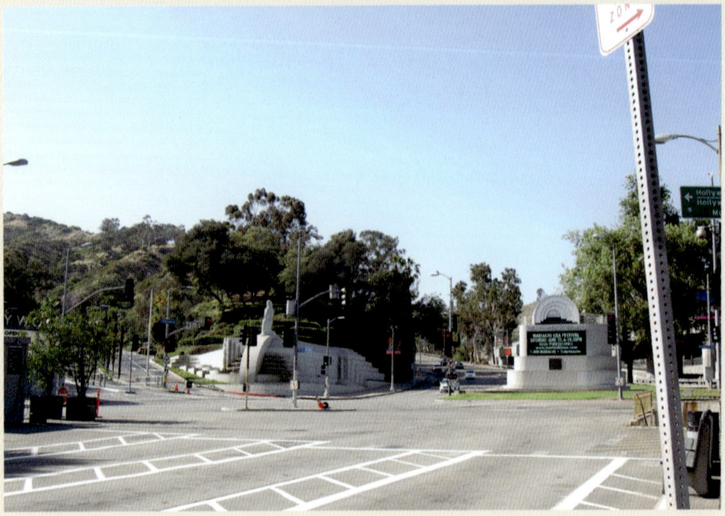

Hollywood Bowl entrance and Cahuenga Pass remain in close proximity to each other. The entrance to the Hollywood Bowl is located at 2301 North Highland Avenue.

The Cahuenga Pass cuts through the Santa Monica Mountains and acts as a connector for Hollywood and the San Fernando Valley. Entertainment has been heard coming out of the Hollywood Bowl amphitheater for many decades. In 1927, the venue received its first shell, covering its stage.

THEN

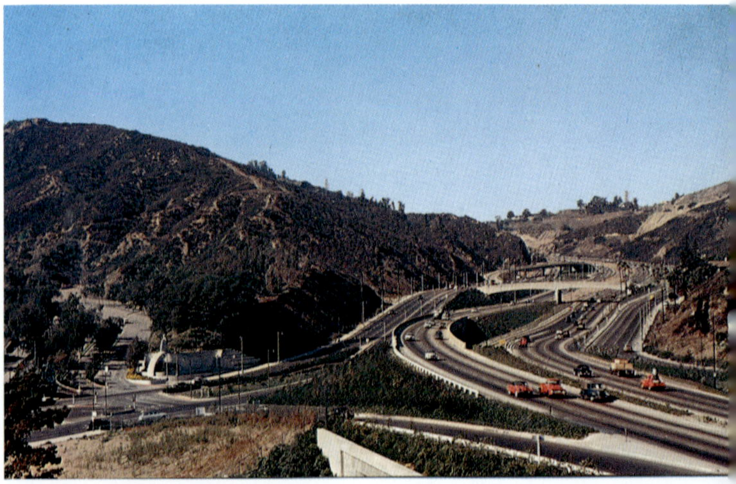

Hollywood Freeway links the Civic Center with Hollywood and the San Fernando Valley; showing an entrance to the Hollywood Bowl.

NOW

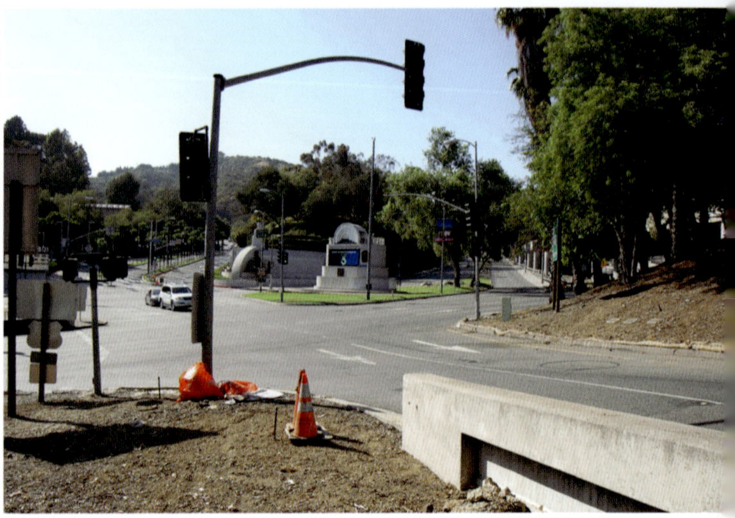

Hollywood Freeway continues to link the Civic Center with Hollywood and the San Fernando Valley. The entrance to the Hollywood Bowl is on the left. An on-ramp to the southbound Hollywood Freeway is on the immediate right.

The Streamline Moderne-style fountain (lower left in "then" view, center in "now" view) that greets visitors to the Hollywood Bowl was built in 1940.

THEN

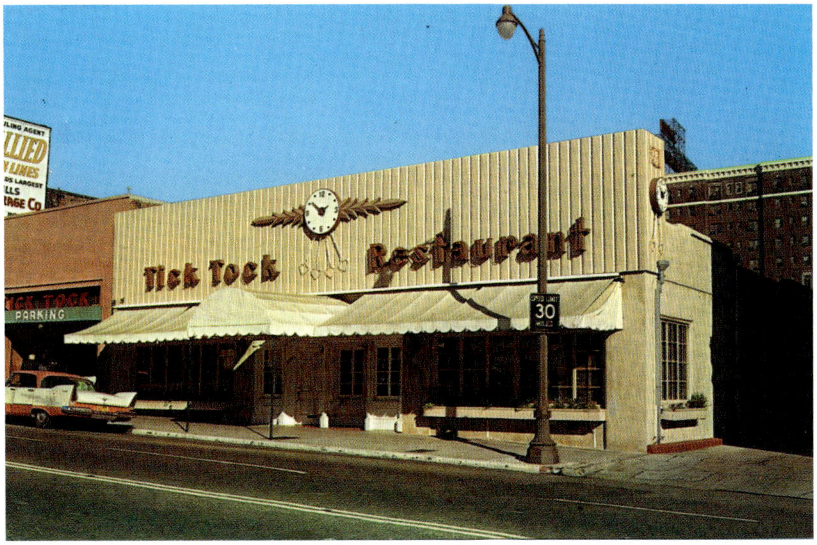

The Tick Tock Restaurant.

NOW

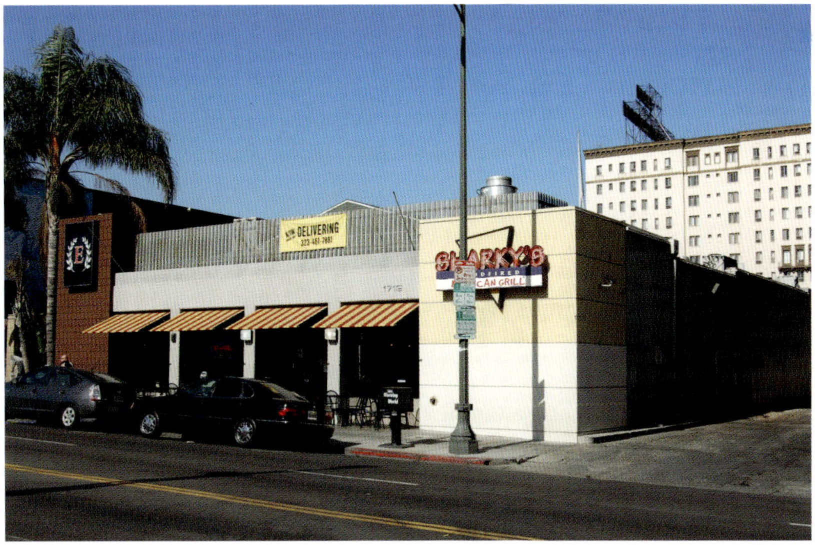

The Tick Tock Restaurant was located at 1716 North Cahuenga Avenue. The building remains, but the establishment has closed.

When the Tick Tock Restaurant was in operation, it boasted of having an antique clock collection on the premises.

THEN

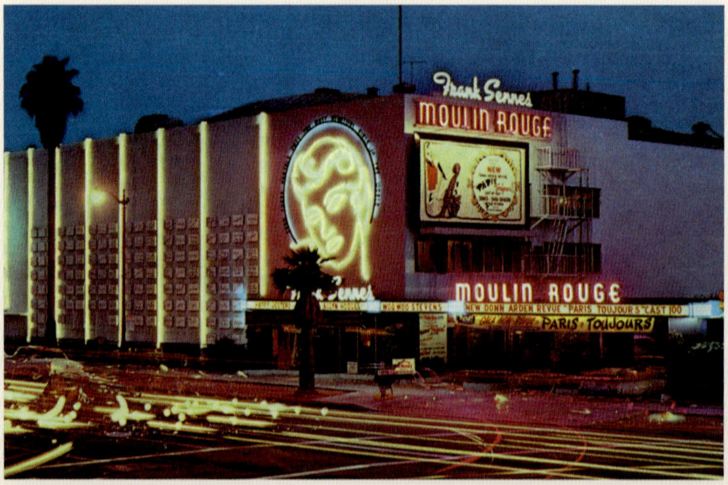

Moulin Rouge Theatre-Restaurant.

THEN

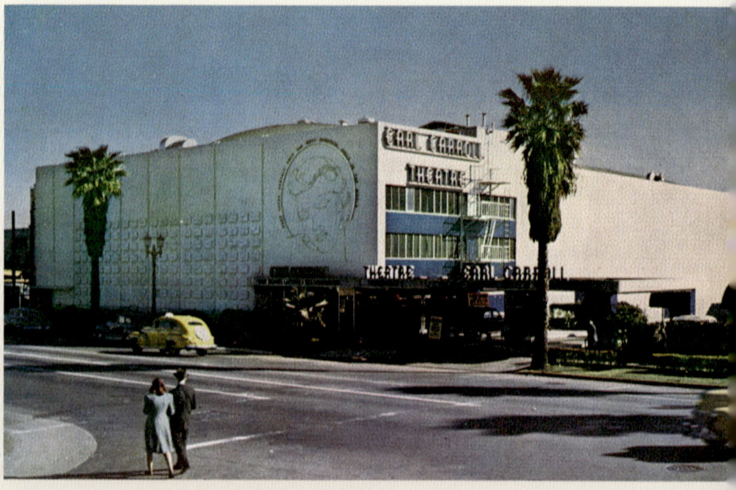

Moulin Rouge Theatre-Restaurant.

NOW

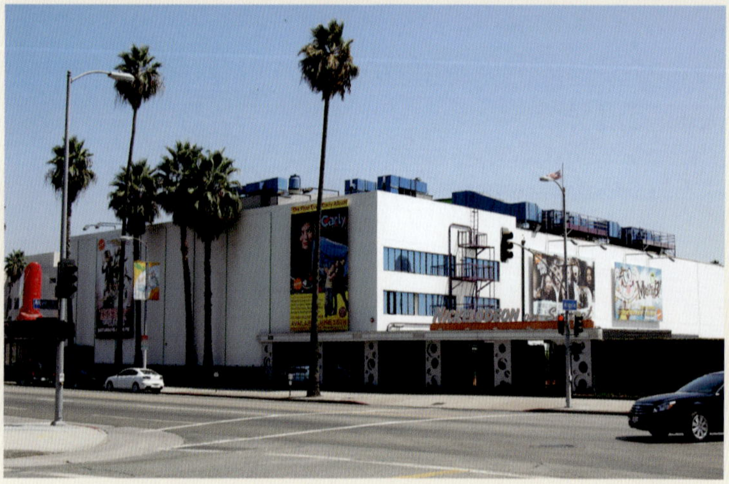

The Earl Carroll Theatre-Restaurant was located at 6230 Sunset Boulevard. It became the Moulin Rouge Theatre-Restaurant, but this too closed its doors. The building still stands.

The Earl Carroll Theatre-Restaurant opened in 1938. The building was famous for its outside "Wall of Fame." The "Wall" featured the self-inscribed names of many actors and actresses, including Joan Bennett and Don Ameche. The building would later become the Moulin Rouge Theatre-Restaurant. Still later, it would become the entertainment venue called Kaleidoscope.

THEN

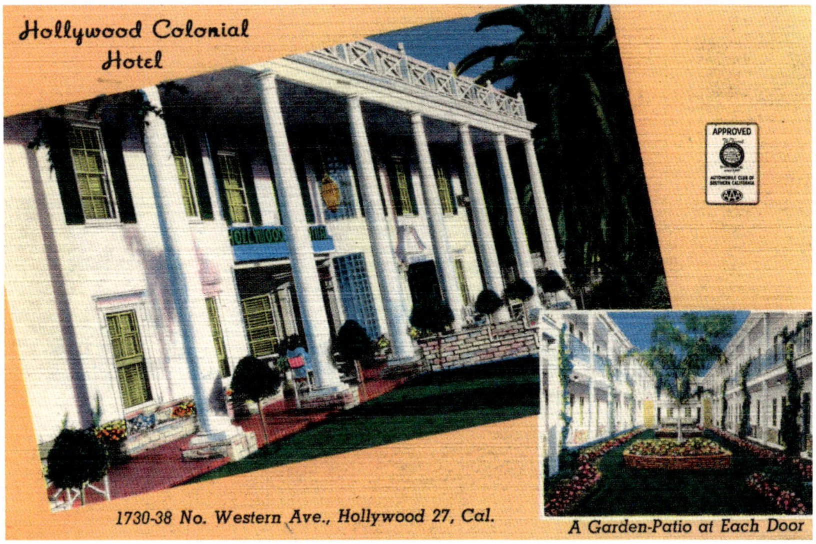

Hollywood Colonial Hotel.

NOW

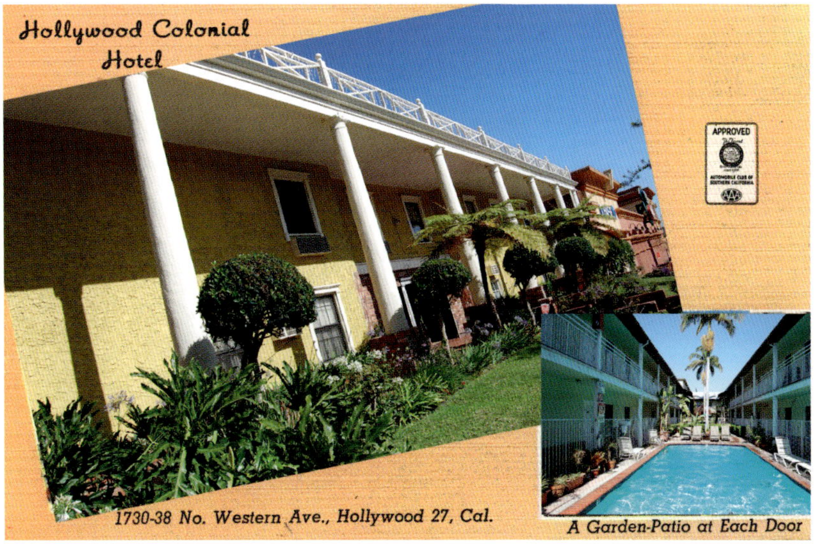

Hollywood Colonial Hotel was located at 1730 North Western Avenue. The building remains as a hotel, but now operates under a different name. Today, a pool has partially replaced a garden patio. (Note: Postcard views are recreated by the author, not the hotel.)

THEN

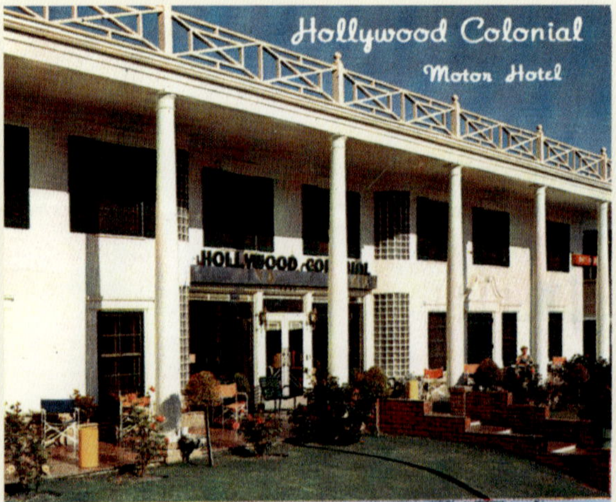

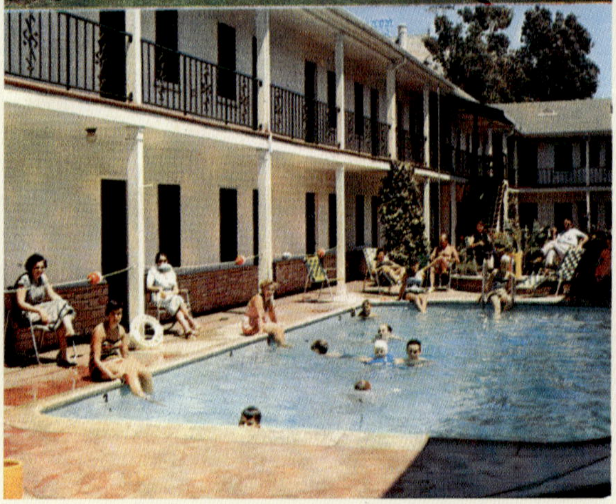

Hollywood Colonial Motor Hotel. (Note: This is same property as the Hollywood Colonial Hotel postcard.)

NOW

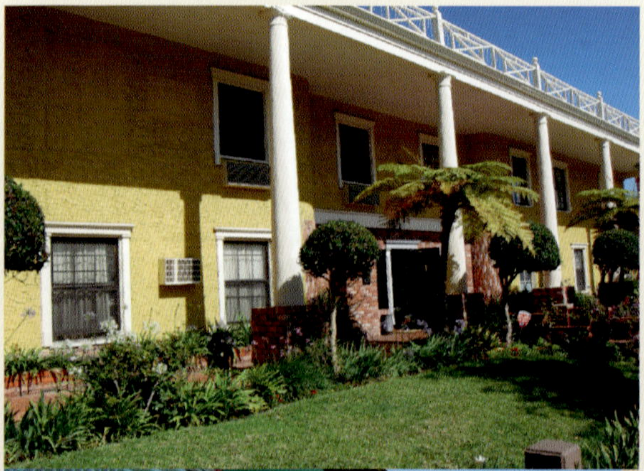

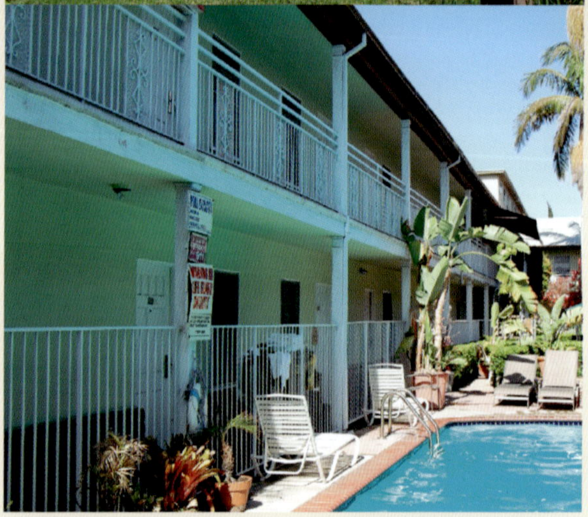

The Hollywood Colonial Motor Hotel exterior and inner pool areas remain relatively unchanged today in terms of physical structure. However, the property is now a hotel of another name. (Note: The postcard views are recreated by the author, not by the hotel.)

The back of the Hollywood Colonial Motor Hotel postcard advertises the property as "A Garden Spot in Hollywood."

THEN

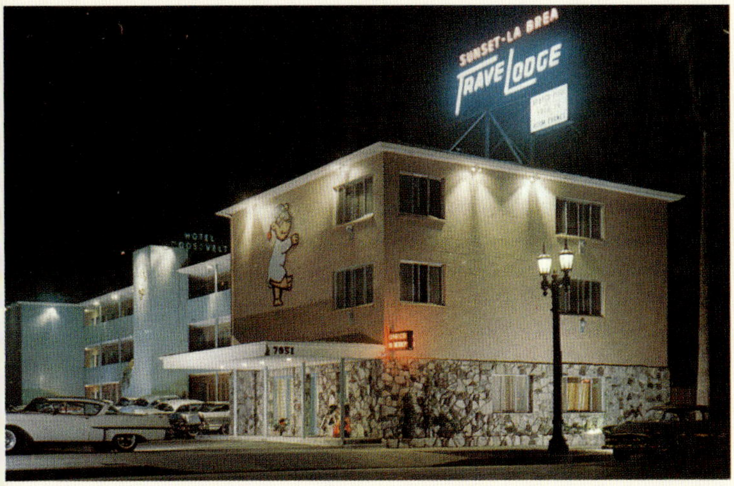

Sunset-La Brea Travelodge.

NOW

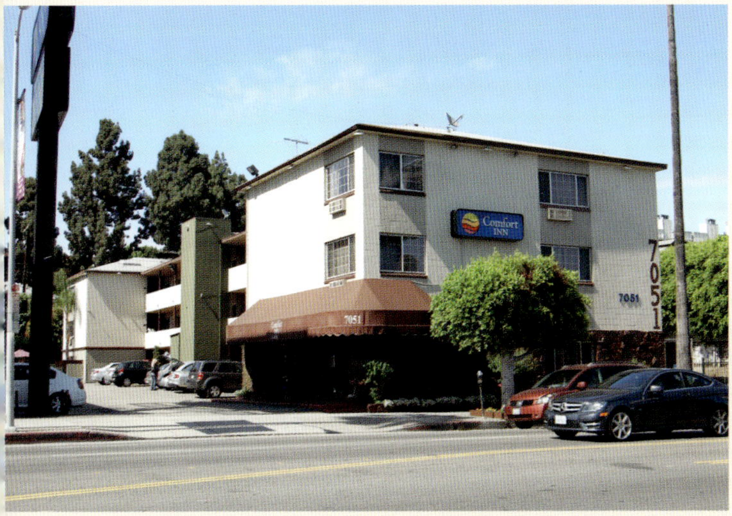

The Sunset-La Brea Travelodge was located at 7051 Sunset Boulevard. The building remains a hotel, but carries a different name.

When it was taken, the postcard photograph of the Sunset-La Brea Travelodge was meant as an advertising vehicle. With the passing of decades, the postcard view has morphed into a memory-invoking piece. The streetlamps and automobiles recall a bygone era.

THEN

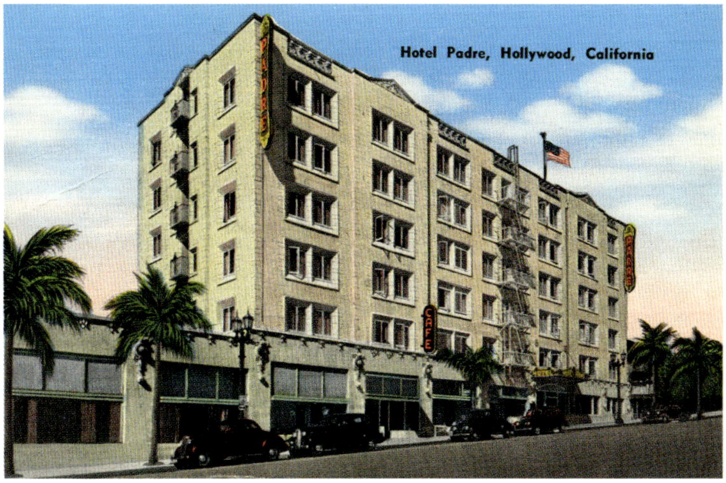

Hotel Padre.

NOW

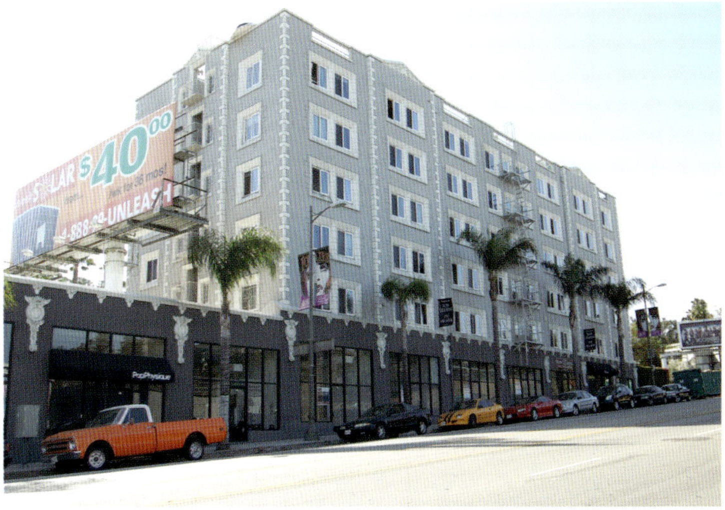

Hotel Padre was located at 1963 North Cahuenga Boulevard. The building stands, but it is no longer a hotel.

Located just south of the Hollywood (101) Freeway, per the back of the postcard, the property is near "Hollywood shops, theatres, Motion Picture Studios, and the Hollywood Bowl."

THEN

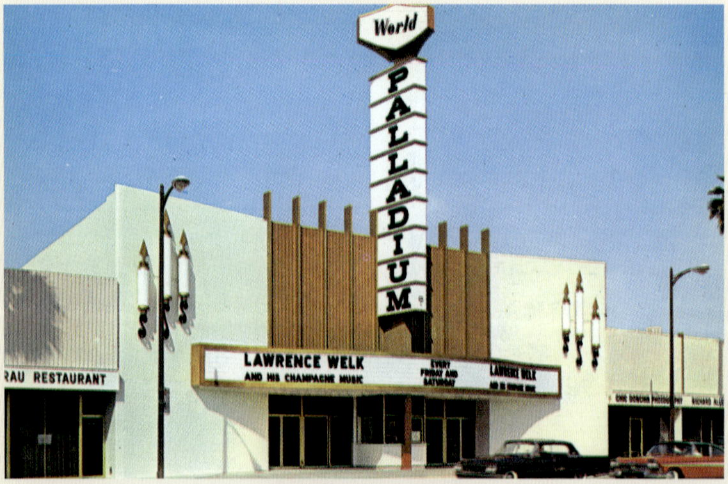

World Palladium.

NOW

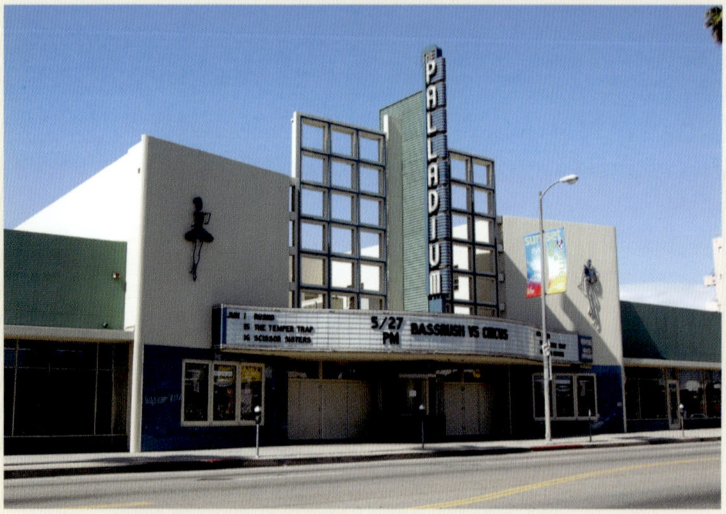

World Palladium was located at 6215 Sunset Boulevard. The Palladium, aka Hollywood Palladium, remains an entertainment venue, though its name has changed throughout its history.

The Palladium opened in 1940 and, as the marquee shown in the "then" view attests to, Lawrence Welk and his Champagne Music were heard here. In 1961, Welk began taping his popular television show (*The Lawrence Welk Show*) here. Other performers have also played music, though of a different era, at the Palladium, including Bob Dylan and Prince.

THEN

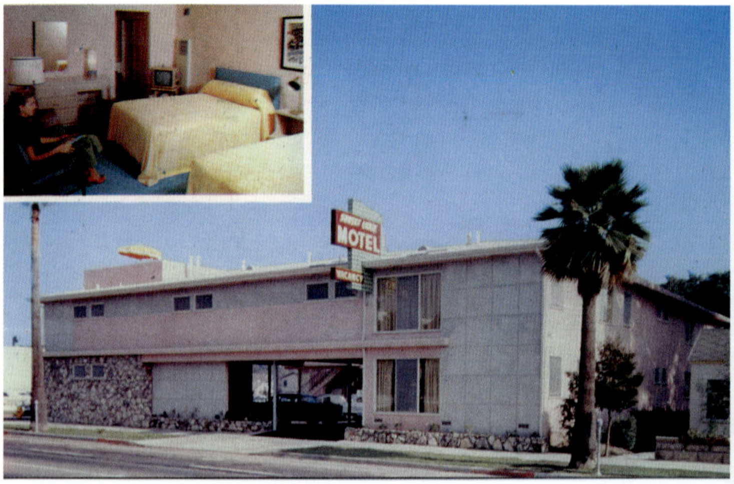

Sunset-Lodge Motel.

NOW

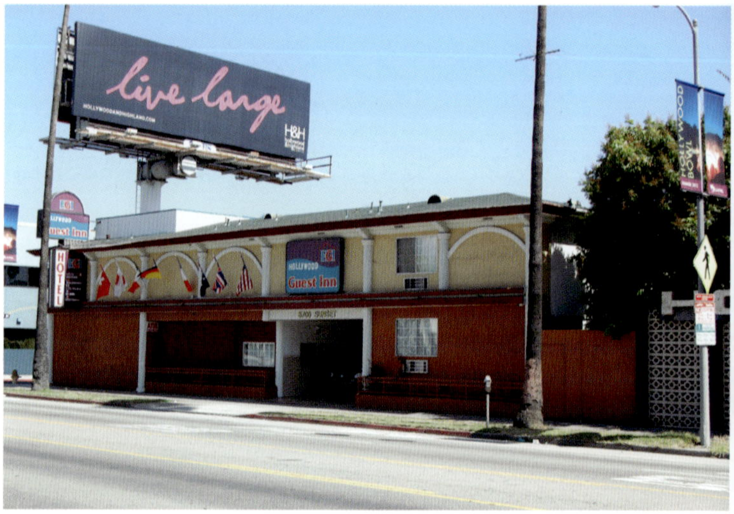

The Sunset-Lodge Motel was located at 6700 Sunset Boulevard. The building remains a hotel, but operates under a different name.

The two palm trees fronting the Sunset-Lodge Motel in the "then" view have grown in size as the "now" photograph shows. The television screens that can be found in the rooms of the hotel property there today have probably also grown in size since the postcard was published.

THEN

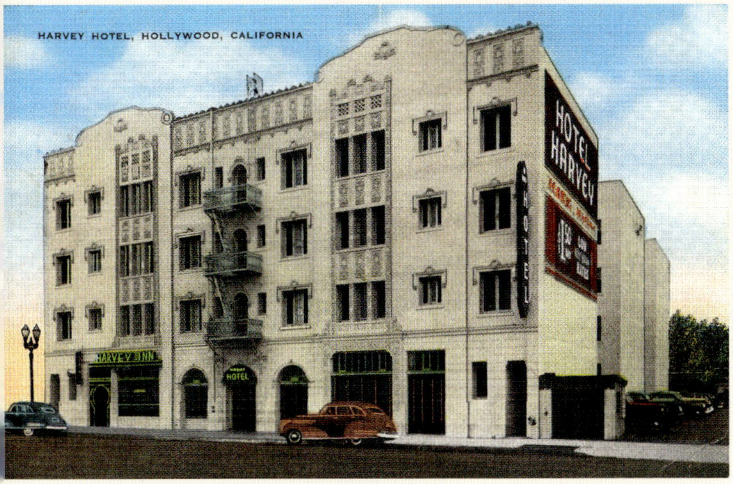

Harvey Hotel.

THEN

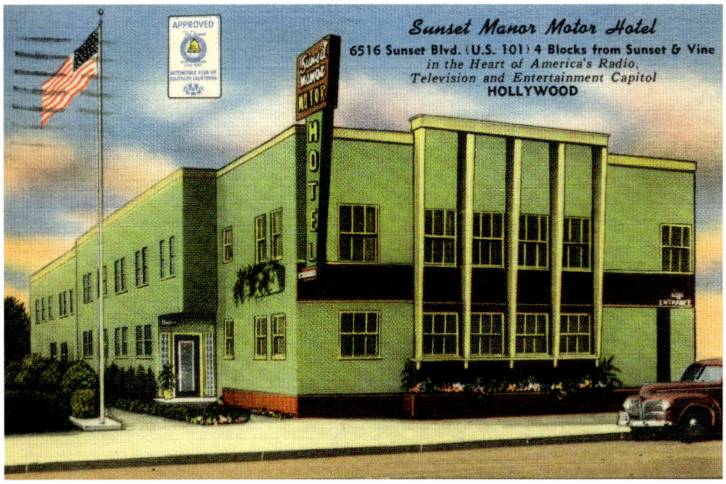

Sunset Manor Motor Hotel.

NOW

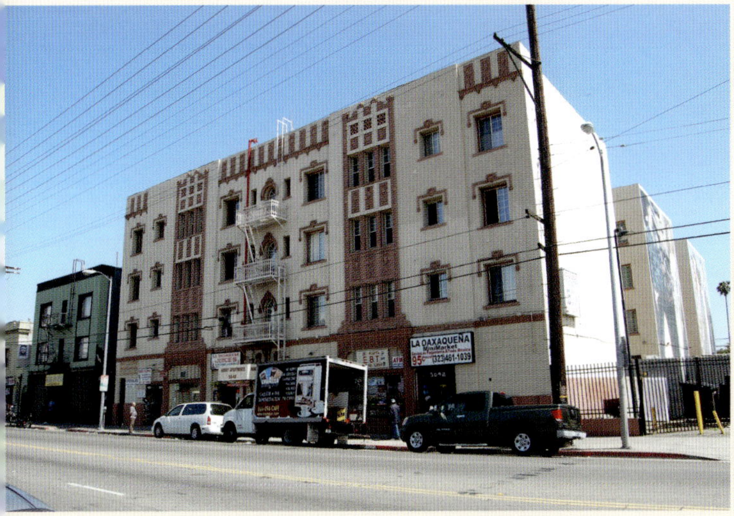

The Harvey Hotel was located at 5640 Santa Monica Boulevard. While the building remains, it is no longer a hotel.

NOW

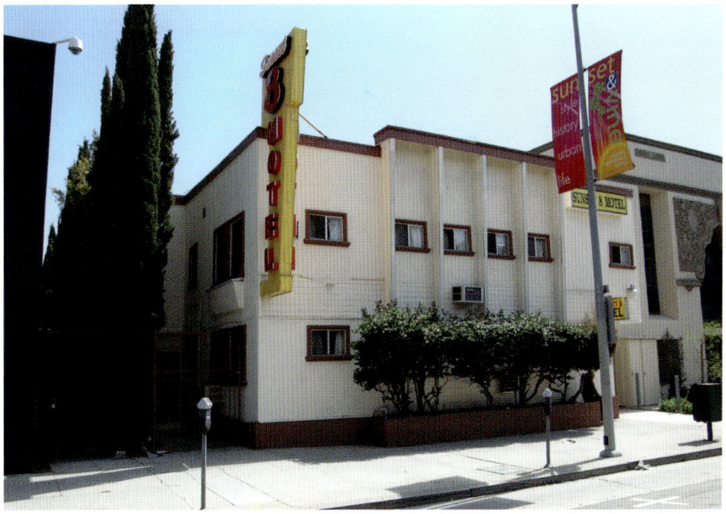

Sunset Manor Motor Hotel was located at 6516 Sunset Boulevard. Though the structure still stands, it houses a hotel of another name.

When it was a hotel property, it advertised having "200 rooms, 200 baths." The building dates back to the 1920s.

The back of the Sunset Manor Motor Hotel postcard advertises "26 new, deluxe, fully carpeted units." It also states that the hotel's offerings include electric heat, radios, and television.

THEN

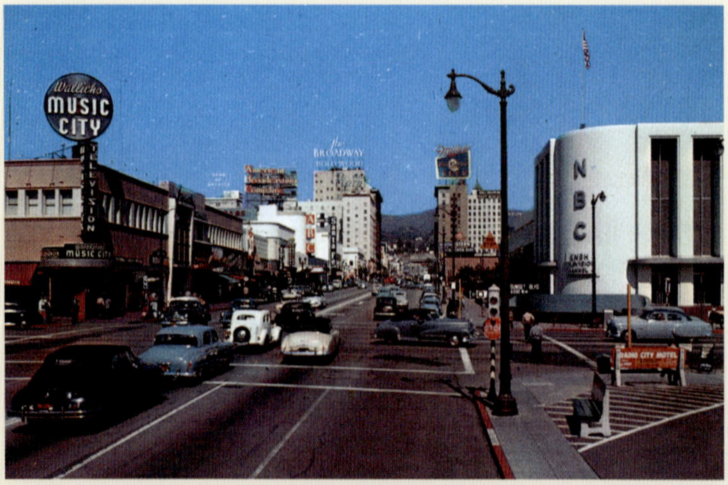

Sunset and Vine.

NOW

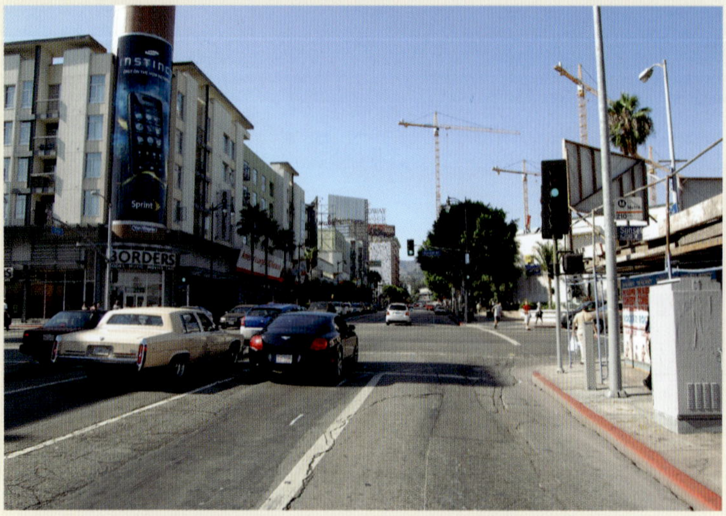

Sunset and Vine. Looking north on Vine Street just before it meets Sunset Boulevard, this intersection has seen some building changes.

The "then" and "now" views of the intersection of Sunset and Vine features some retail relics. The Wallach's Music City, shown in the postcard "then" view (left), is no more. Where the music store once stood, a Borders bookstore was located there, as seen in the "now" view of 2008. Borders has since gone out of business.

THEN

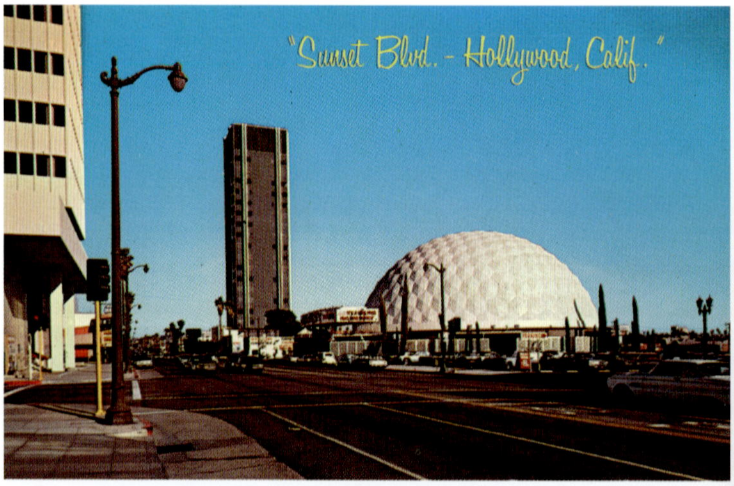

Sunset Boulevard.

NOW

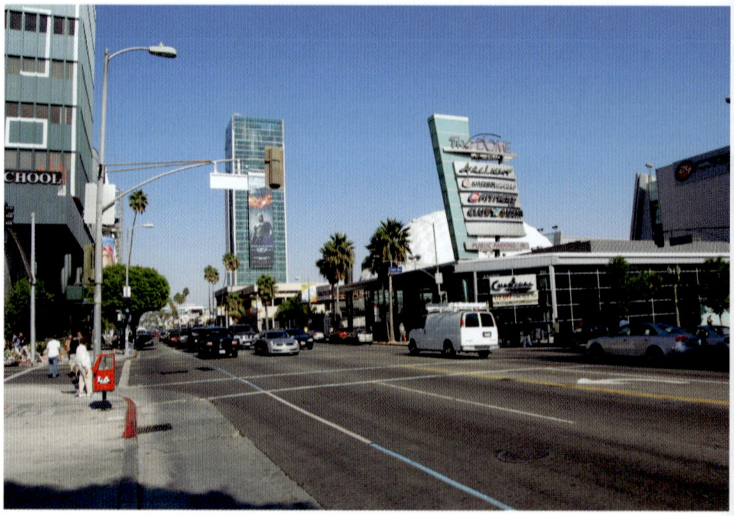

Sunset Boulevard, looking east just before it meets Ivar Avenue. The Arclight Cinerama Dome is showing on the right side, at 6360 Sunset Boulevard.

Sunset Boulevard is over twenty-two miles long, ending on its western-most end at the sands of the beach in Pacific Palisades.

CHAPTER 6

MARINA DEL REY

THEN

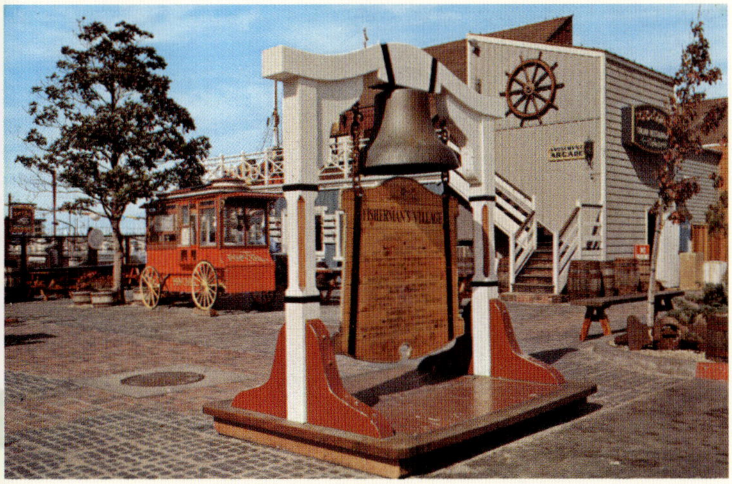

Fisherman's Village, Marina del Rey.

NOW

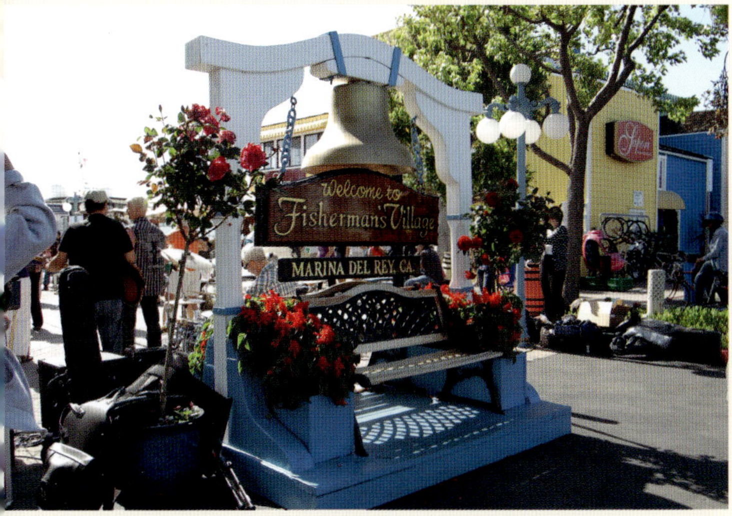

Fisherman's Village in Marina del Rey still has a bronze bell at its entrance. The yellow restaurant building that sits to the bell's right is located at 13723 Fiji Way.

Fisherman's Village was built to emulate a New England fishing village. The area has quaint buildings dominant with yellow, blue, and red colors. The village restaurants line the blue waters of the village's adjacent marina.

THEN

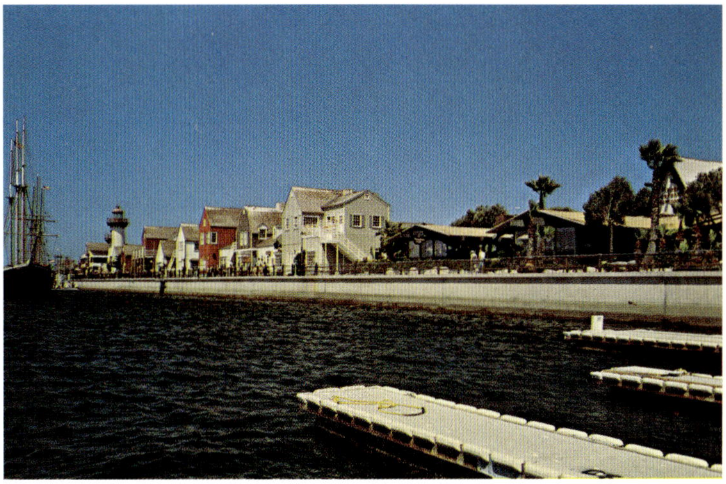

Fisherman's Village, Marina del Rey.

NOW

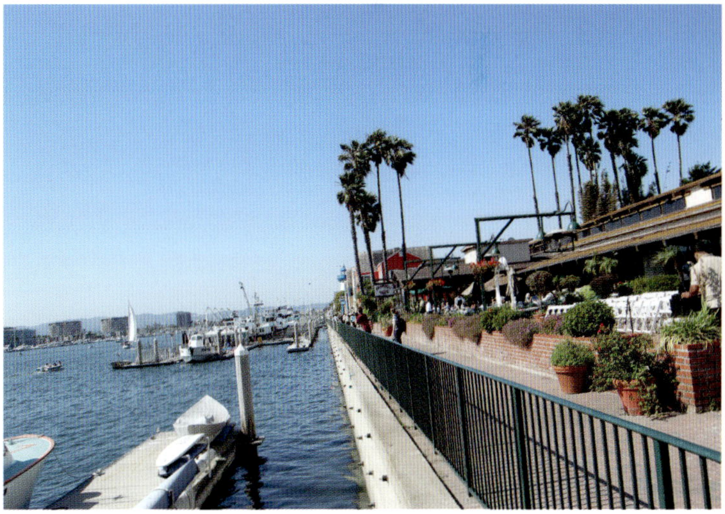

Fisherman's Village in Marina del Rey. The restaurant to the immediate right is at 13813 Fiji Way. (Note: View is from sidewalk along the water. The postcard view is from out on a dock area not accessible.)

Marina del Rey offers a multitude of waterside walkways, boat-watching, and the ever-present, dock-hogging seagulls.

THEN

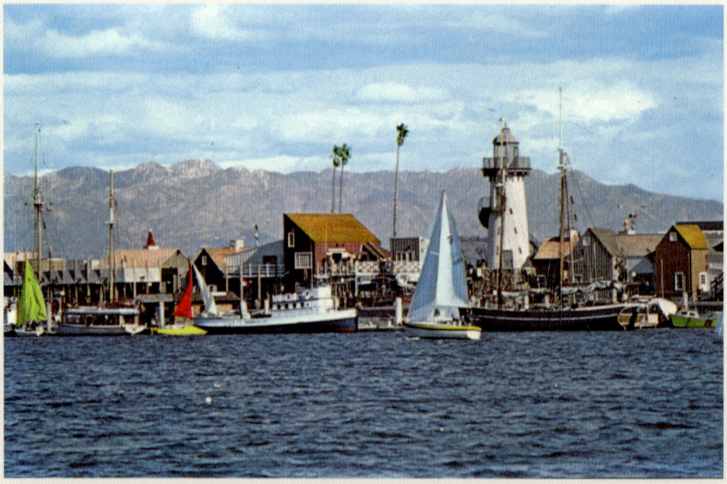

Fisherman's Village in Marina del Rey.

NOW

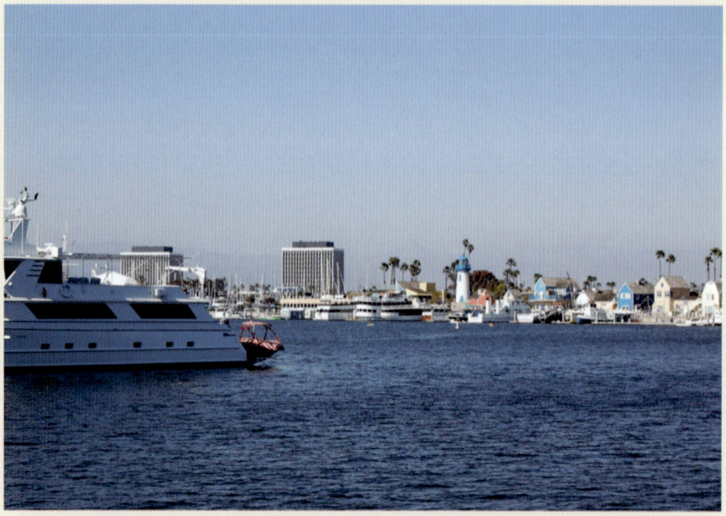

Fisherman's Village in Marina del Rey. The lighthouse (center of view here, blue and white) remains at guard over the village. It stands close in proximity to the bronze bell that welcomes visitors to the village. (Note: View is from a point along the shoreline opposite Fisherman's Village. The "then" view is much closer to the village, probably taken from a boat or with a camera utilizing a more powerful zoom lens.)

The boats may have changed, but the strip of buildings that make up Fisherman's Village have not changed much in recent decades. The marina itself opened in the 1960s.

THEN

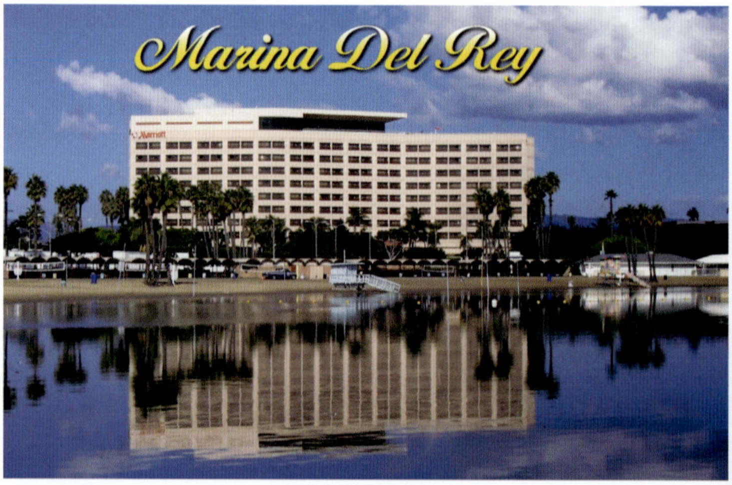

Marina del Rey.

NOW

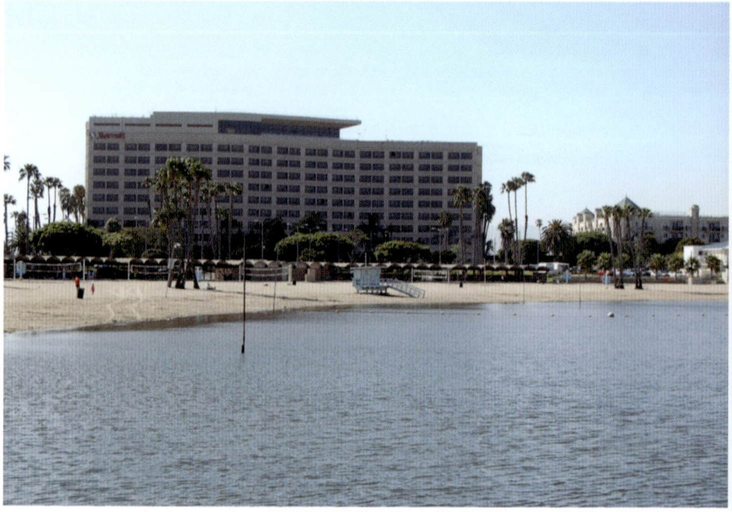

Marina del Rey. A hotel at 4100 Admiralty Way remains prominent here with the marina in the foreground.

In Marina del Rey, one is never far from the water, as both the "then" and "now" views show. The sandy beach in the "now" view is enclosed with a pedestrian sidewalk.

THEN

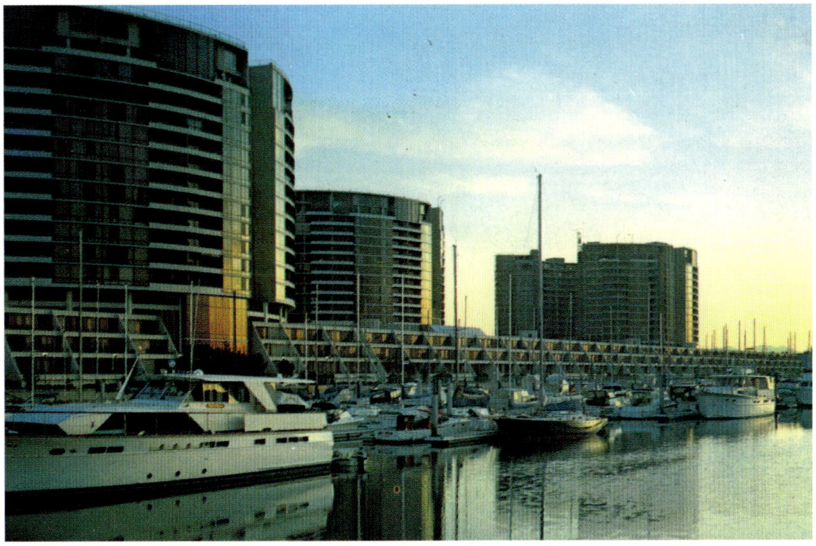

Marina del Rey.

NOW

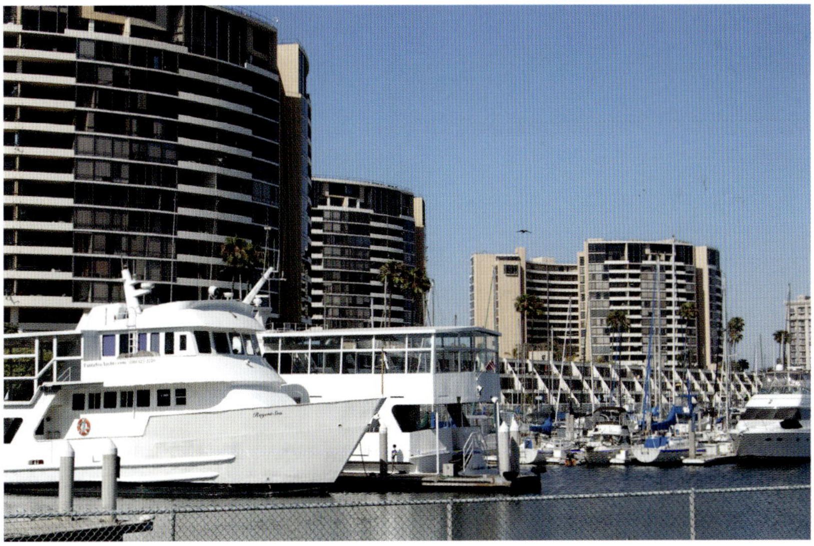

Marina del Rey. View is from a lot adjacent to Palawan Way. It is on the marina side, or south side, of where Palawan Way meets Admiralty Way.

Circular residential towers stand adjacent to yet another part of the extensive maze of water bodies that the Marina del Rey offers.

THEN

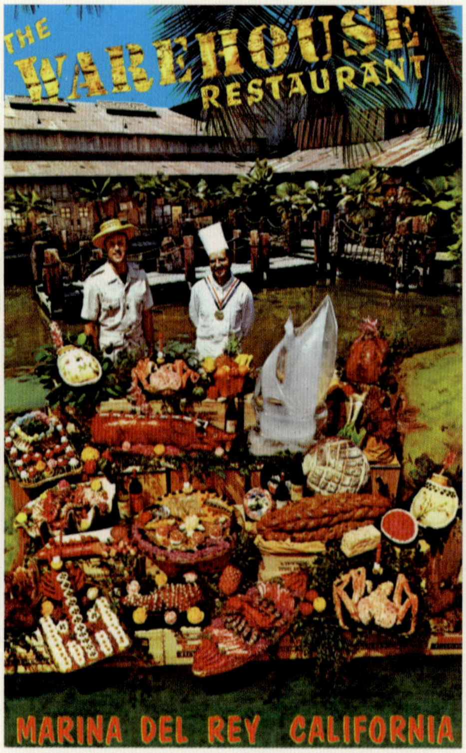

THEN

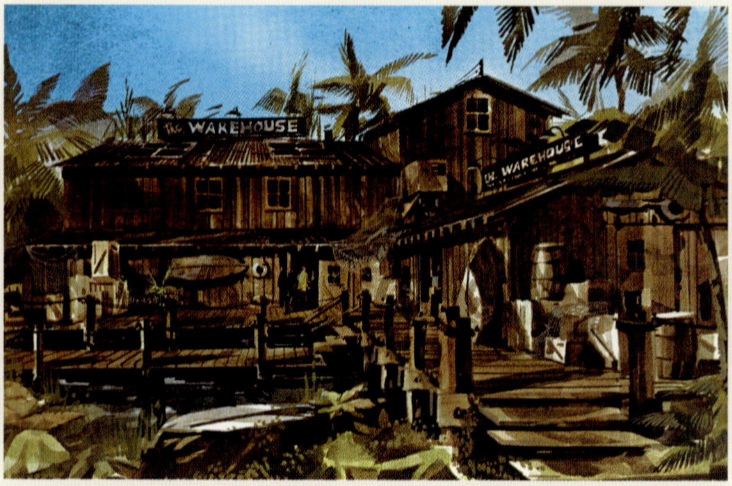

The Warehouse Restaurant.

NOW

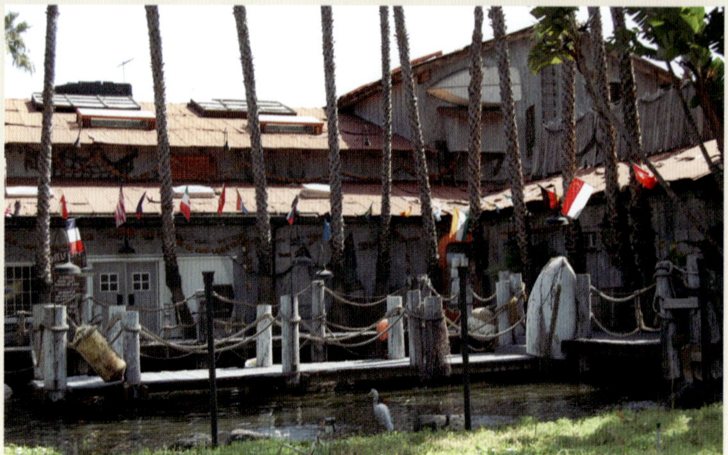

The Warehouse Restaurant is still open for business at 4499 Admiralty Way.

The South Seas atmosphere of the Warehouse Restaurant mixes well with the community life of Marina del Rey. The eating establishment has been here for over four decades.

CHAPTER 7
OCEAN PARK

THEN

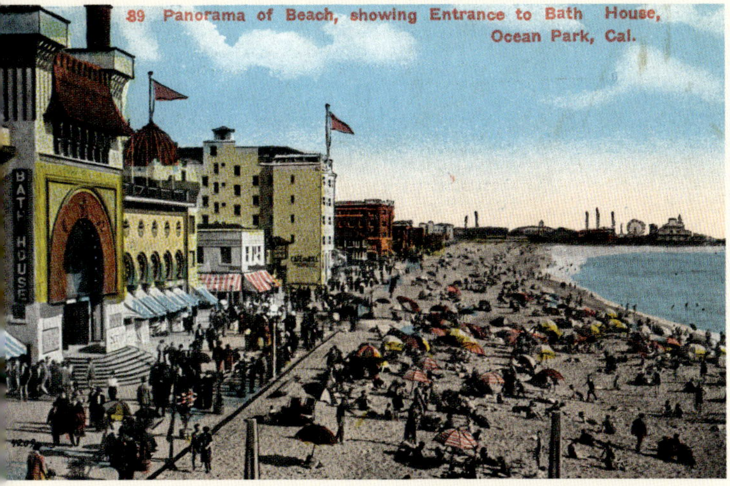

Panorama of beach, entrance to Bath House, Ocean Park.

THEN

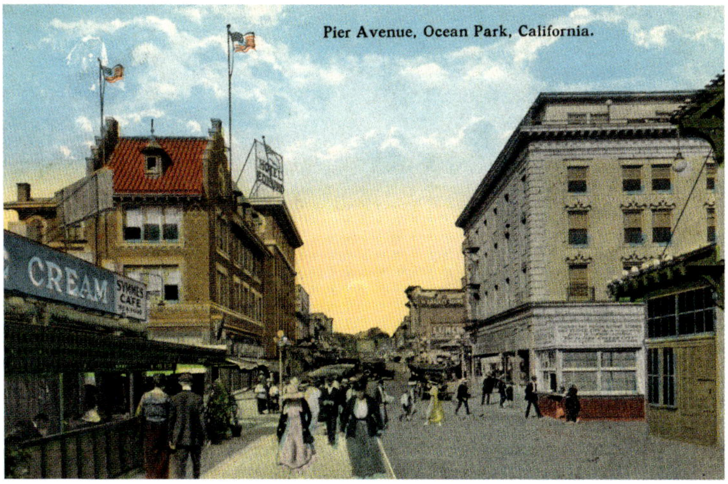

Pier Avenue, Ocean Park.

NOW

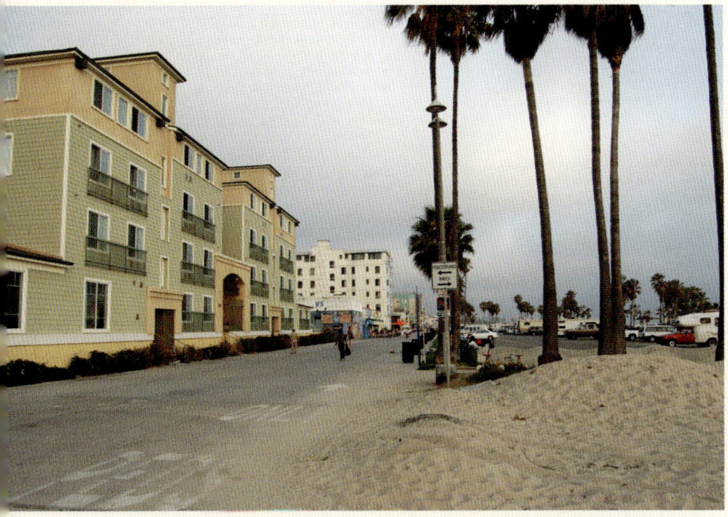

Panorama of beach in Ocean Park. The Bath House has been replaced by modern structures. The Ocean Park Association describes Ocean Park as having "a funky, artsy feel, similar in manner to its neighbor, Venice Beach." Abbot Kinney, the founder of Venice, first invested in OCean Park before he built his creations in Venice.

NOW

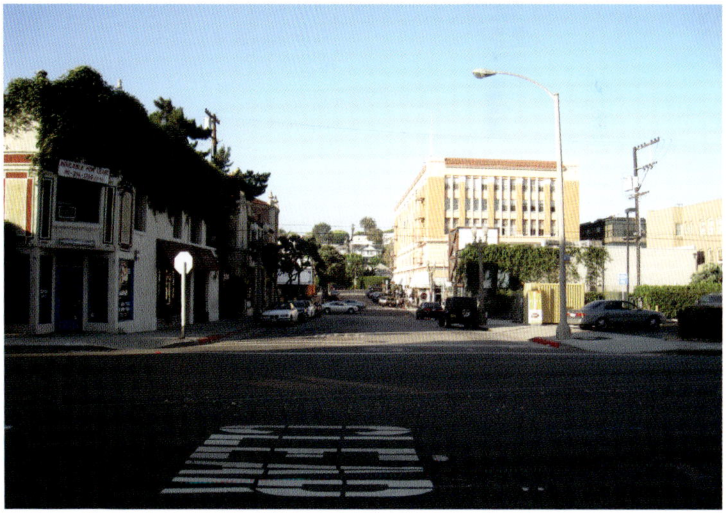

Pier Avenue, Ocean Park, looking east on Pier Avenue where it meets Neilson Way. (Note: The author does not make a claim to lining up the "then" and "now" views. There are too many unknowns to make a definitive conclusion. It is known that the prominent building on the right in the postcard view was at one time listed as being the Ocean Park Hotel at 110 Pier Avenue. If that address is placed on Pier Avenue today, the hotel would have stood close to the southeast corner of Pier Avenue and Neilson Way. The Hotel Edmund, with is signage on top of it, can be seen on the left side of the postcard view. This hotel was listed at 111 Pier Avenue in its time. If that address is placed on Pier Avenue today, it would not be far from the northeast corner of Pier Avenue and Neilson Way.)

CHAPTER 8

PACIFIC PALISADES

THEN

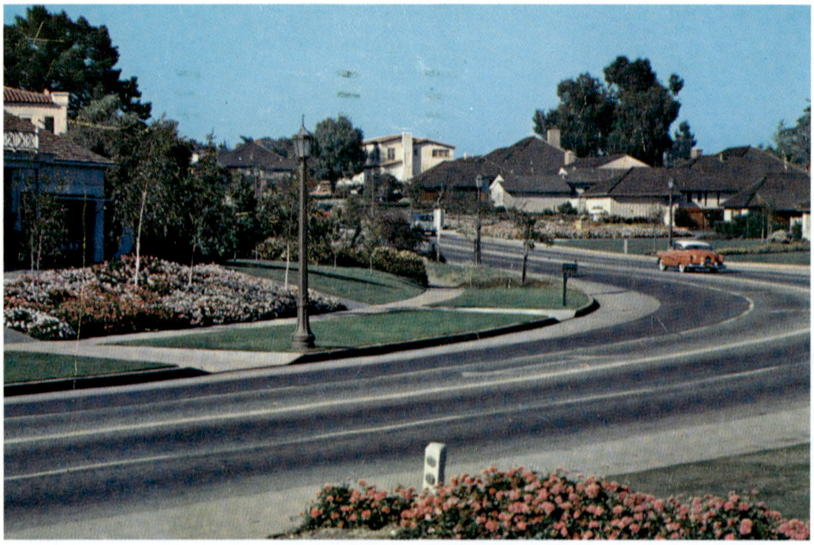

Sunset Boulevard, Pacific Palisades.

NOW

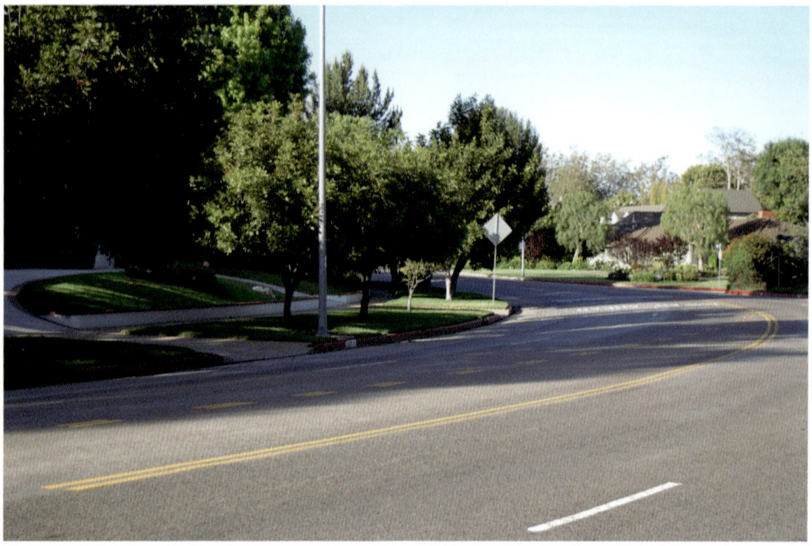

Sunset Boulevard, Pacific Palisades. This view is looking east on Sunset, just east of Amalfi Drive.

Pacific Palisades was founded in 1922.
Many movies stars have made it their home, including
Tom Cruise, Goldie Hawn, and Sylvester Stallone.

THEN

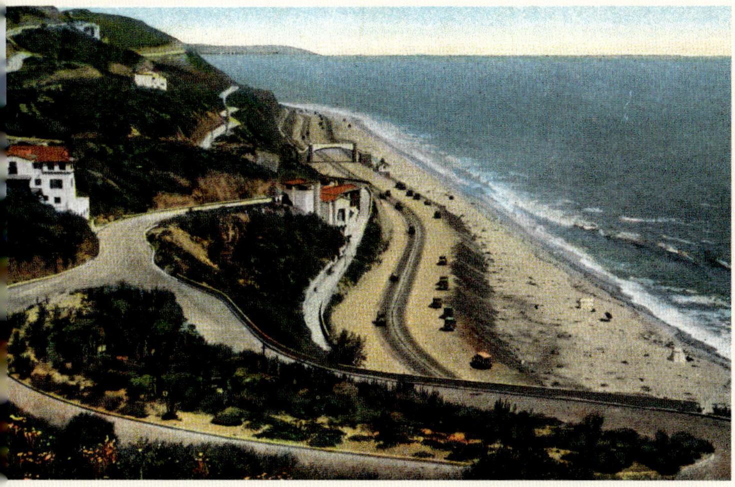

[Pacific] Coast Highway at Castellammare.

THEN

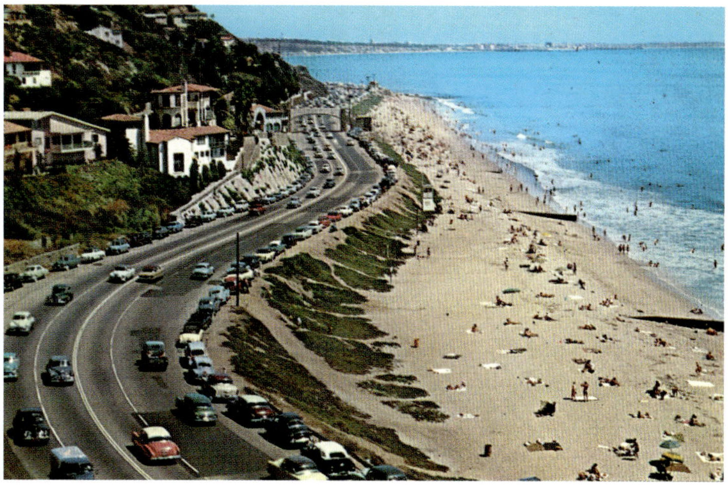

Pacific Coast Highway at Castellammare.

NOW

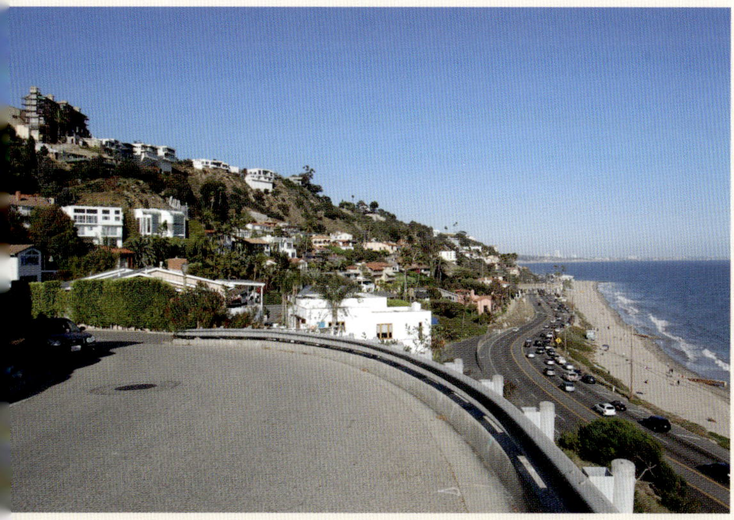

Pacific Coast Highway at Castellammare, a neighborhood of Pacific Palisades. Looking south over Pacific Coast Highway as it curves along the ocean on the right, the view is from Porto Marina Way just as it passes Lecco Lane for the second time coming up from Pacific Coast Highway.

NOW

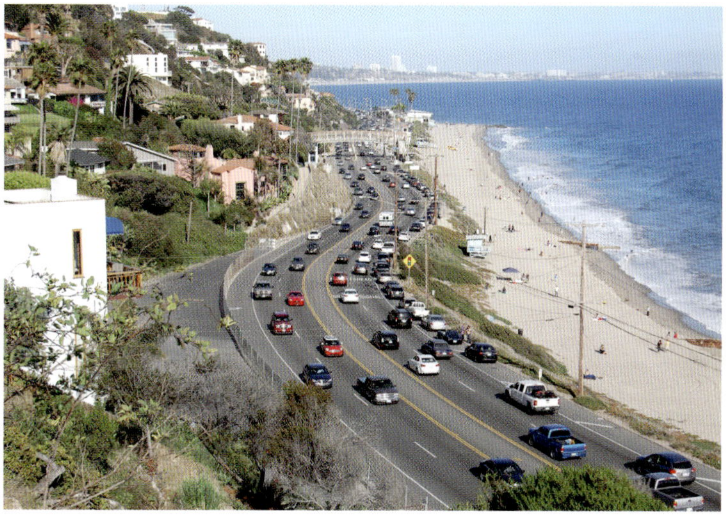

Pacific Coast Highway at Castellammare, looking south over the highway. The bridge extending over Pacific Coast Highway in the far distance here is just south of where Porto Marina Way meets Pacific Coast Highway.

Many of the bluff-hugging homes of Castellammare (Italian for "castle by the sea") have views of the Pacific Ocean. Castellammare is a community that traces its development to the 1920s.

CHAPTER 9

PARKS

THEN

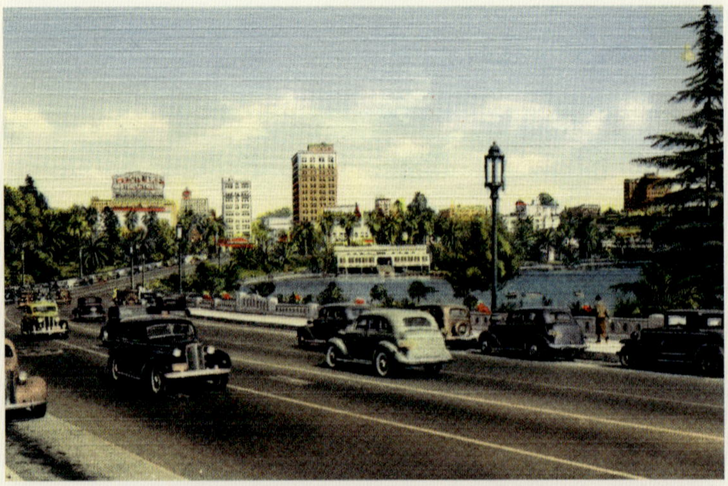

Wilshire Boulevard looking through Westlake Park. The park is now called MacArthur Park.

NOW

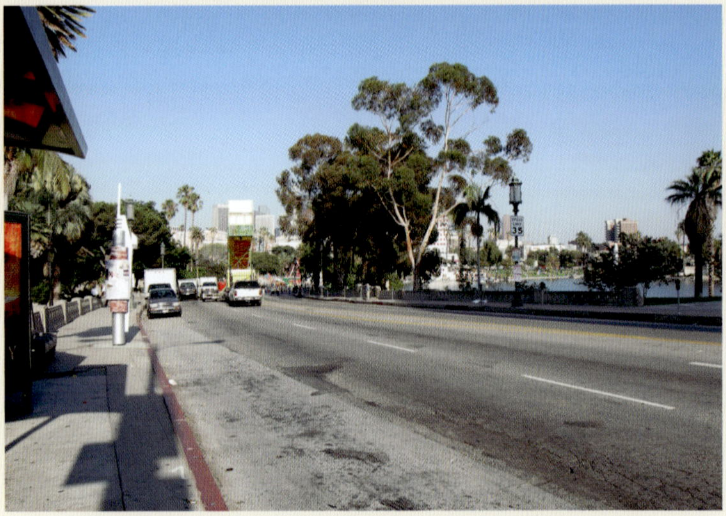

Wilshire Boulevard looking through MacArthur Park (seen on the right here), formerly called Westlake Park. View is looking east on Wilshire Boulevard.

THEN

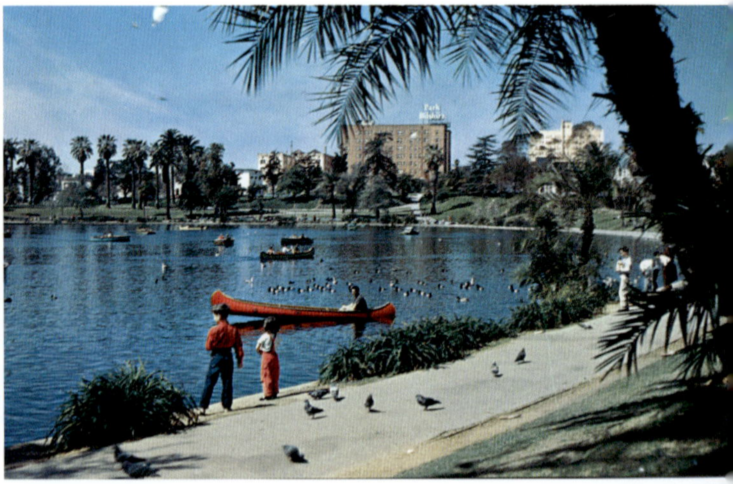

MacArthur Park.

NOW

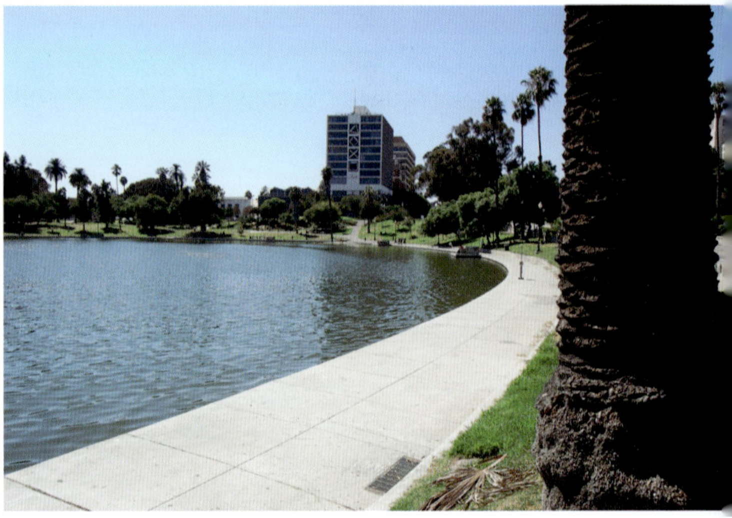

MacArthur Park. View is an area of the park south of Wilshire Boulevard.

Busy Los Angeles can easily fade away after stepping into one of its parks. Nearly 150 parks are managed by the Los Angeles County Department of Parks and Recreation. The parks of Los Angeles have been celebrated through postcards for decades.

THEN

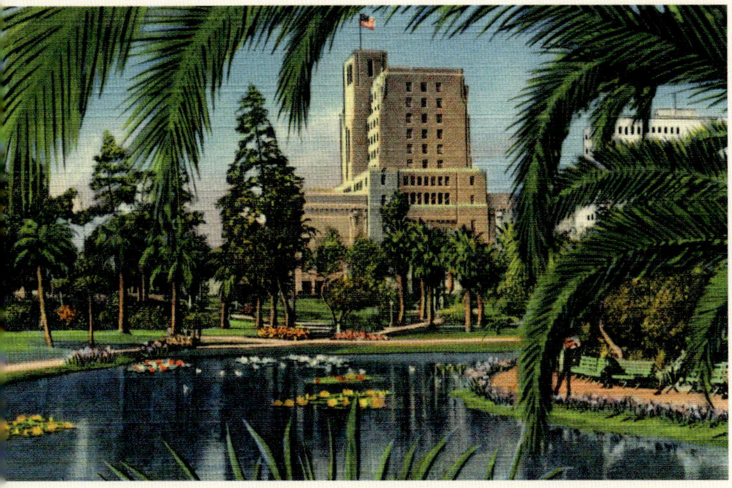

Elks Club from General Douglas MacArthur Park.

NOW

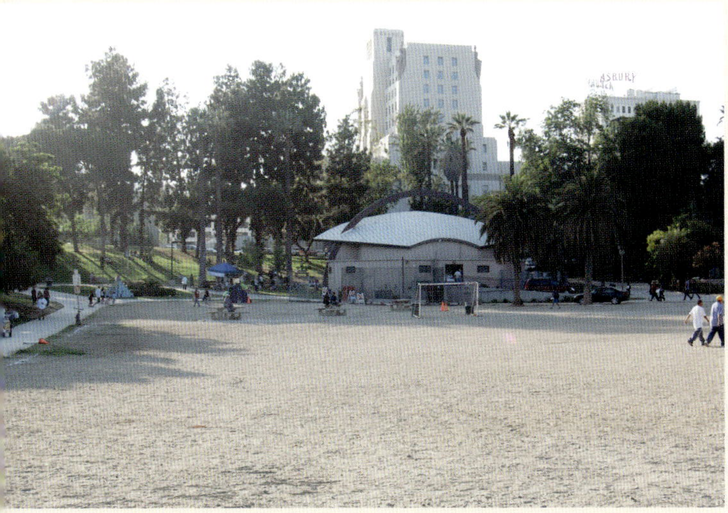

The Elks Club building from the postcard view remains, but it no longer houses the club. The building stands at 607 Park View Street. View is from an area of the park north of Wilshire Boulevard.

MacArthur Park has changed some of its water bodies to dry land areas.

THEN

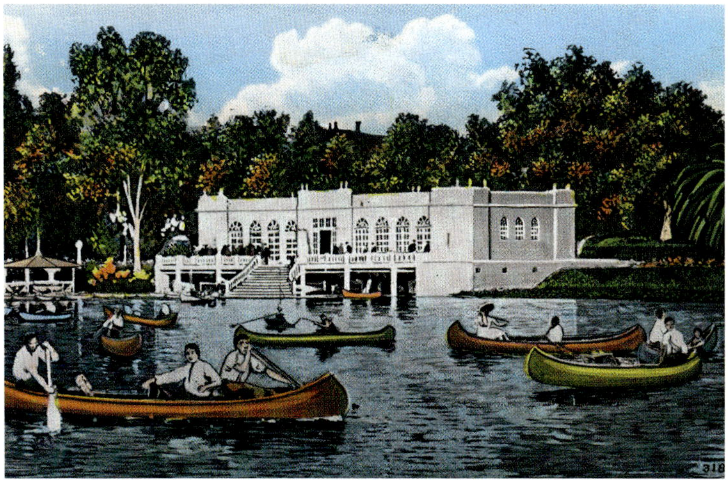

Boathouse and café, Westlake Park. The park is now called MacArthur Park.

NOW

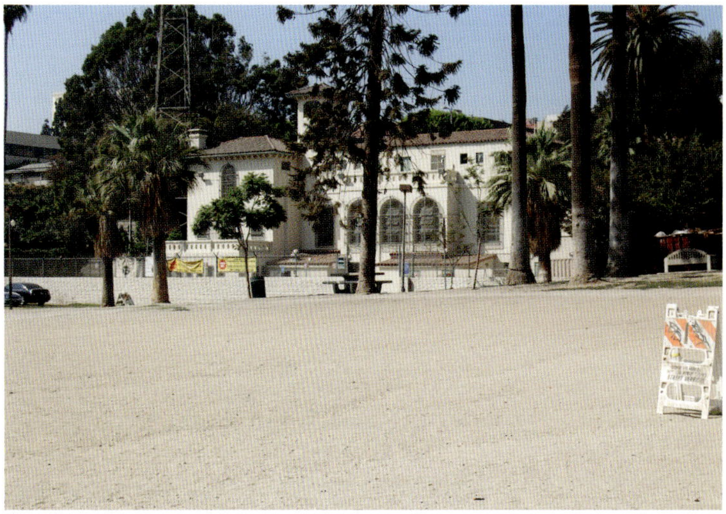

A boathouse in this now dry-land area of MacArthur Park is no longer needed. View is from an area of the park north of Wilshire Boulevard.

Park boaters were frequently pictured in vintage postcards.

THEN

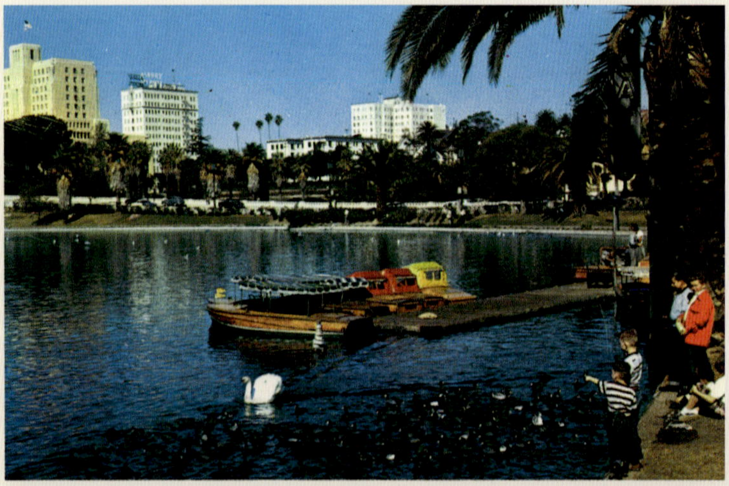

MacArthur Park's boat docks.

NOW

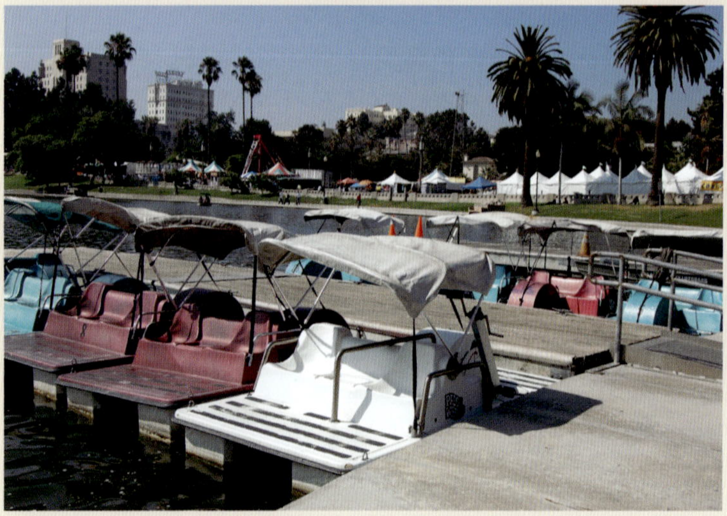

MacArthur Park's boat docks. View is from an area of the park south of Wilshire Boulevard.

Beginning in the 1930s, Wilshire Boulevard (center in both postcard and now views) cut into MacArthur Park (then Westlake Park).

THEN

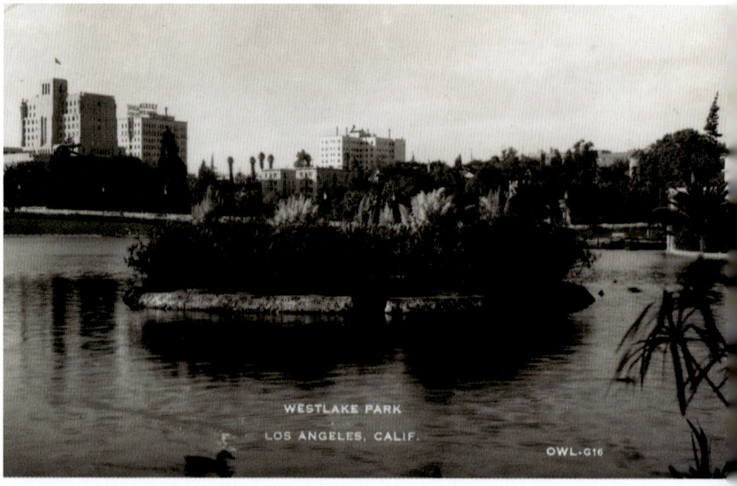

Westlake Park. The park is now MacArthur Park.

NOW

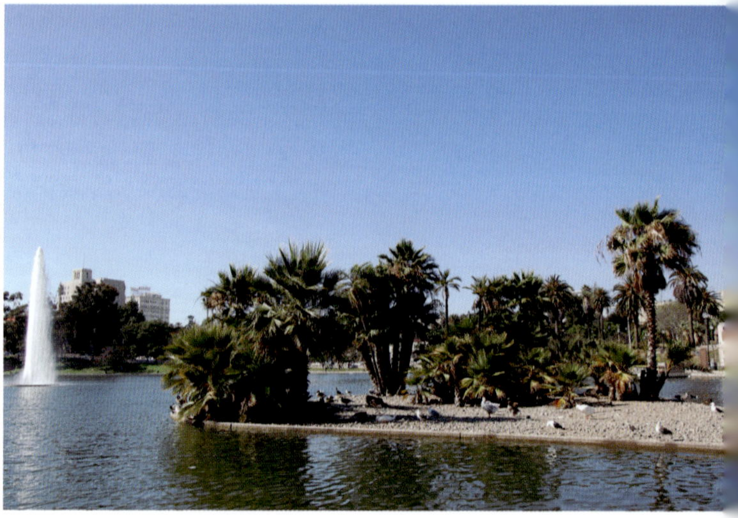

MacArthur Park lake remains on its south of Wilshire Boulevard territory. Part of an island in the park is in the foreground, but the author does not know if any portion of it dates back to the time of the postcard's printing. Many of the buildings in the background of the postcard view can be seen when standing near where this current-era photograph was taken. View is from a point close to West 7th Street, looking toward Wilshire Boulevard.

MacArthur Park is named after a hero of World War II, General Douglas MacArthur.

THEN

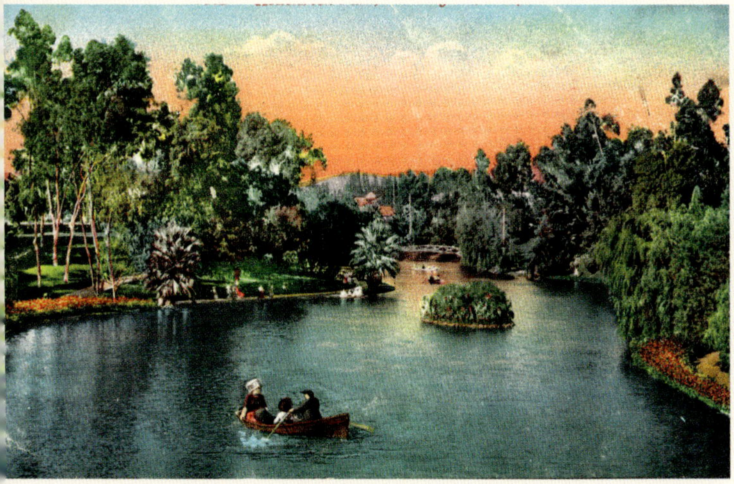

Hollenbeck Park.

NOW

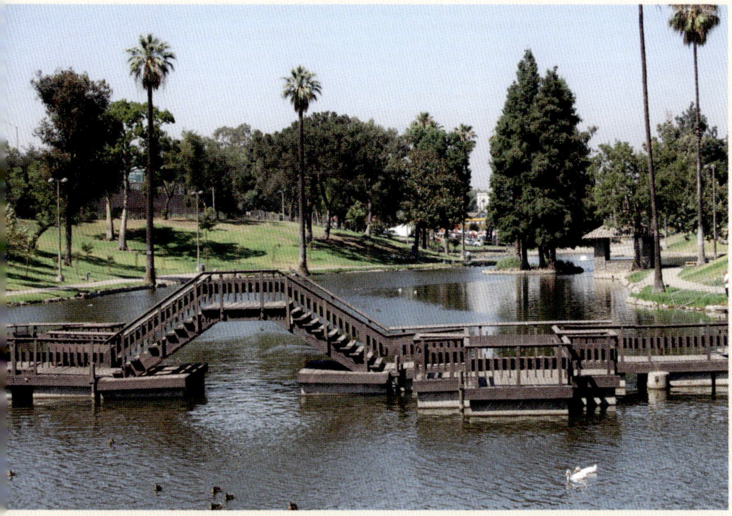

Hollenbeck Park's body of water remains close in shape to its corresponding "then" view. This view is looking north towards the direction of East 4th Street. The "then" view seems to have been taken from a bridge located about where this bridge is. The bridge was not accessible at the time this photograph was taken and so the photograph was taken a short distance south of it.

THEN

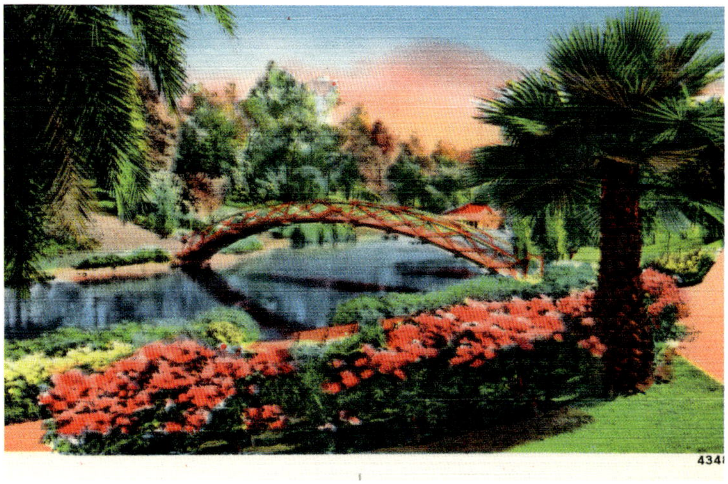

Restful beauty in Hollenbeck Park.

NOW

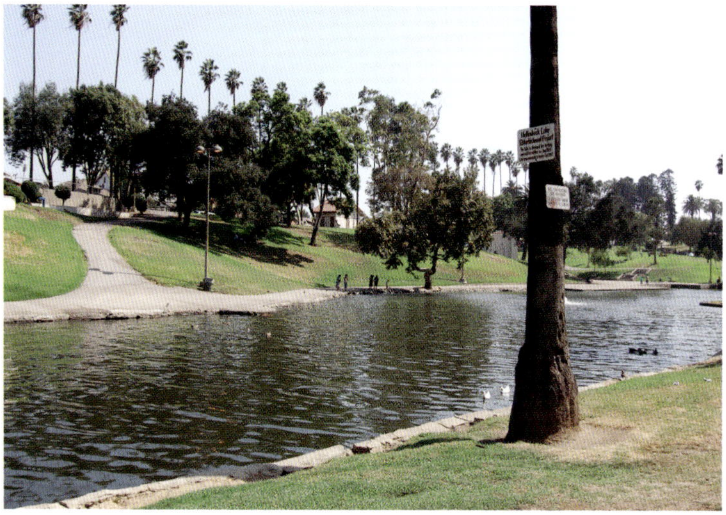

Restful beauty in Hollenbeck Park remains, save for the bridge that is no longer part of this area of the park. There is also no longer boating in the park, which takes up twenty-six acres.

THEN

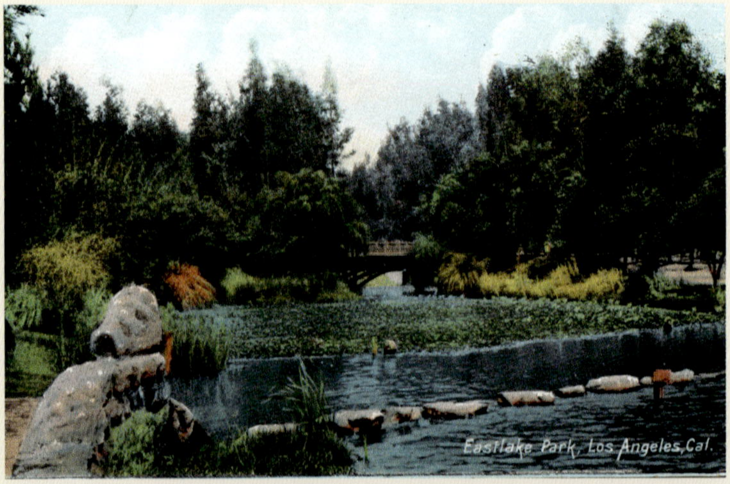

Eastlake Park.

THEN

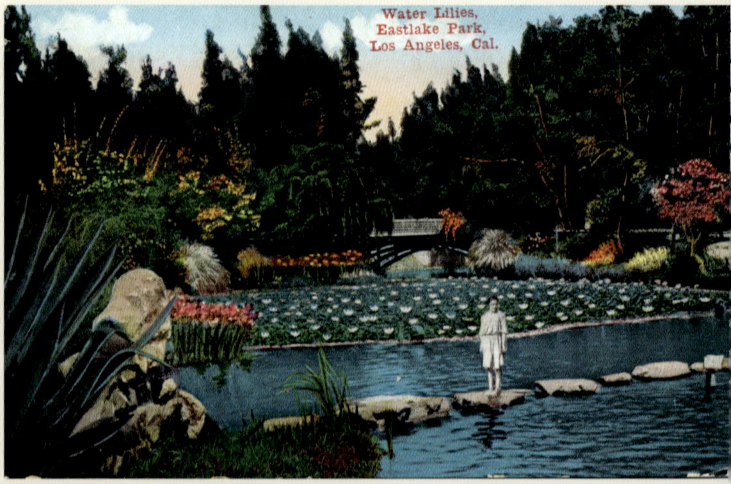

Water lilies in Eastlake Park.

NOW

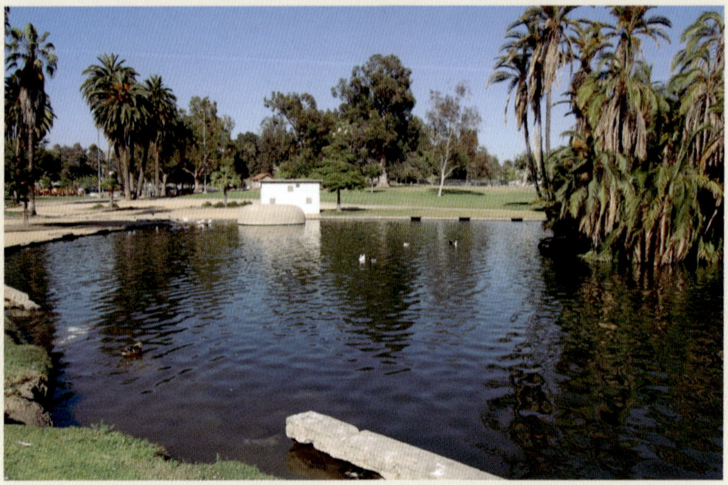

Eastlake Park is now named Lincoln Park.

Eastlake Park, now Lincoln Park, once had stepping stones running across its lake (as seen in the "then" views. The author makes no claim that the "now" view is exactly where the stepping stones were once located, but, from his research, it seems a good probability that the stones reached the shoreline close to where the cement (center, foreground) along the water's edge comes to a stop. In vintage postcard views of parks, a now long-gone water activity particular to that given park can often be seen playing out.

THEN

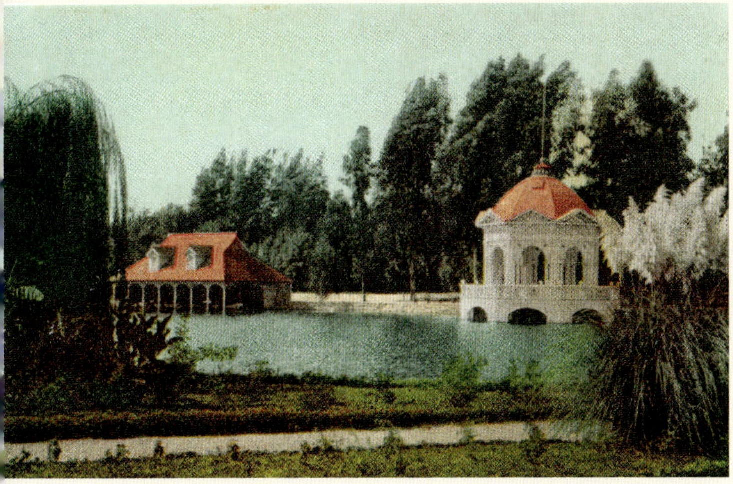

Eastlake Park. The park is now Lincoln Park.

NOW

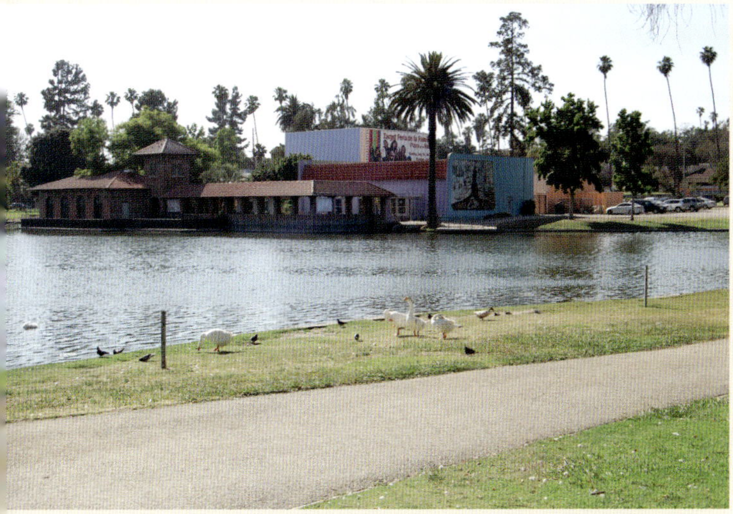

Lincoln Park, formerly Eastlake Park, has replaced the structures shown in the "then" view. For example, the Bandstand over the lake is gone; however, the ducks can be seen in both the "then" and "now" views of the park, as well as in other vintage postcard views.

THEN

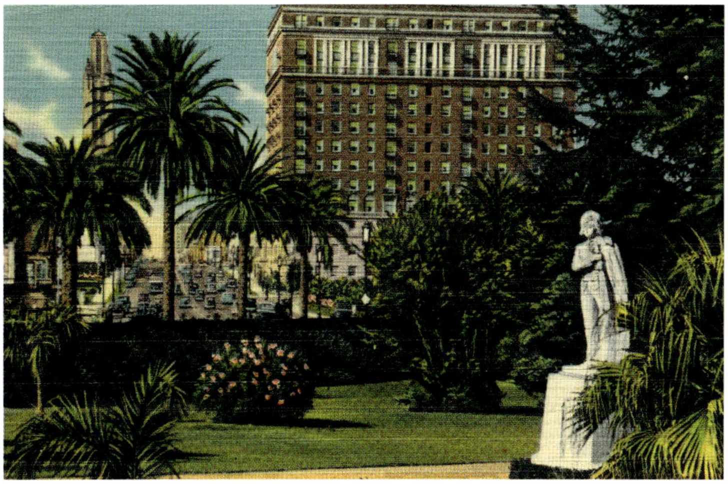

Lafayette Park.

NOW

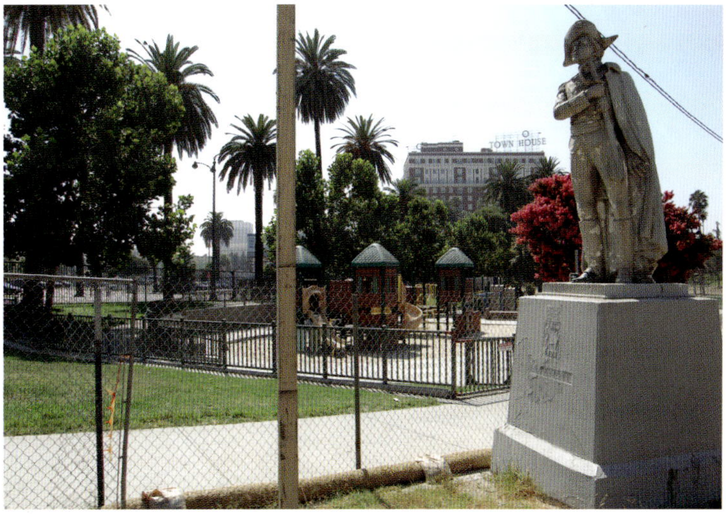

Lafayette Park is shown here near its Wilshire Boulevard border. A statue of French-born General Marquis de Lafayette stands guard over the southeast corner of the park. View is looking west with Wilshire running along the left.

CHAPTER 10

SANTA MONICA

THEN

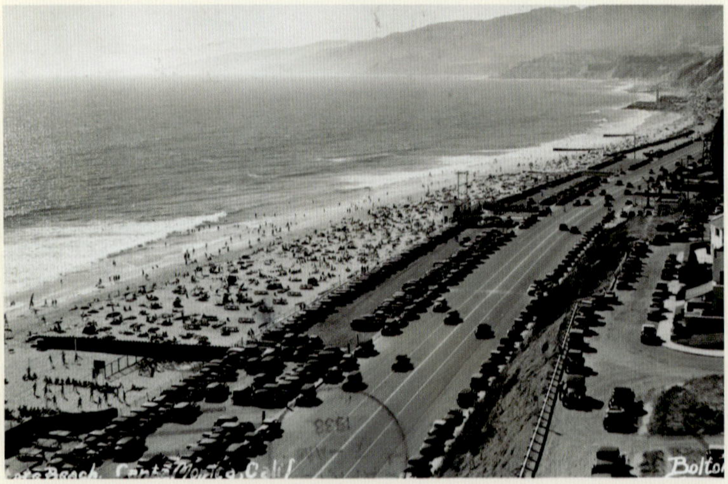

Santa Monica State Beach.

NOW

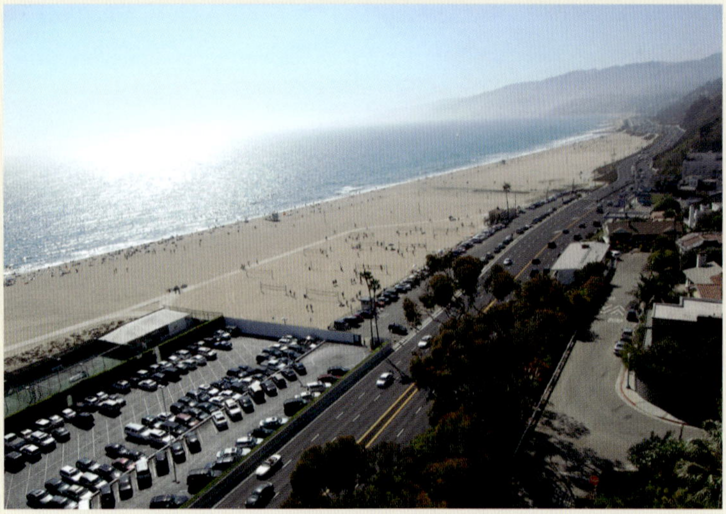

Santa Monica State Beach runs along Pacific Coast Highway. It runs into Will Rogers State Beach on its northernmost point. The two beaches meet close to where the Santa Monica Canyon empties into the Pacific Coast Highway. The houses in the foreground on the right sit inside the Santa Monica Canyon. View is from a building adjacent to the north end of Palisades Park.

The Pacific Ocean is the crown jewel of Santa Monica. Though the landscape around it may change, the ocean remains a constant.

THEN

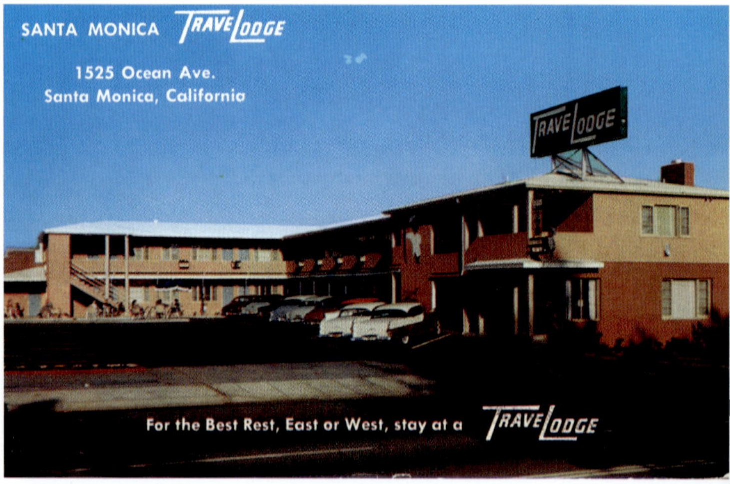

Travelodge.

NOW

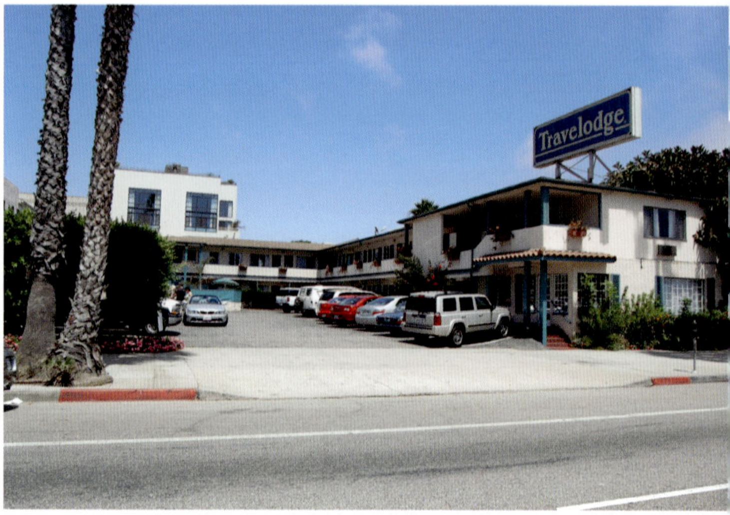

Travelodge remains at 1525 Ocean Avenue.

Ocean Avenue provides Santa Monica with plenty of hotels, restaurants, and residential complexes. The avenue stretches from Adelaide Drive (north end) to Pico Boulevard (south end).

THEN

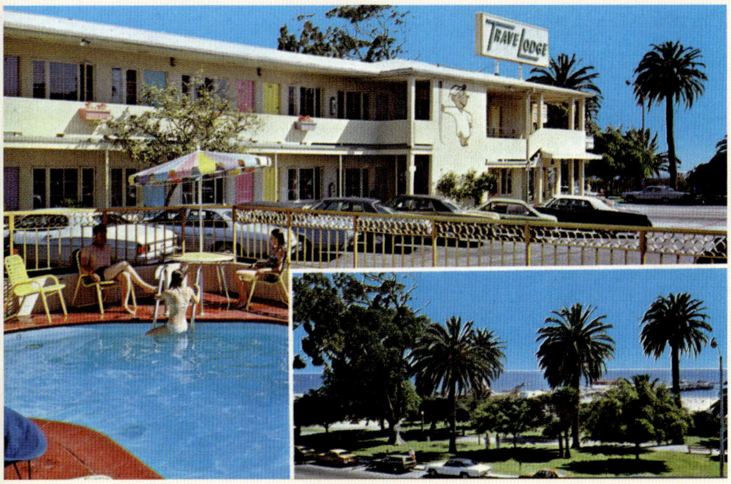

Travelodge.

THEN

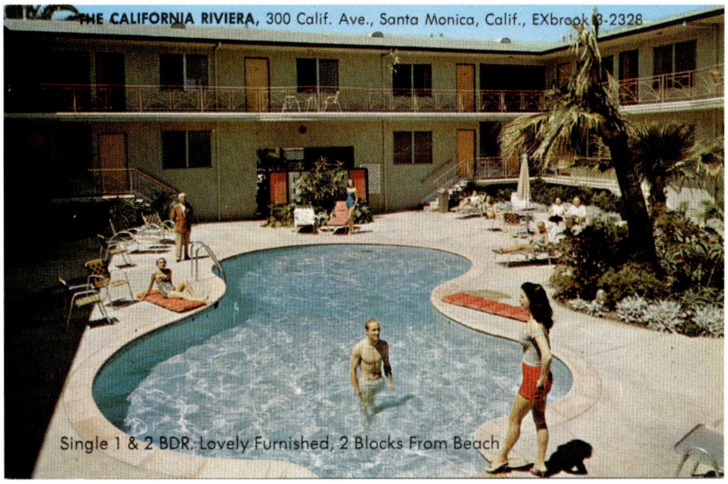

The California Riviera [apartments].

NOW

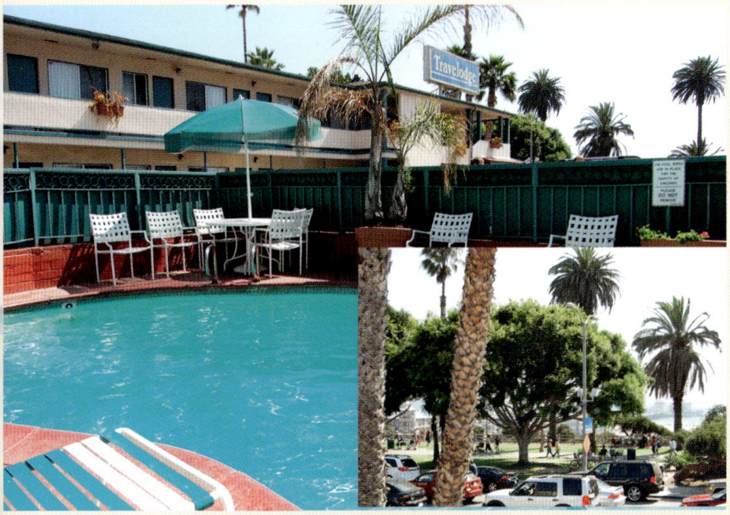

The property sits at 1525 Ocean Avenue. A view of the nearby Pacific Ocean shows in the bottom right corner and can be compared to the one in the postcard view. (Note: Postcard views are recreated by the author, not by the hotel.)

NOW

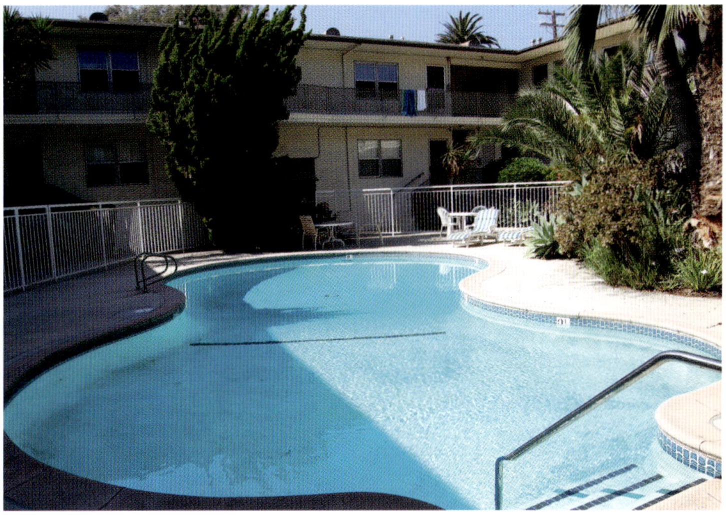

The California Riviera apartment complex was located at 300 California Avenue. The property remains an apartment complex and the building still carries the California Riviera signage, but it may have a different official name. (Note: Postcard pool view is recreated by the author, not by the current building owner.)

The inset photo on both the Travelodge views show the nearby Santa Monica Municipal Pier stretching out over the Pacific Ocean. Since 1909, the pier has been a presence in Santa Monica. It draws millions of visitors annually.

Poolside scenes often display memory-enticing stimuli. An item as simple as a lounge chair can recall certain eras.

THEN

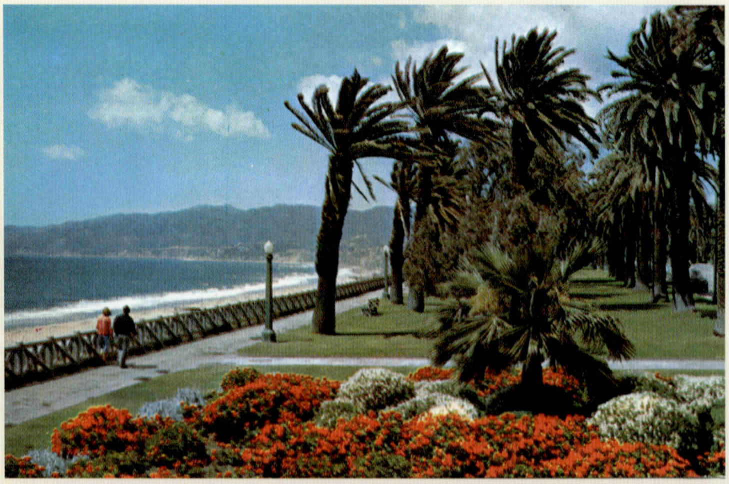

Palisades Park.

NOW

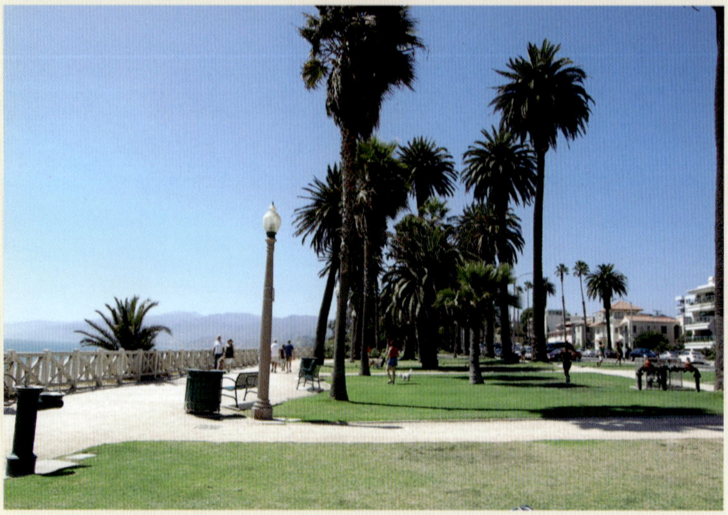

Palisades Park is located along Ocean Avenue. It overlooks Pacific Coast Highway. View is looking north toward the Santa Monica Mountains.

All of the land that makes up Palisades Park was donated to the city of Santa Monica beginning in 1892 by Senator John P. Jones and Colonel Robert S. Baker. Senator Jones is the founder of Santa Monica.

THEN

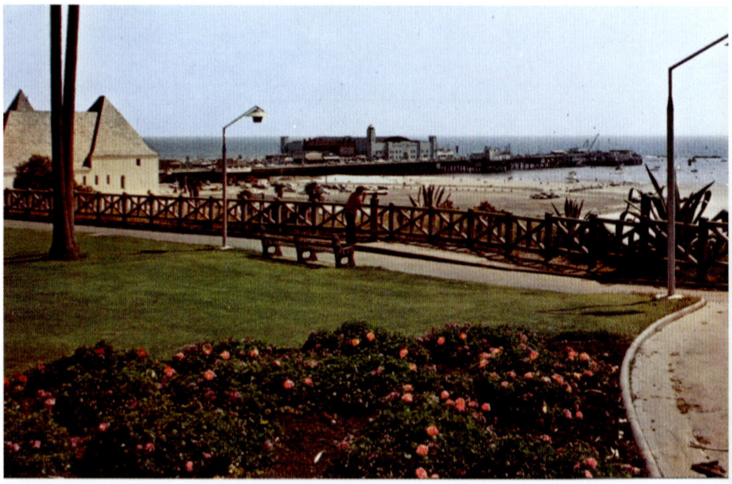

Santa Monica Municipal Pier.

NOW

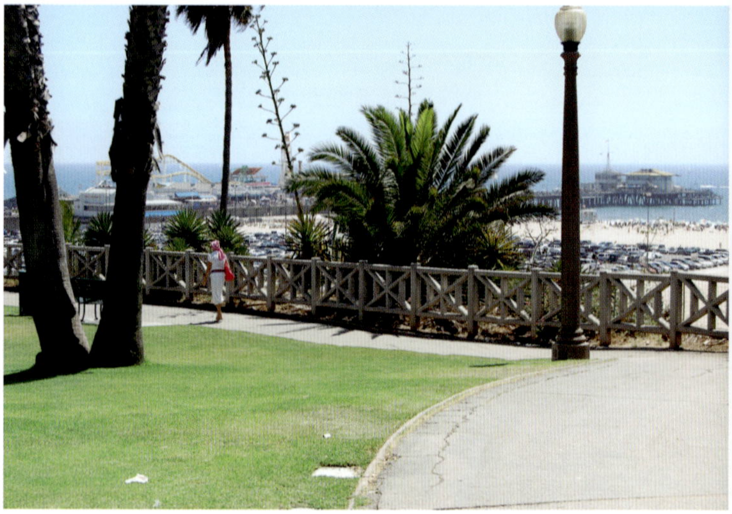

Santa Monica Municipal Pier is viewed here from Palisades Park.

Palisades Park has foot paths, palm trees, and cliff-top views of the Pacific Ocean.

THEN

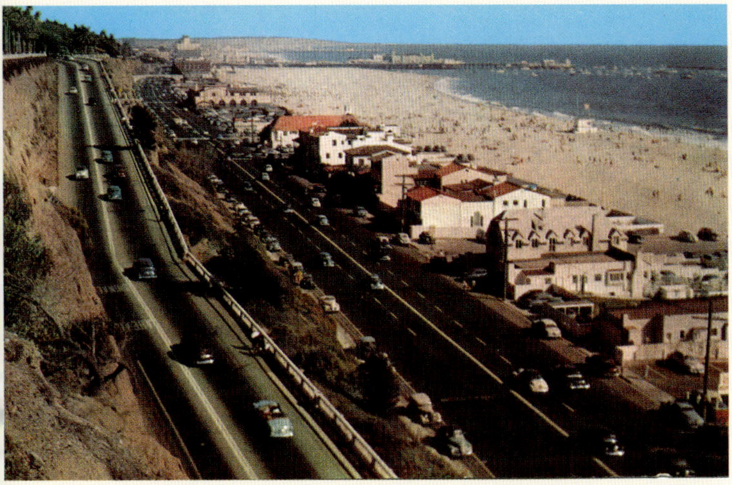

Palatial beach homes below the Palisades.

NOW

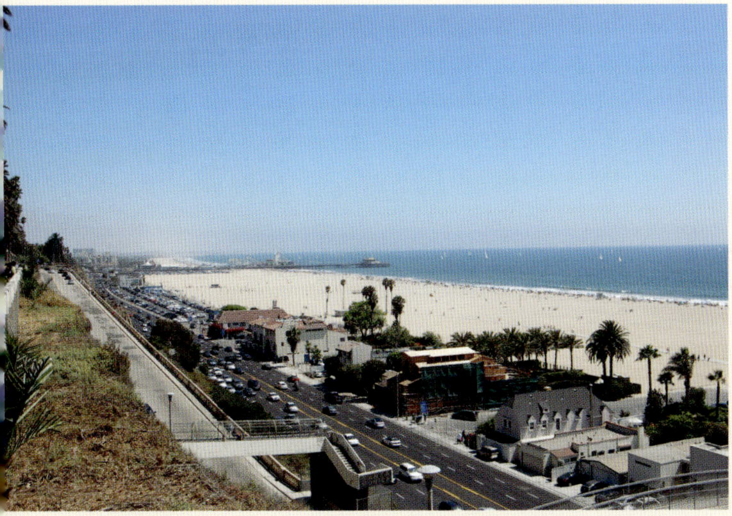

Palatial beach homes remain along this strip of the Pacific Coast Highway. View is from a vantage point in Palisades Park and looking south on the highway, which is the road next to the houses.

Bebe Daniels, Marion Davies, and Peter Lawford were among the many Hollywood stars that had beach houses along Palisades Beach Road, a stretch of the Pacific Coast Highway.

THEN

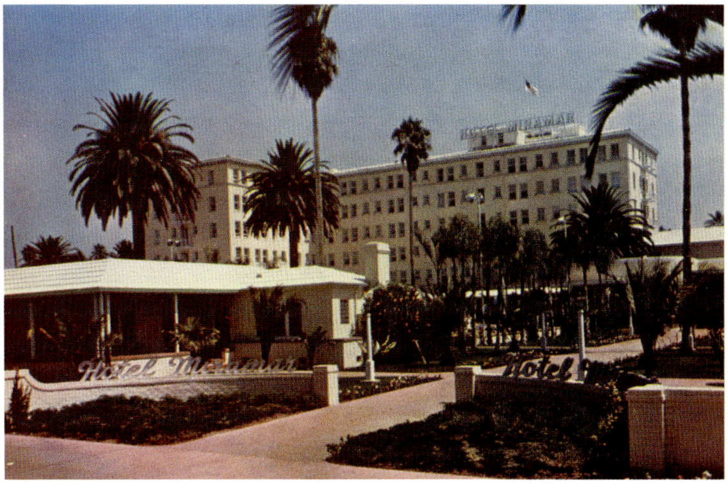

Hotel Miramar.

NOW

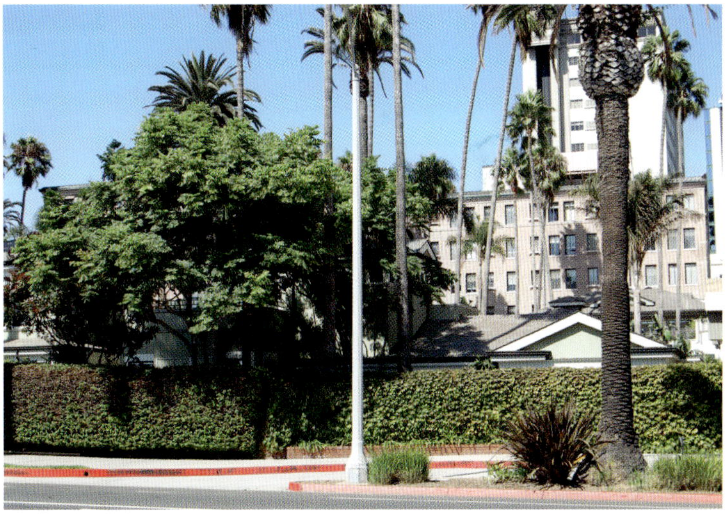

Hotel Miramar remains, but it's now called the Fairmont Miramar Hotel and Bungalows. When the postcard was printed ("then" view), the hotel had at least one entrance off Ocean Avenue. Here is that same view today: the Ocean Avenue entrance is no longer. View is from Ocean Avenue, between California Avenue and Wilshire Boulevard.

The Hotel Miramar began its operations in 1921, and Hollywood came to visit often. For some years, beginning in the mid-1920s, the silent actress Greta Garbo made the hotel her home.

THEN

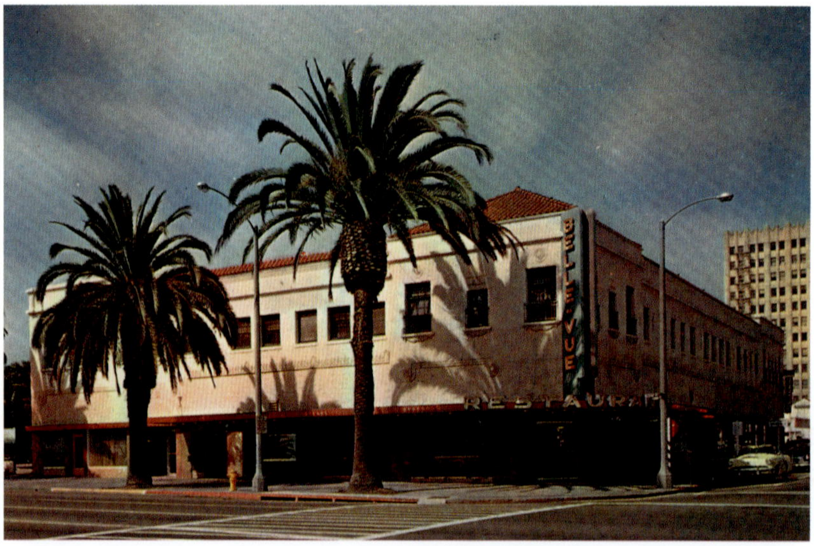

Belle-Vue French Restaurant.

NOW

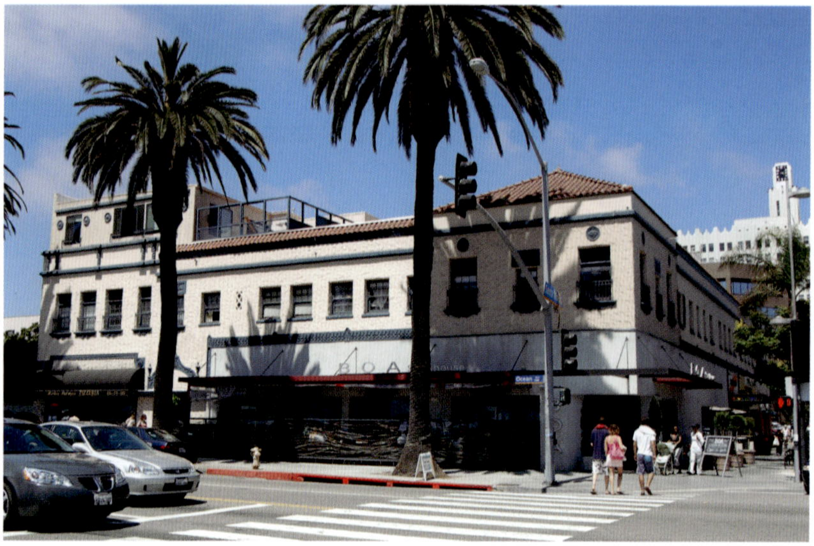

Belle-Vue French Restaurant was located at the northeast corner of Ocean Avenue and Santa Monica Boulevard. A restaurant of another name now occupies the property.

The Bay City's Guaranty Building of 1929 looms in the background in the former location of Belle-Vue French (right in both the "then" and "now" views). The high-rise Art Deco structure was designed by Walker and Eisen.

THEN

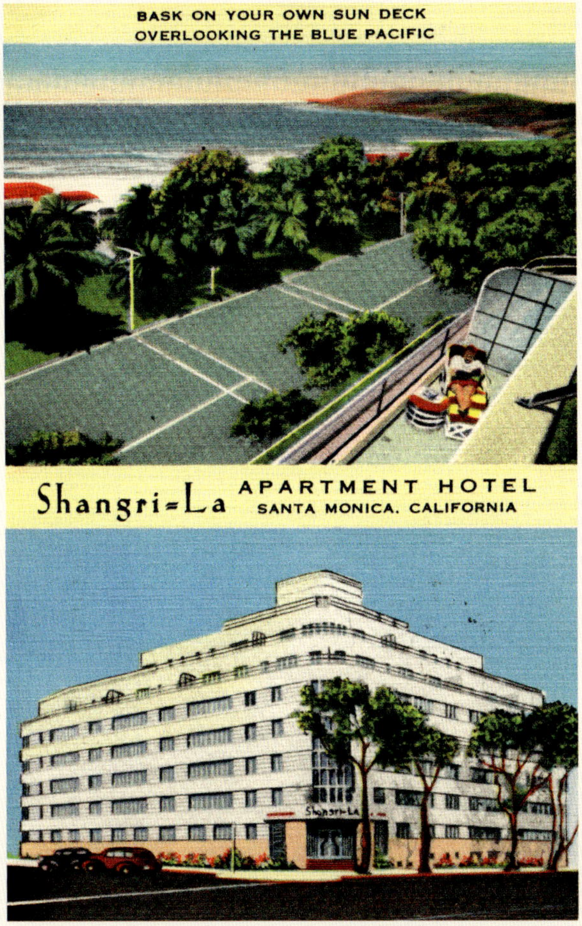

Shangri-La Apartment Hotel.

NOW

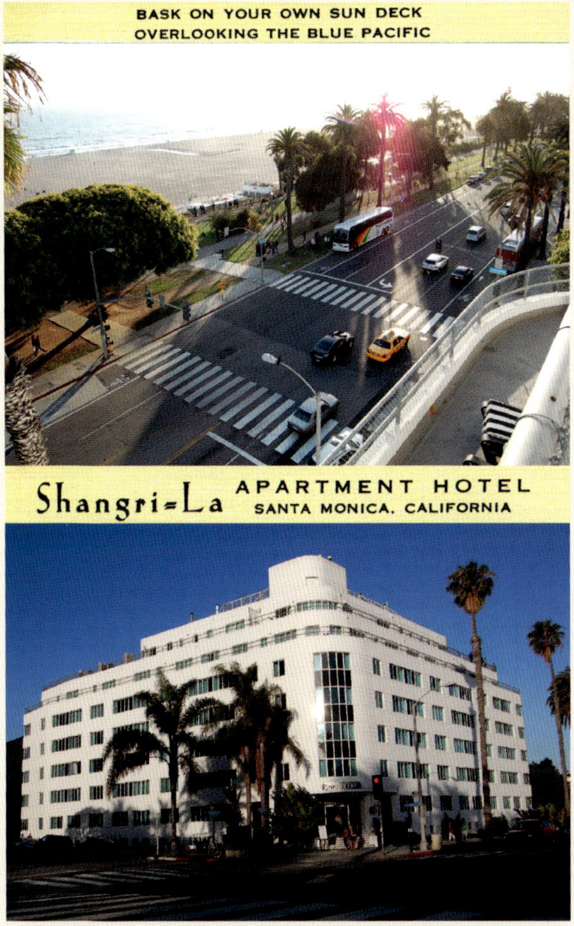

The Hotel Shangri-La, formerly called Shangri-La Apartment Hotel, is located at 1301 Ocean Avenue. (Note: Postcard views are recreated by the author, not by the hotel.)

The Hotel Shangri-La is an Art Deco structure built in 1939. It has a view of the Pacific Ocean.

THEN

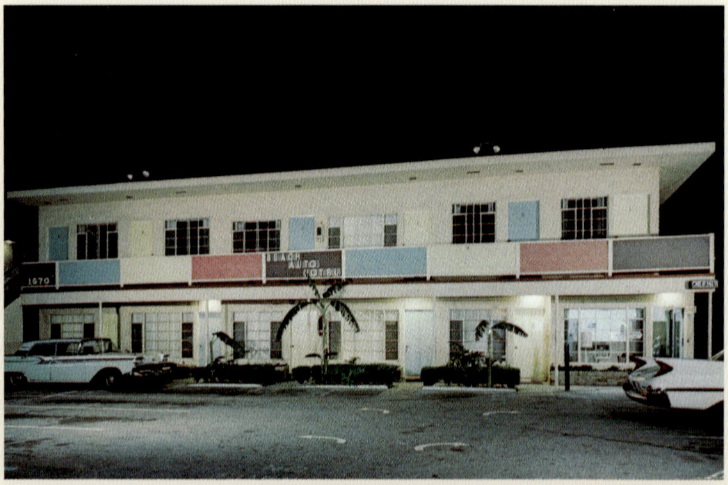

Beach Auto Hotel.

NOW

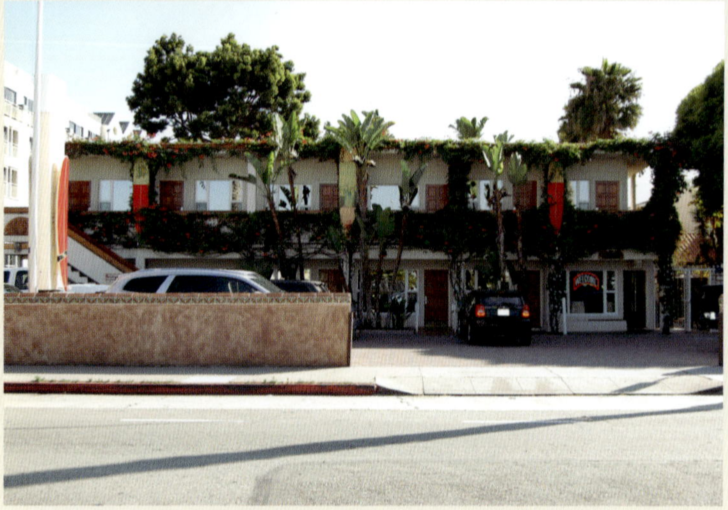

The Beach Auto Hotel was located at 1670 Ocean Avenue. The property remains a hotel, but now goes by another name.

An ocean breeze coming from behind, wood doors, tropical foliage, and surf boards are part of this hotel property of today. Gone are the pastel colors, old cars, and oil-stained parking spaces of the Beach Auto Hotel in the postcard view.

THEN

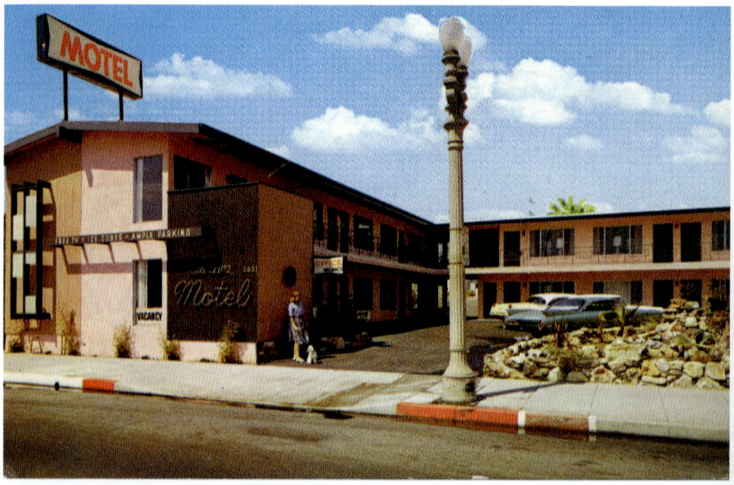

Sea Shore Motel.

NOW

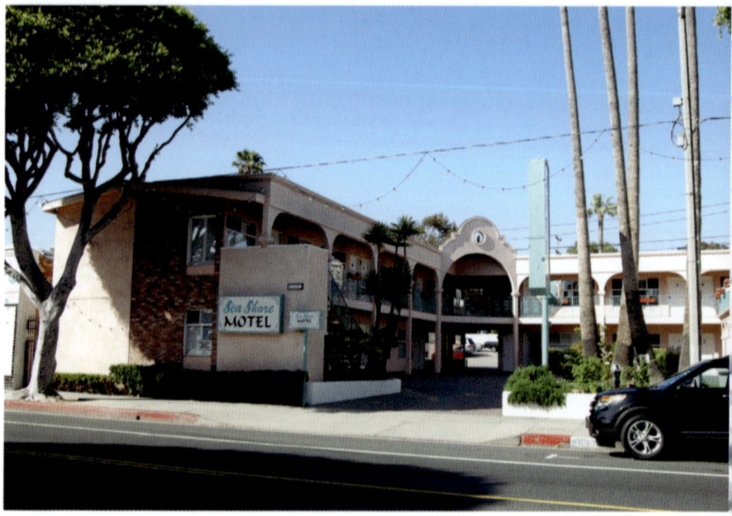

Sea Shore Motel remains at 2637 Main Street.

The Sea Shore Motel is part of the busy Main Street of Santa Monica. Motels, hip shops, boutiques, and food make Main Street one of Santa Monica's top drawing jewels.

THEN

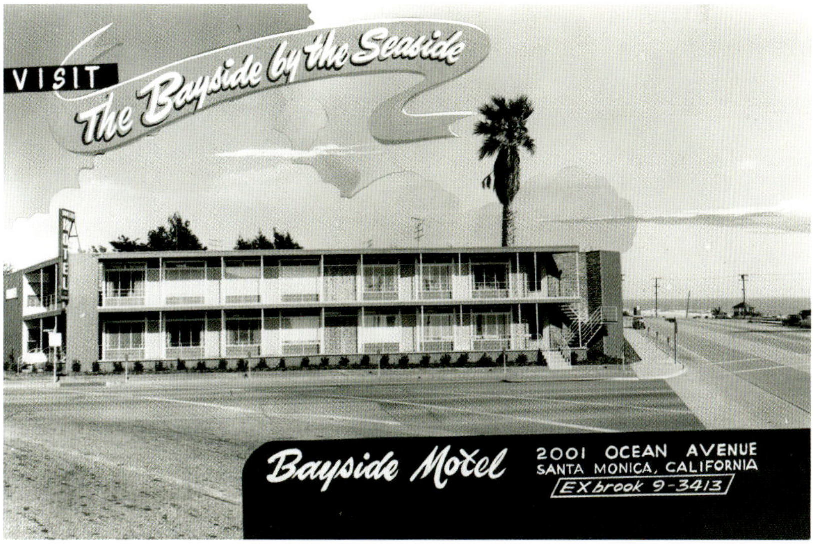

Bayside Motor Hotel.

NOW

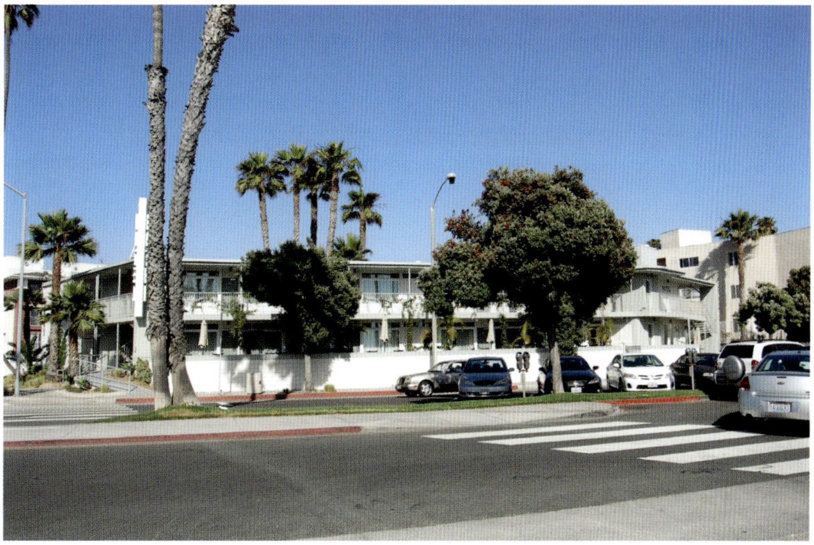

The Bayside Hotel, formerly Bayside Motor Hotel, remains at 2001 Ocean Avenue.

Buildings and parking spaces have cropped up around the Bayside Hotel property since the postcard view. The building dates to the 1950s.

CHAPTER 11
VENICE

THEN

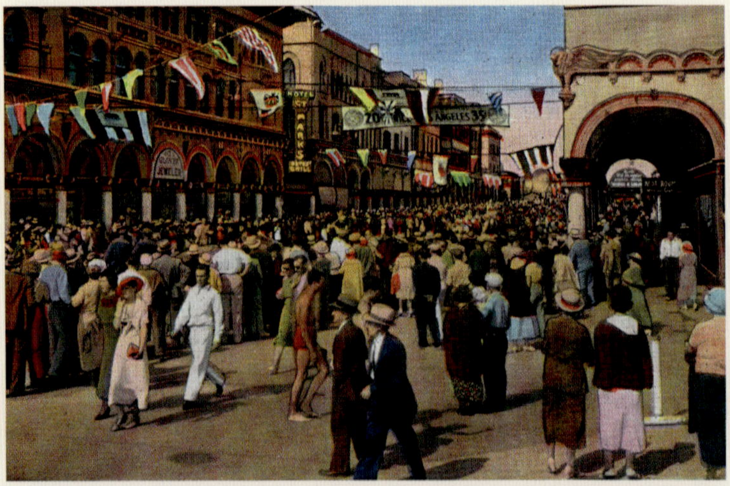

A crowded day at Venice.

THEN

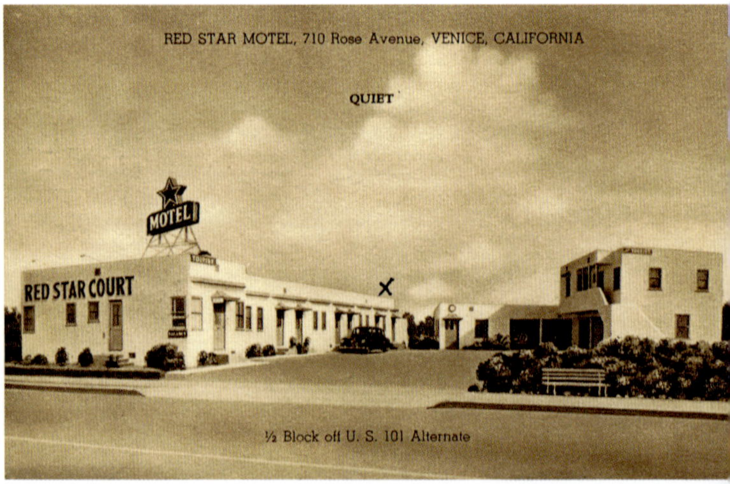

Red Star Motel.

NOW

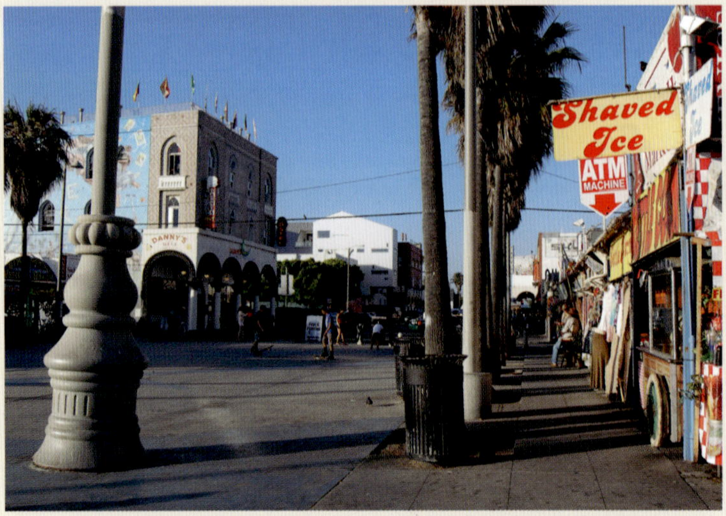

Venice has lost some of its signature buildings. The St. Mark Hotel, on the immediate left in the "then" postcard view, no longer stands. View is looking east on Windward Avenue from Ocean Front Walk.

NOW

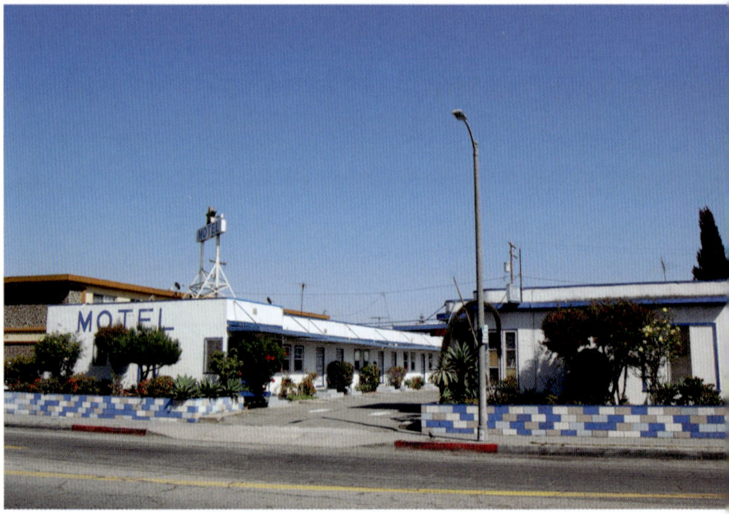

The Red Star Motel is now the Golden Star Motel. It is located at 710 Venice Avenue. In the immediate right, an addition to the property is apparent when compared to the "then" postcard view.

Venice has several decades of subcultural history behind it. The Beat generation has been here. Hippies have been attracted to Venice, and even the rock band The Doors called Venice their birthplace. It is about canals, ocean air, and funky musicians that entertain the throngs of visitors walking its sandy beach-close sidewalks.

CHAPTER 12
WEST ADAMS

THEN

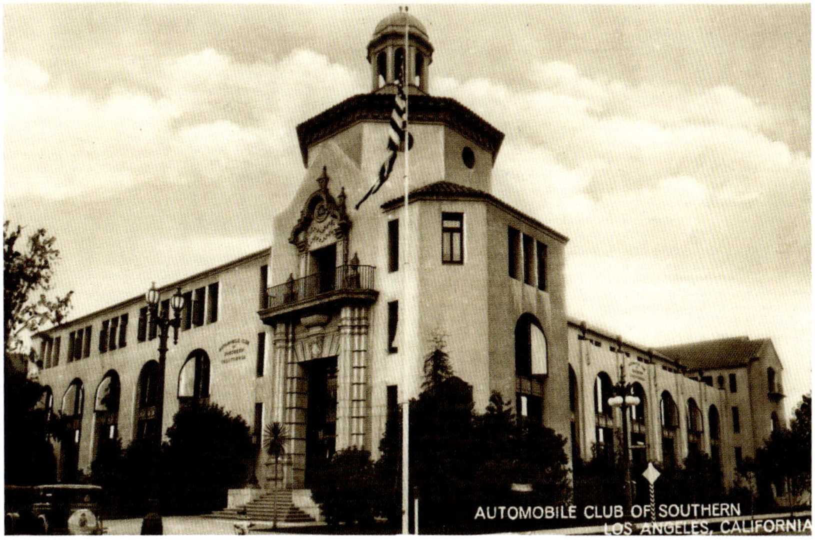

Automobile Club of Southern California.

NOW

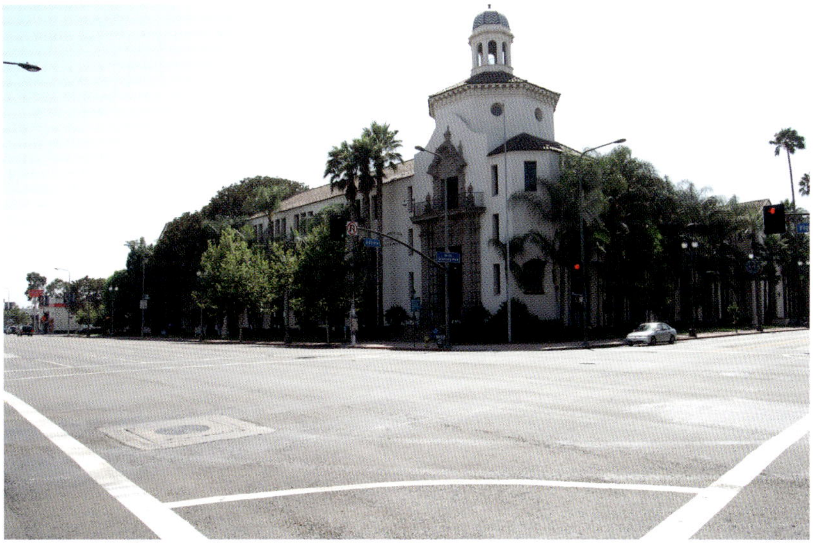

The Automobile Club of Southern California (AAA) remains at 2601 South Figueroa Street..

The Automobile Club of Southern California (AAA) building was built in the early 1920s. It is an example of the Spanish Colonial Revival style of architecture.

THEN

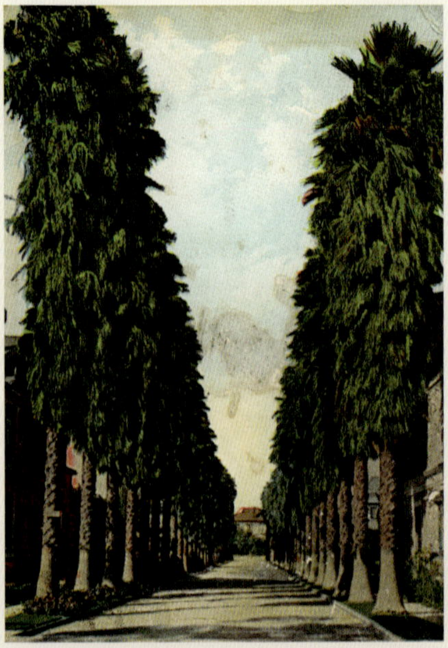

Palm Drive near Adams Street and Grand Avenue.

NOW

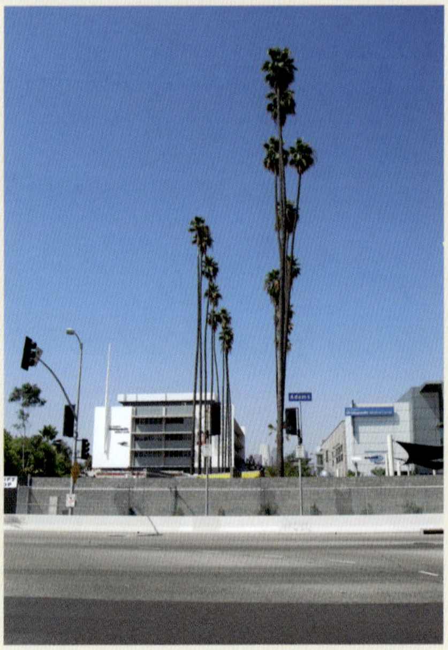

Cars that exit the northbound Harbor (110) Freeway at West Adams Blvd. are greeted with palm trees that once lined Palm Drive when it intersected Adams. Palm Drive is no longer on the map here, but the wall across Adams is the estimated spot where the postcard view begins.

If palm trees could talk? Oh, the West Adams history lessons they could offer.

THEN

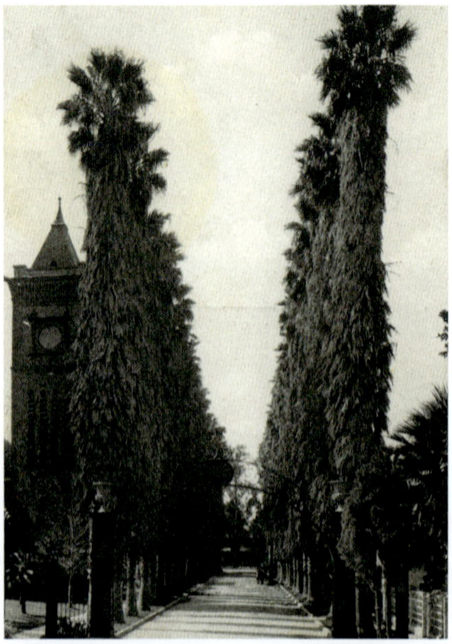

Palm Drive, looking toward West Adams Boulevard (formerly West Adams Street).

NOW

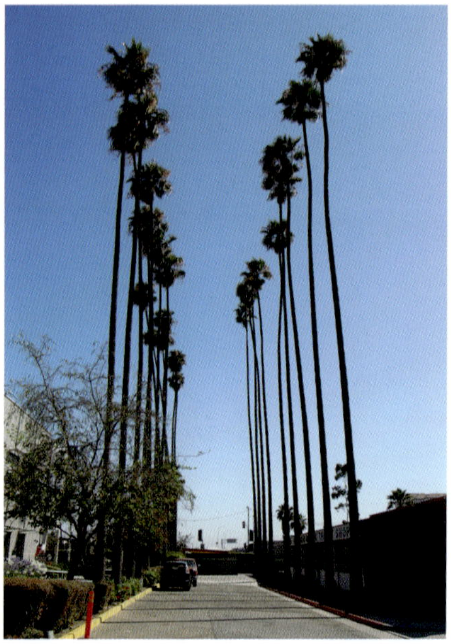

Palm trees line what once was Palm Drive. This pathway would meet West Adams Blvd. at the far end of this view but for a wall. View is from inside a complex of medical buildings, one being listed at 2400 South Flower Street. An entrance to the medical grounds is on 23rd Street, east of Flower Street.

The palm trees standing proud despite having Palm Drive taken from them.

THEN

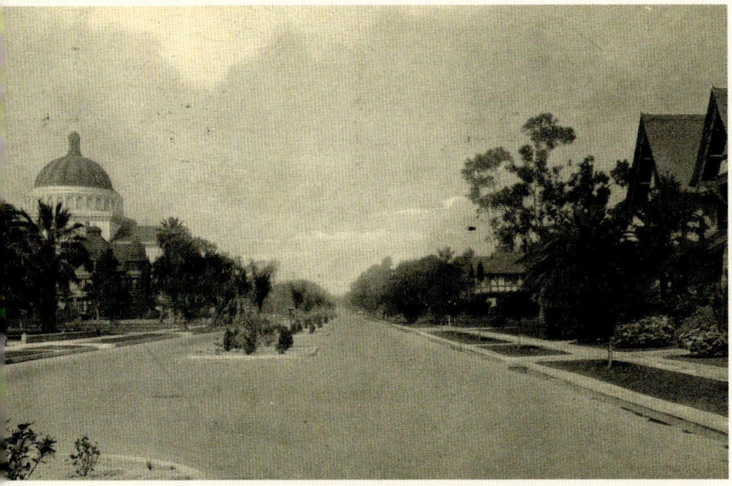

West Adams Street. (Note: The street is now West Adams Boulevard.)

NOW

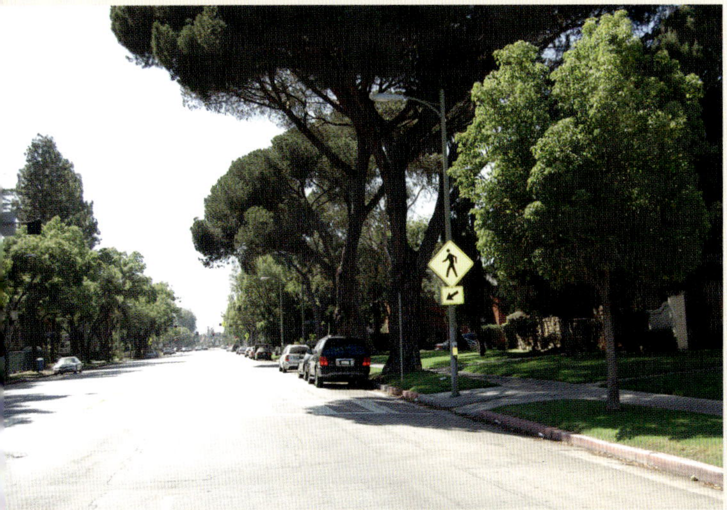

Looking west on West Adams Boulevard. In the "then" view, both the house (immediate right) and church (far left) remain standing, but foliage obscures them in this view. The church structure was once home to the Second Church of Christ Scientists. It is located at 946-948 West Adams Boulevard.

One of the older communities of Los Angeles, the West Adams District is a museum of architectural homes. Entering on the east at Figueroa, one is immediately aware that they are inside a unique area of vintage homes. Turn into any of the immediate side streets and a variety of homes styles, such as Victorian and Queen Anne, await you.

THEN

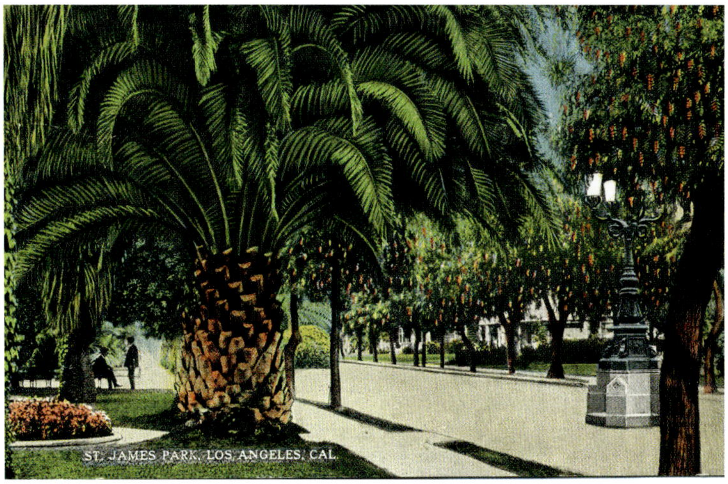

St. James Park.

NOW

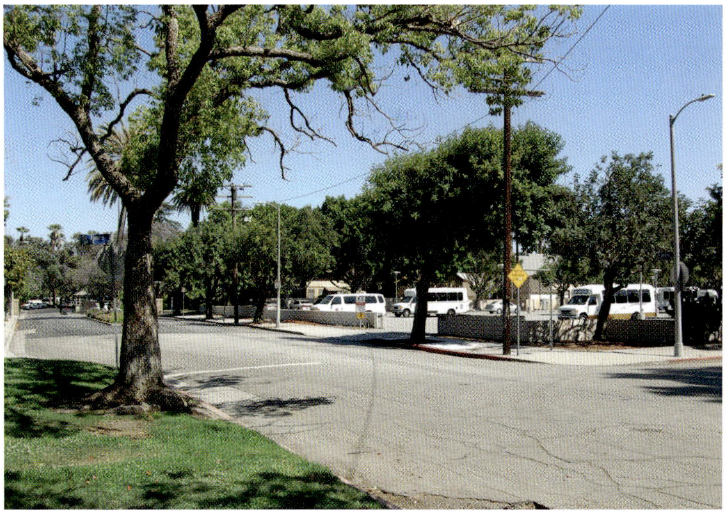

The grass and tree in the left foreground is part of St. James Park. The parking lot across the street sits at the southeast corner of St. James Park W and St. James Place.

The back of the St. James Park postcard states that the park is a private place for "the exclusive use of the residents who reside by the side and is a part of the property of several millionaires whose homes adjoin it." The card describes the park as a "beautiful tropical verdure and palms are much admired and lend distinction to the surroundings." Today, the park is still beautiful and now open to anybody.

THEN

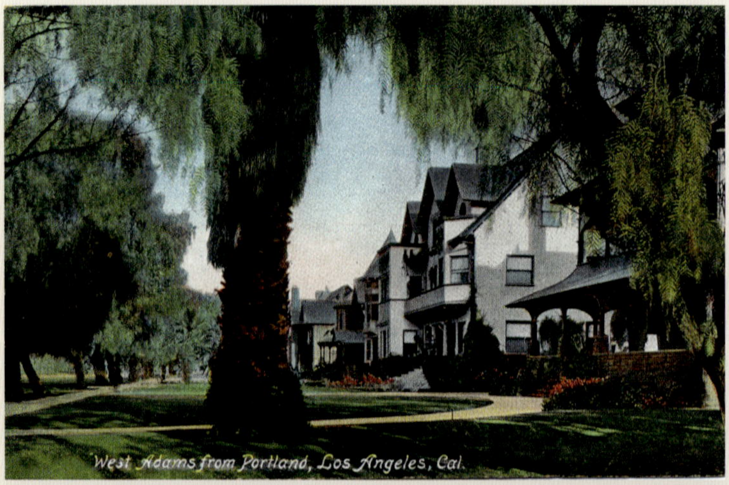

West Adams [Boulevard] from Portland [Street].

NOW

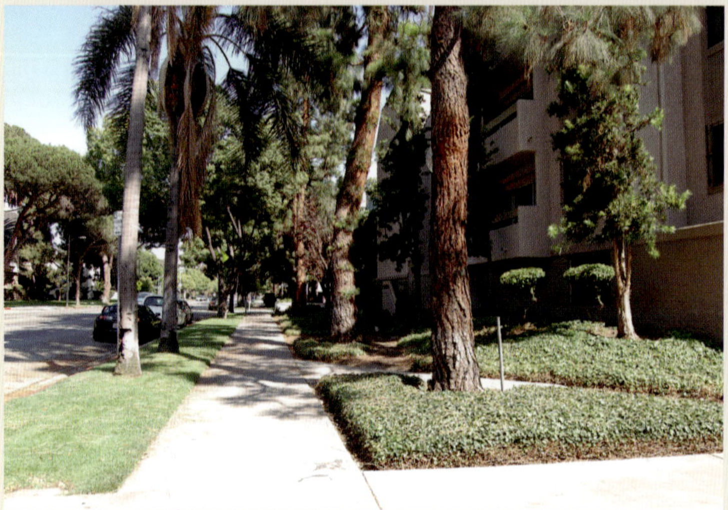

Looking east on West Adams Boulevard from Portland Street. Heading east, one must go a half-block down before coming to a home that resembles the time of the postcard's publishing.

Some of the historic West Adams homes have been met with the wrecking ball. Today, these homes only remain standing in postcards and photographs.

THEN

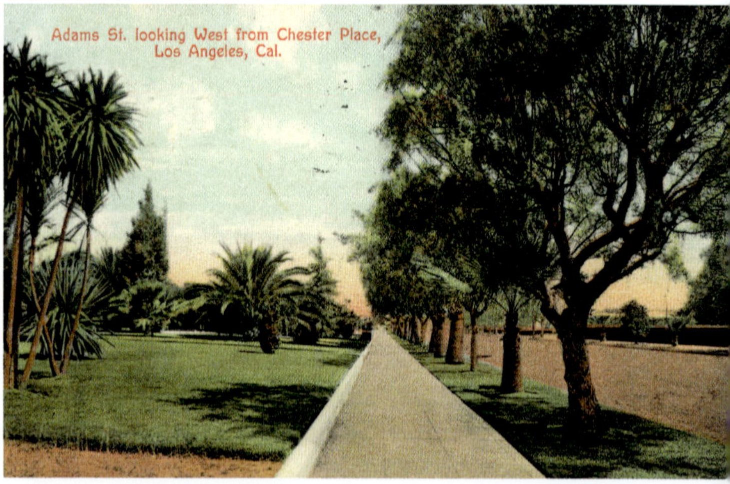

Adams Street looking west from Chester Place. (Note: Adams Street is now West Adams Boulevard.)

NOW

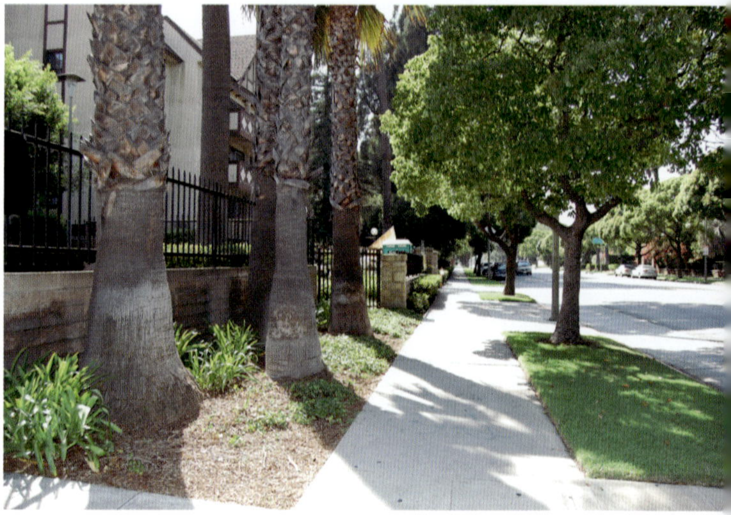

West Adams Boulevard looking west from across the street where Chester Place pours into the Boulevard. There is a gate that limits access to Chester Place from West Adams Boulevard.

Chester Place is a private road and dates back over one hundred years. Decades ago, inside the gates of Chester Place was where a number of wealthy families lived.

THEN

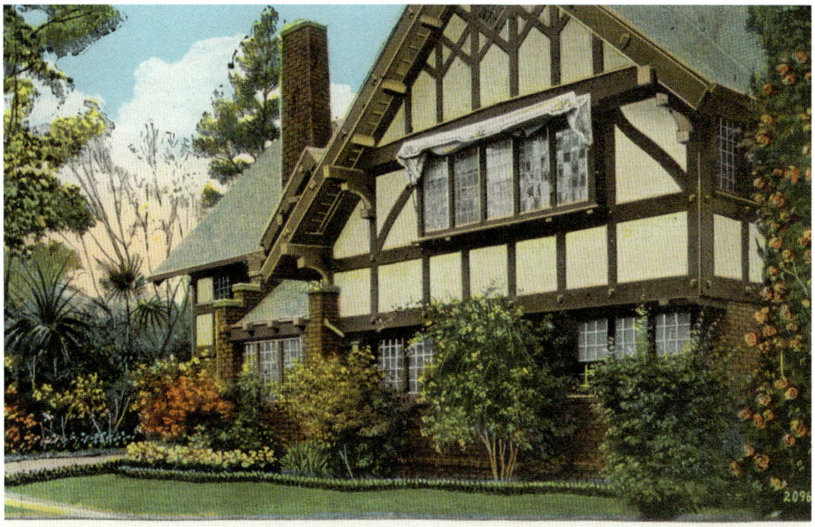

Home of Norma Talmadge. (Note: Card mistakenly states the home is located in Hollywood. It is in the West Adams District.)

NOW

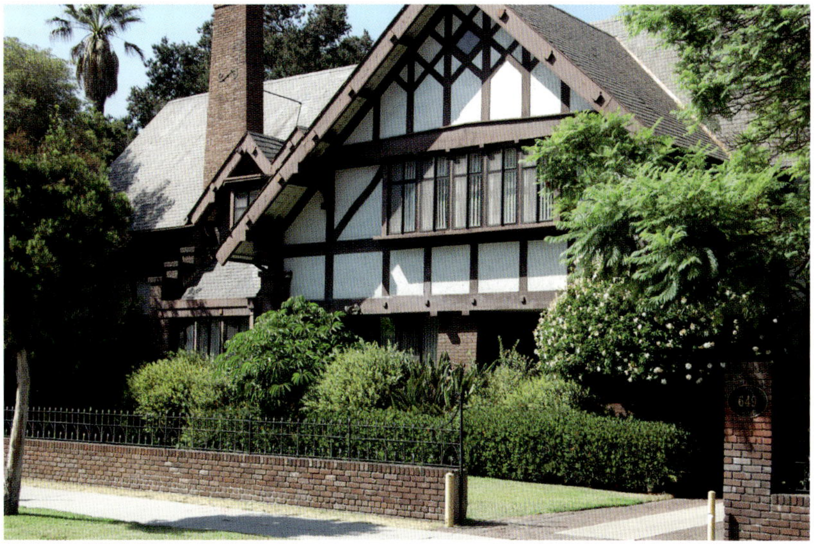

Silent-film actress Norma Talmadge lived at this home, located at 649 West Adams Boulevard, in the early 1920s.

Besides Norma Talmadge, Theda Bara and Roscoe "Fatty" Arbuckle were silent-film players who also once called 649 West Adams Boulevard their home.

CHAPTER 13

WEST HOLLYWOOD

THEN

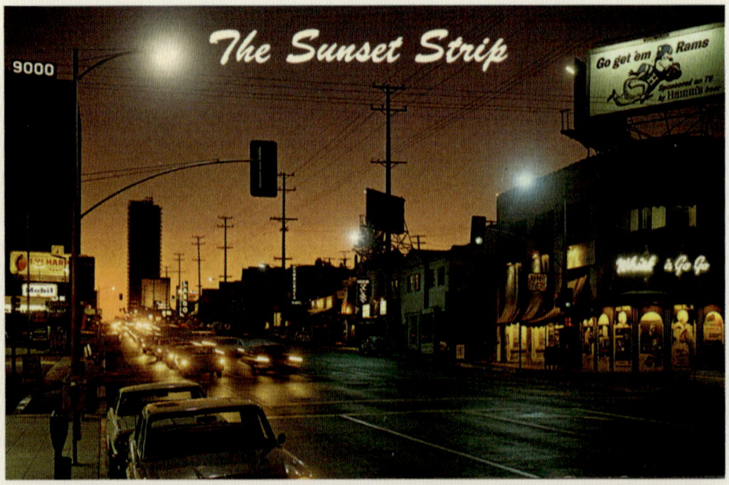

The Sunset Strip.

NOW

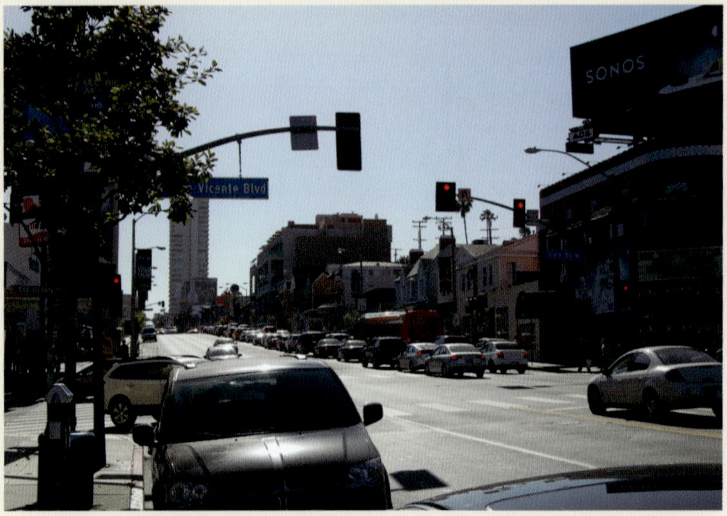

The Sunset Strip, looking west just before it splits San Vicente Boulevard and Clark Street. The Whiskey a Go Go entertainment house in the postcard view, remains in the right side foreground here.

The Sunset Strip is the piece of Sunset Boulevard that falls between Crescent Heights (its east end) and Doheny Drive (its west end). Yes, the Sunset Strip is made up of bustling restaurants and big-name nightclubs, but its claim to fame comes from all the partying that has taken place on it for decades.

THEN

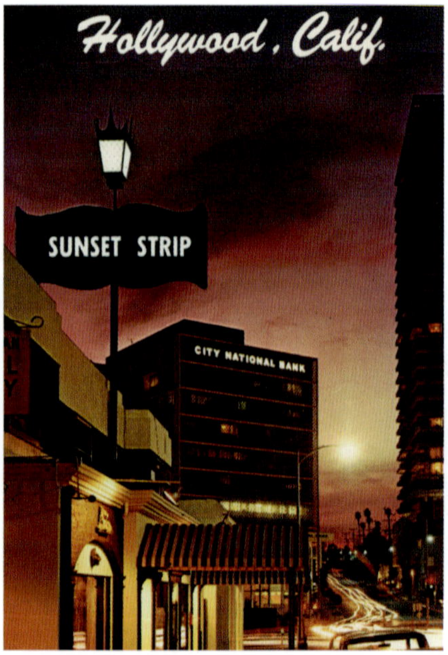

[West] Hollywood, Sunset Strip.

NOW

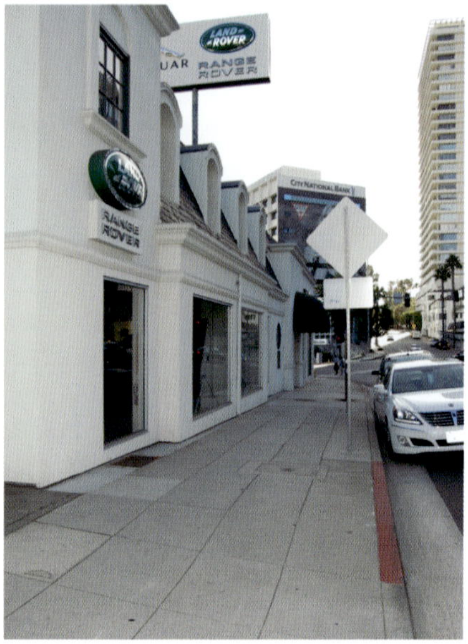

Looking west on Sunset Boulevard just before it splits Corey Avenue and Doheny Road, the Sunset Strip hasn't changed much in terms of physical structures on this corner location.

Besides clubbing at any number of nightspots, one can shop for books or boutique clothing along the Sunset Strip.

THEN

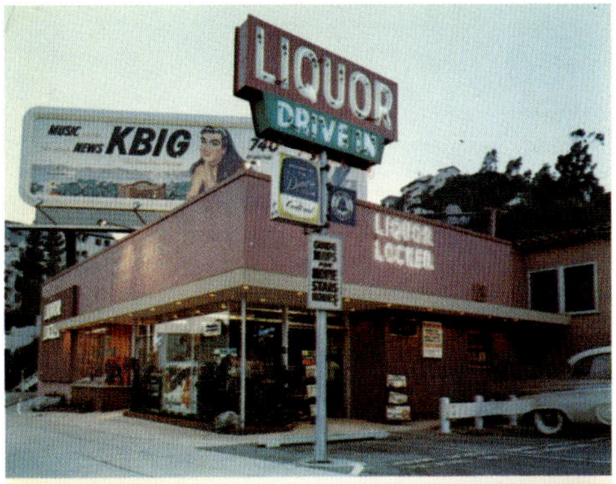

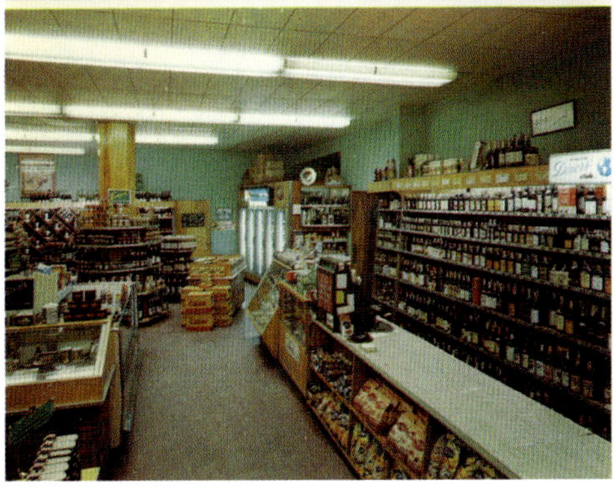

The Liquor Locker.

NOW

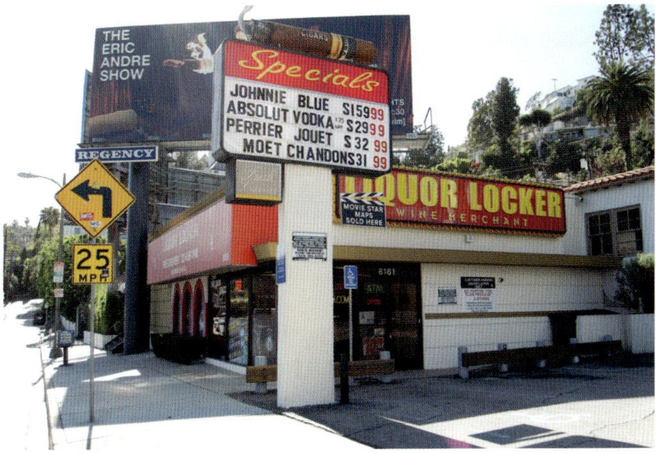

The Liquor Locker remains at 8161 Sunset Boulevard.

Every kind of vintage postcard can
trigger a memory buried inside.

CHAPTER 14

WESTWOOD

THEN

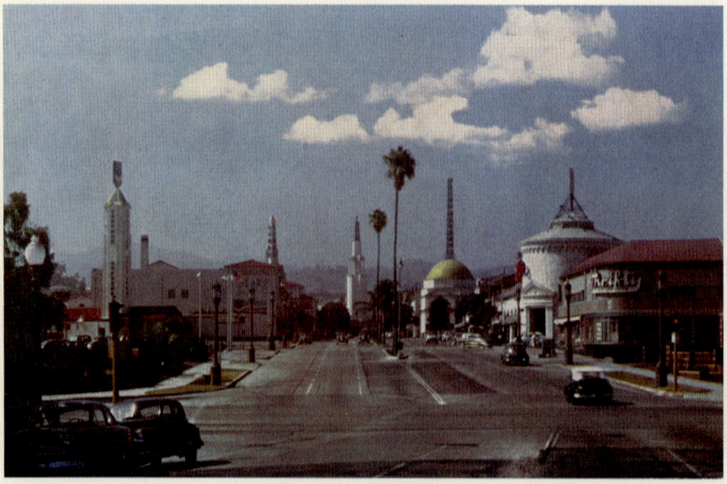

Westwood Village.

NOW

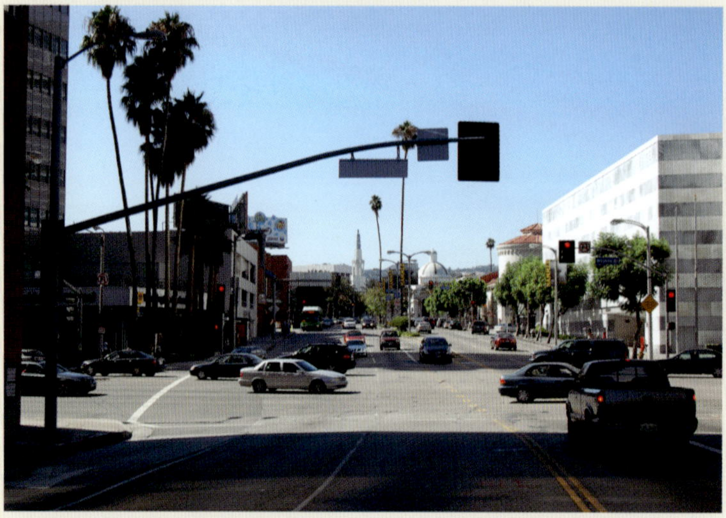

Looking north on Westwood Boulevard, Westwood Village is seen here past the foreground intersection of Westwood and Wilshire boulevards. The Janss Investment Company Building, with its famed dome, still stands. The dome is gold in the postcard view and to the right of the tall palm tree in the center of this view.

Westwood Village is adjacent (south) to the campus of UCLA. It offers students and visitors alike such things as restaurants, movie houses, and sidewalk window shopping.

THEN

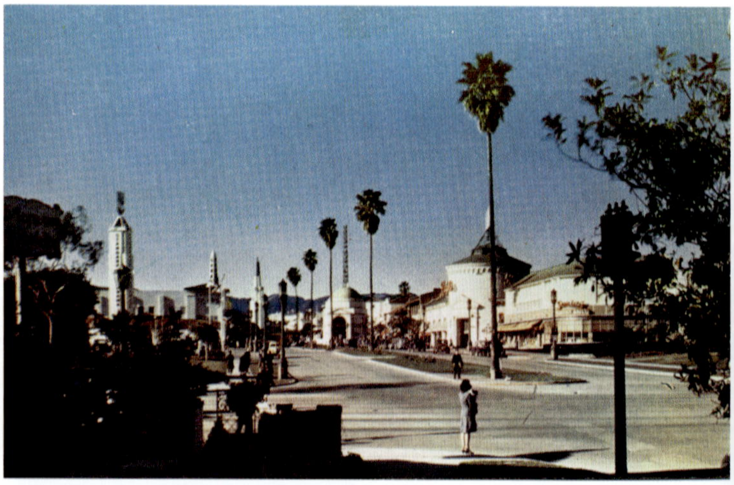

Westwood Village.

NOW

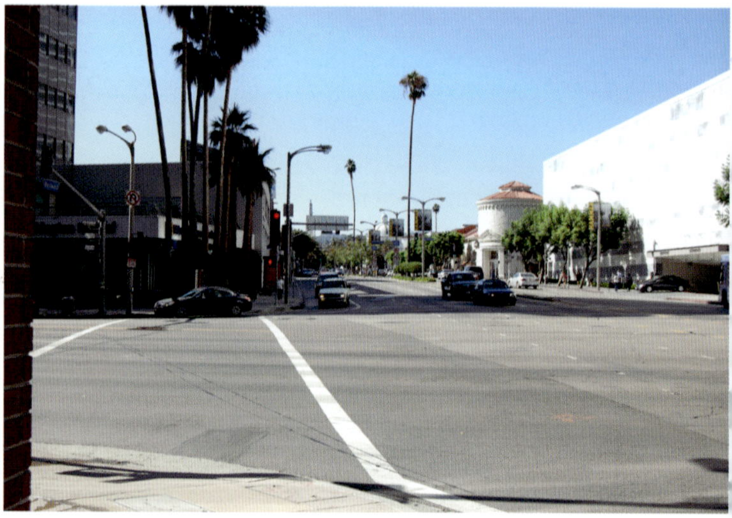

Looking into Westwood Village from the southwest corner of Westwood and Wilshire boulevards.

The master plan to develop Westwood dates back to the 1920s. The sidewalks of Westwood Village have seen years of crowds, as well as times of lean foot traffic.

THEN

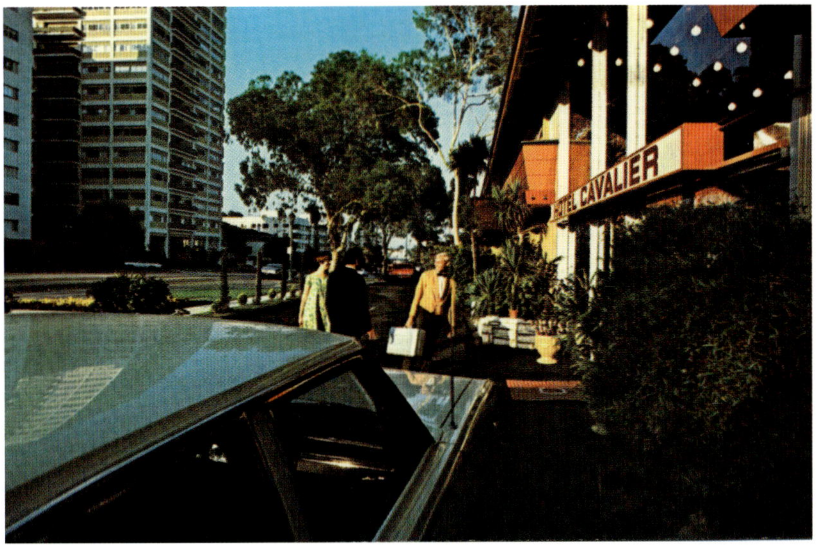

Hotel Cavalier.

NOW

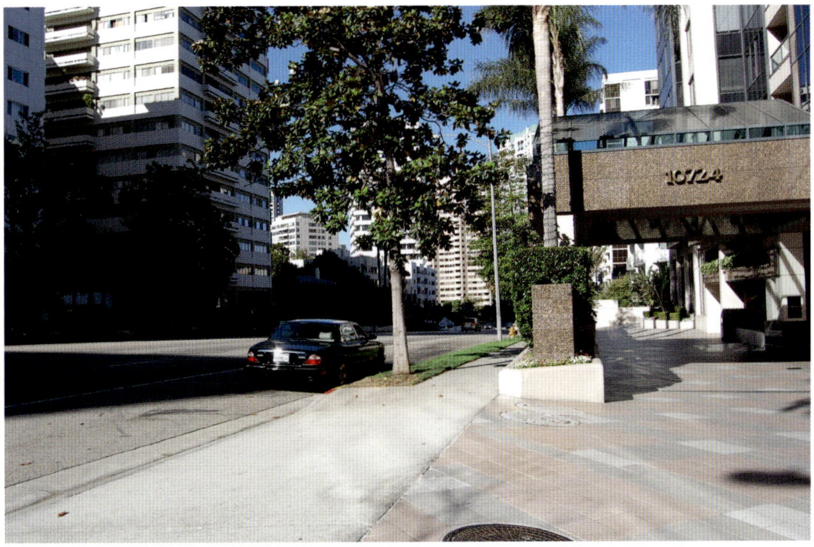

When Hotel Cavalier was operating here, it faced Wilshire Boulevard. It was located at 10724 Wilshire. View is looking east on Wilshire.

The address of 10724 Wilshire Boulevard sits in the Wilshire Corridor, a canyon of mostly high-rise residential buildings that stretch between Westwood Village and Beverly Hills. It has been referred to as the Millionaire Mile due to the high-price points of the condos that make up the corridor.

THEN

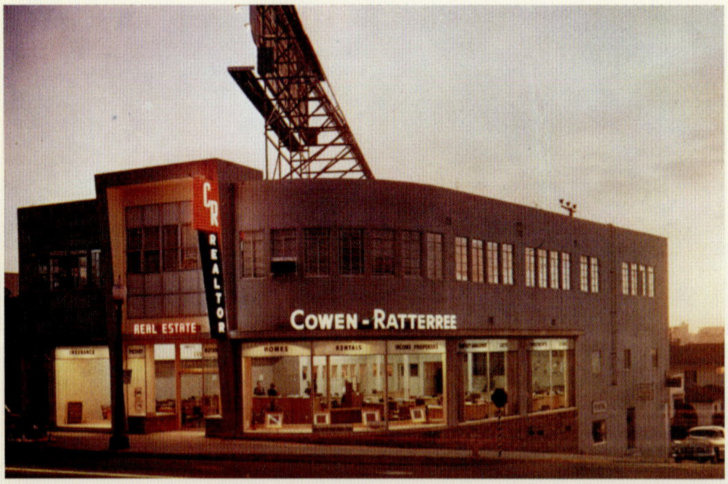

Cowen-Ratterree Realtor.

NOW

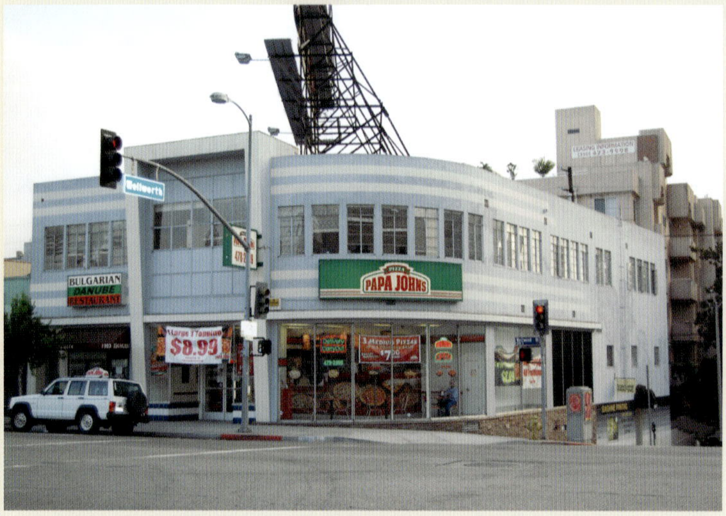

Cowen-Ratterree Realtor was located at 1301 Westwood Boulevard. The building maintains its look from the postcard's era, but no longer houses the realtor.

From real estate sales to pizza flipping. Often it becomes interesting in comparing what business filled a previous business home.

THEN

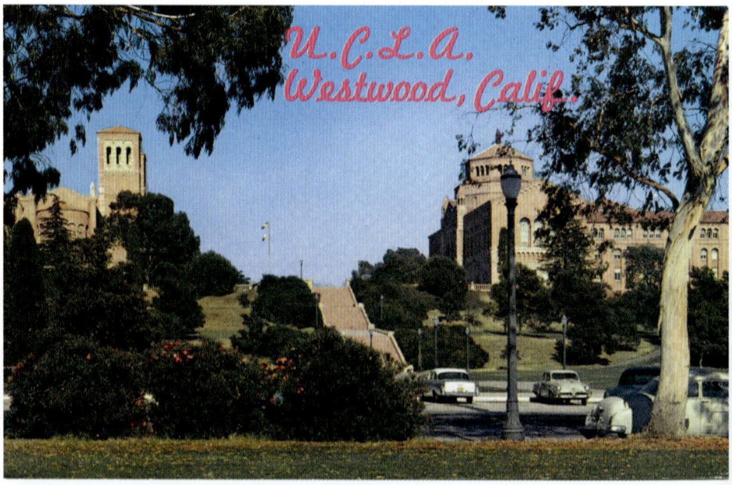

UCLA.

NOW

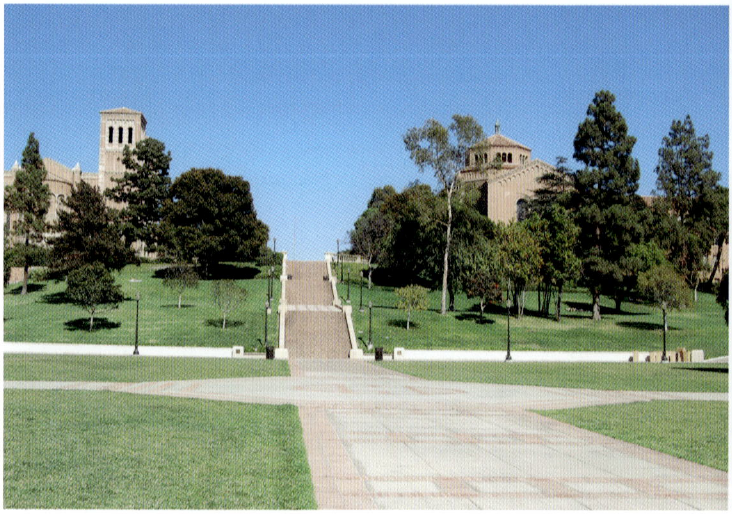

UCLA is perhaps Westwood's most famous property. Royce Hall, a concert hall, is on the left.

The campus of UCLA is often overlooked as simply a walker/jogger paradise, save for attending students.

CHAPTER 15
OUT & ABOUT IN LA

THEN

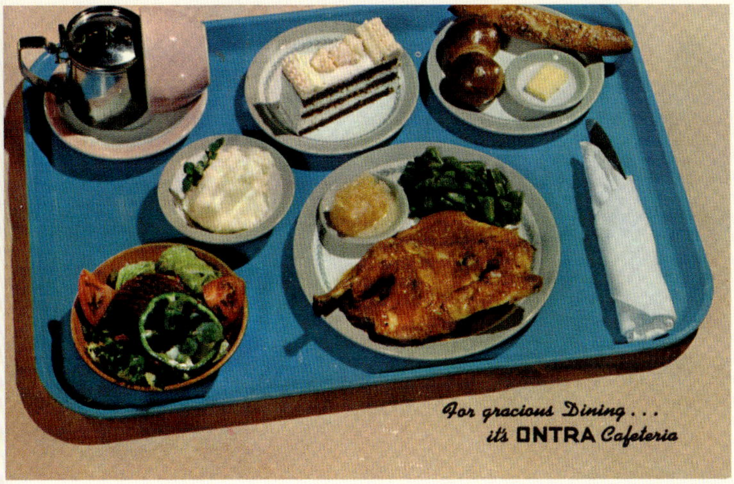

THEN

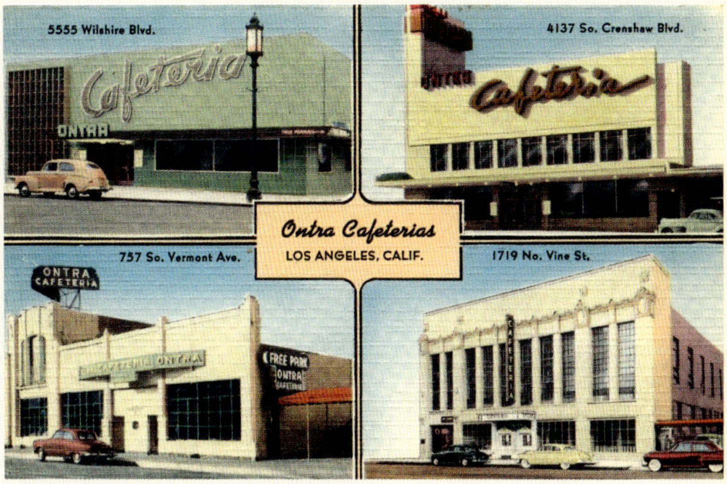

For gracious dining...it's Ontra Cafeteria.

NOW

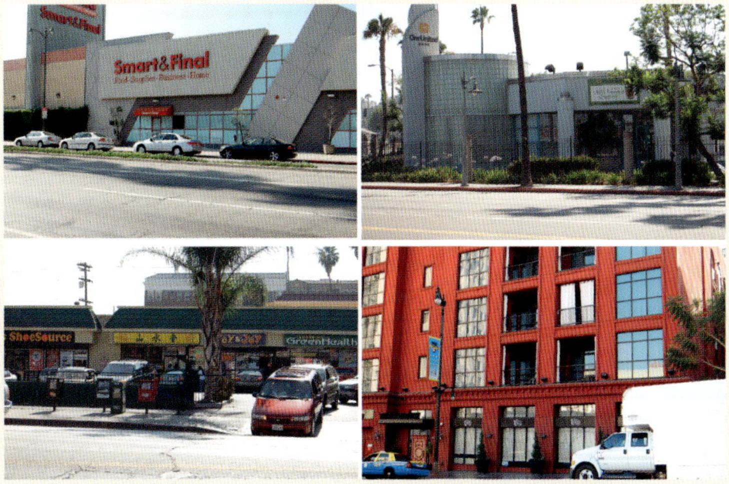

Four former Ontra Cafeterias locations are shown here, each corresponding to their respective postcard view. Beginning clockwise with the top, left location are the Ontra Cafeteria's postcard addresses: 4137 Crenshaw Boulevard, 1719 Vine Street, 757 South Vermont Avenue, and 5555 Wilshire Boulevard.

The Vine Street location of the Hollywood Ontra Cafeteria opened in the 1930s. It was known to serve food to many a movie star.

THEN

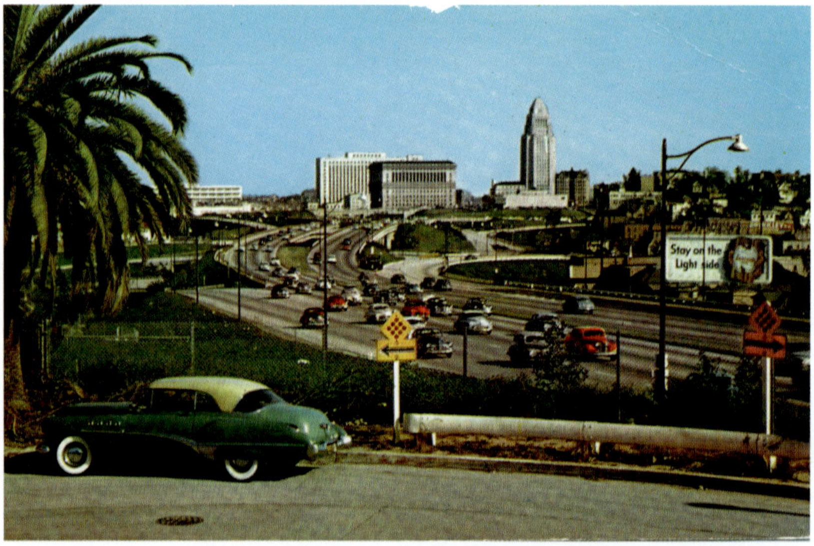

Civic Center from Hollywood Freeway.

NOW

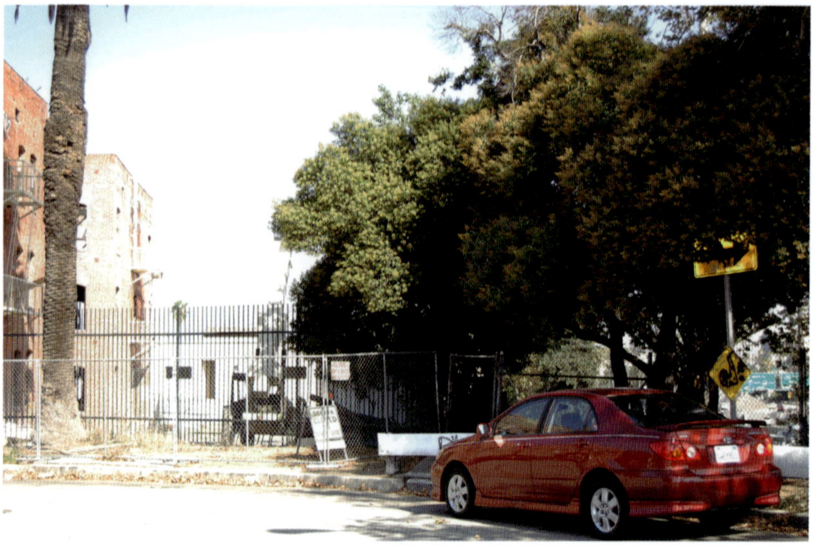

The Civic Center is blocked from view here due to foliage. A small piece of the Hollywood (101) Freeway can be seen just above the lower right corner in this photograph. View is from where Boston and Boylston streets meet.

Where Boston and Boylston streets meet is inside the Angelino Heights area, where one can experience numerous Victorian homes.

THEN

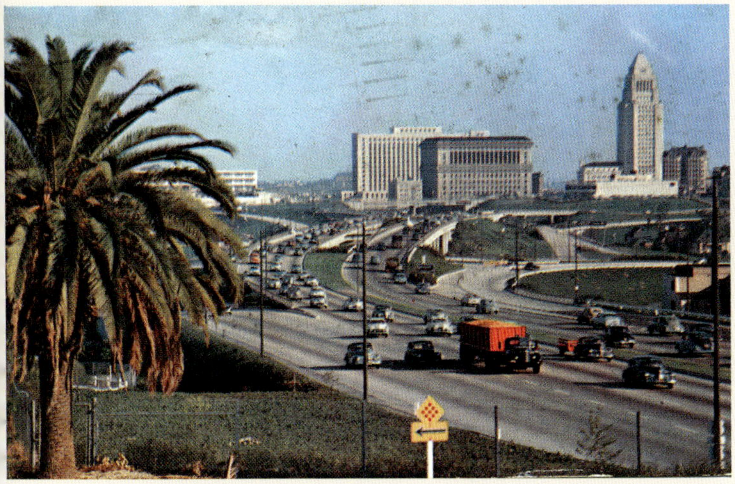

Hollywood Freeway linking Civic Center with Hollywood and the San Fernando Valley.

THEN

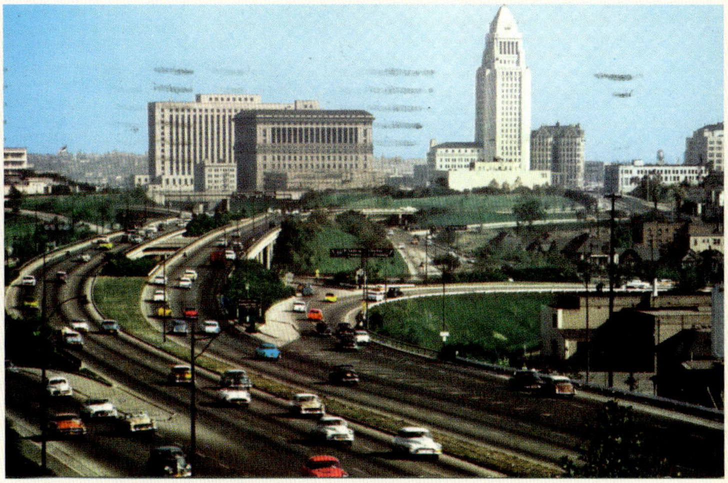

Hollywood Freeway looking toward Civic Center.

NOW

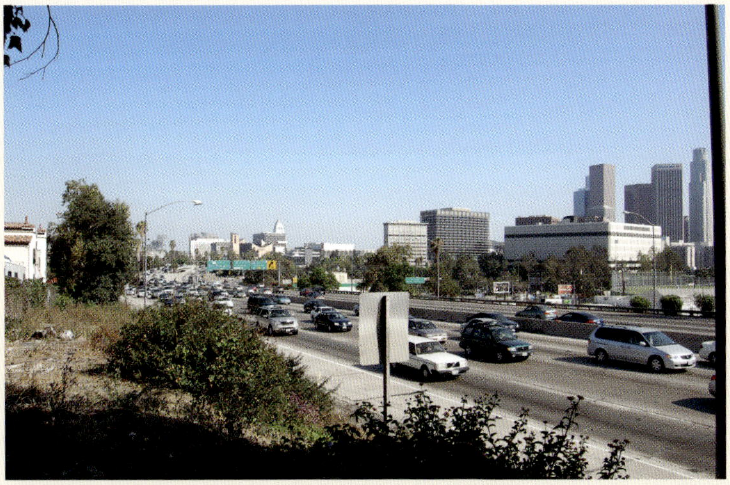

The Civic Center — tall, pointed building in center — can be seen from the vantage point of the side of the Hollywood (101) Freeway. View is from land adjacent to where Boston and Boylston streets meet.

Los Angeles freeways provide any car passenger with ample building-watching opportunities.

THEN

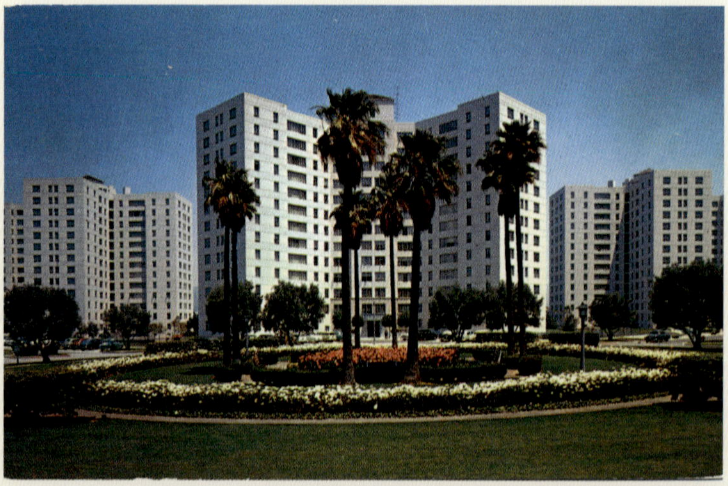

Park La Brea.

NOW

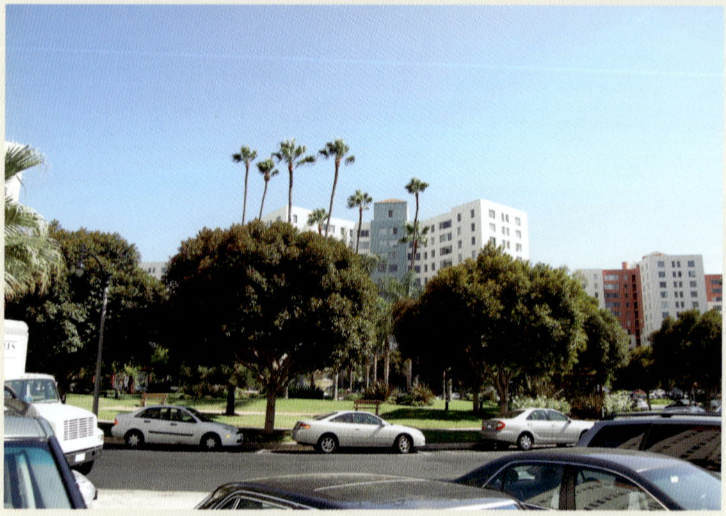

Park La Brea is a gated apartment complex of tall buildings. Tower 39 is the center building. It is only one of the many towers inside the grounds. Park La Brea has an entrance at 6200 West 3rd Street, between Fairfax Avenue and Hauser Boulevard.

Covering 160 acres, Park La Brea is a maze of tall, mid-century apartment buildings. The complex offers over 4,000 units and has a resort-like feel to it. Actor Charlton Heston once called Park La Brea home.

THEN

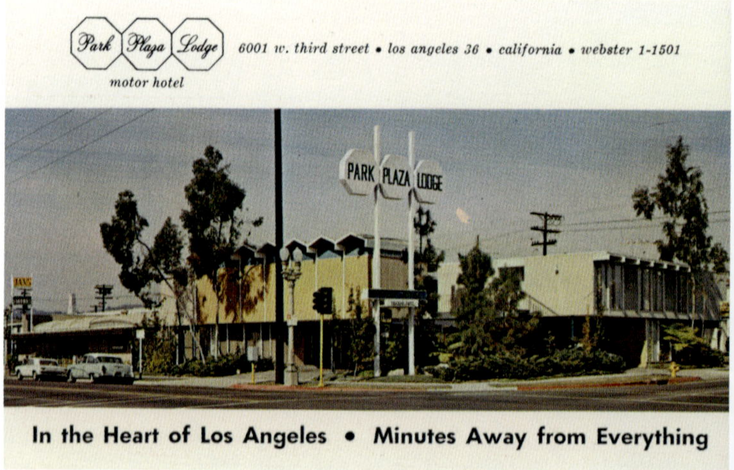

Park Plaza Lodge.

NOW

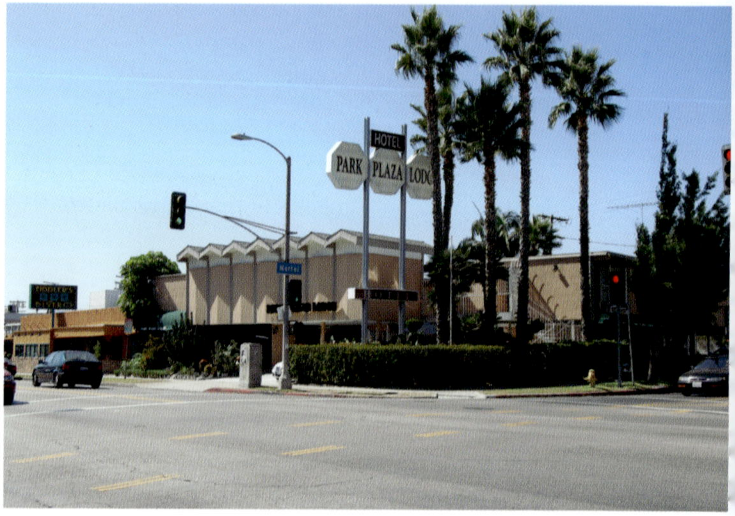

Park Plaza Lodge Hotel, formerly called Park Plaza Lodge, remains at 6001 West 3rd Street.

Park Plaza Lodge Hotel has been a presence on the northwest corner of Martel and 3rd for decades. The cars and the size of the trees are seemingly the only difference between the "then" and "now" views.

THEN

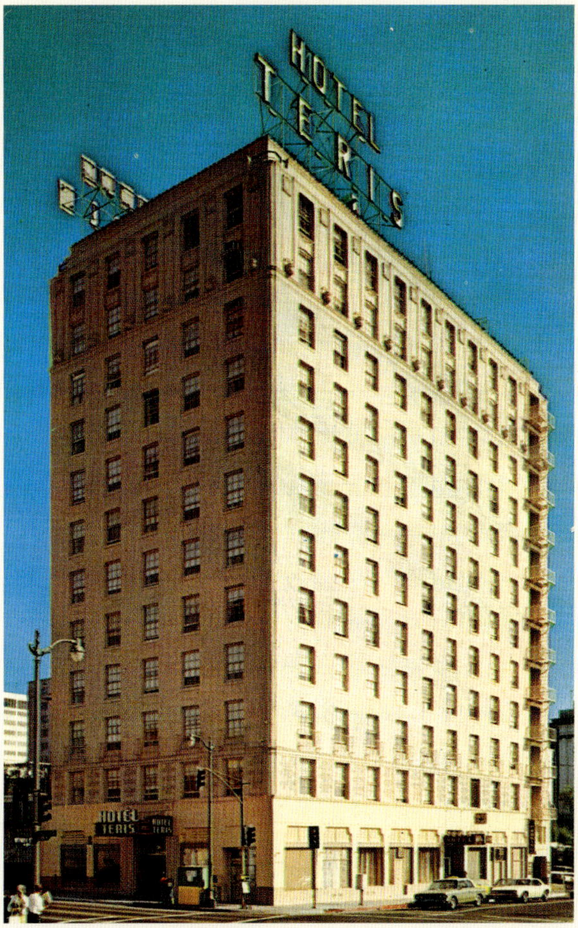

Hotel Teris.

NOW

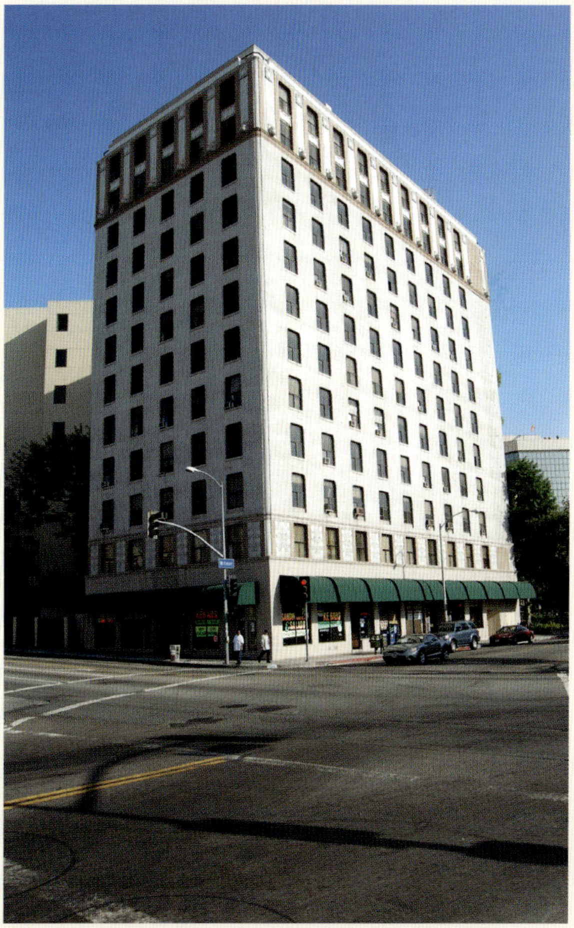

Hotel Teris was located at 1254 West 6th Street. The hotel is no longer here.

The Hotel Teris advertised itself, per the back of the postcard, in part as offering "250 moderately priced rooms with Private Baths – Television – Cafe – Cocktail Lounge – Drive-in Garage."

THEN

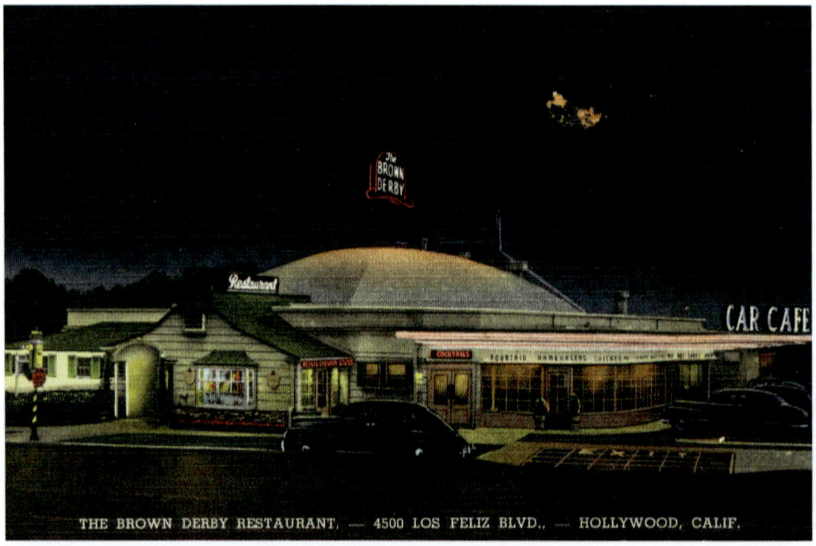

The Brown Derby Restaurant.

NOW

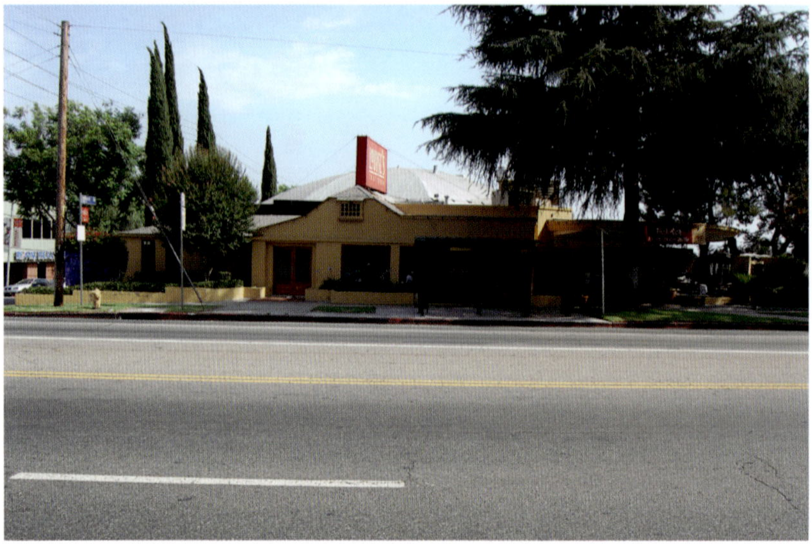

The Los Feliz location of the Brown Derby Restaurant chain stood at 4500 Los Feliz Boulevard; it shut its doors in 1960. All of the Brown Derby restaurants are now closed.

THEN

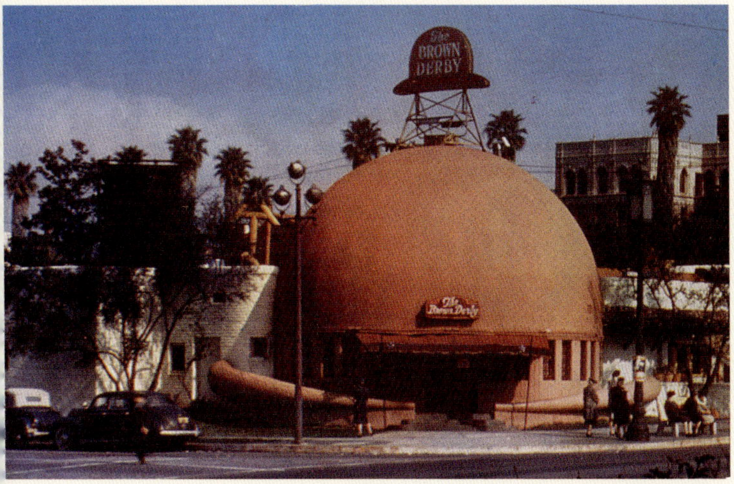

THEN

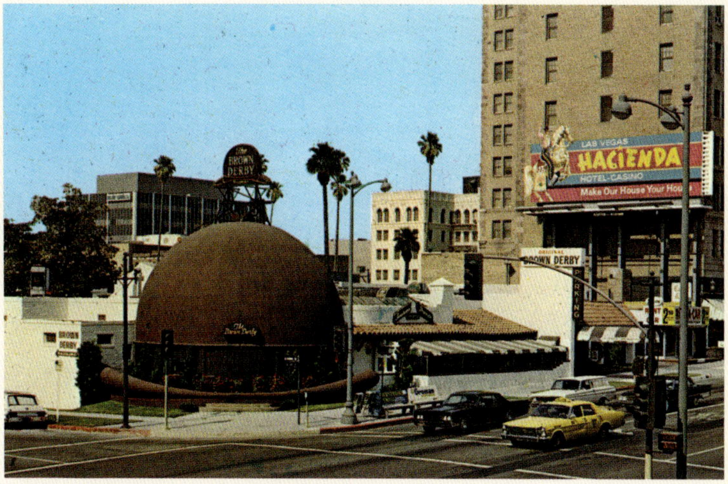

The Brown Derby Restaurant.

NOW

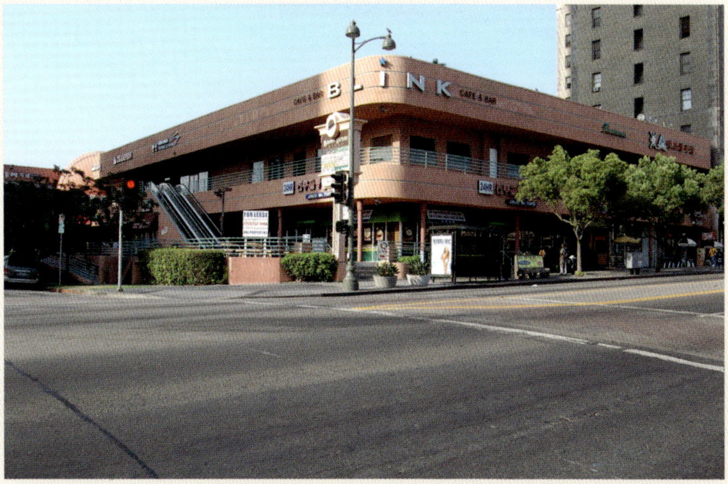

The first Brown Derby Restaurant location stood here on the northeast corner of Alexandria Avenue and Wilshire Boulevard. Once a place where Hollywood stars were often seen eating, the Brown Derby restaurants are no more in Los Angeles.

THEN

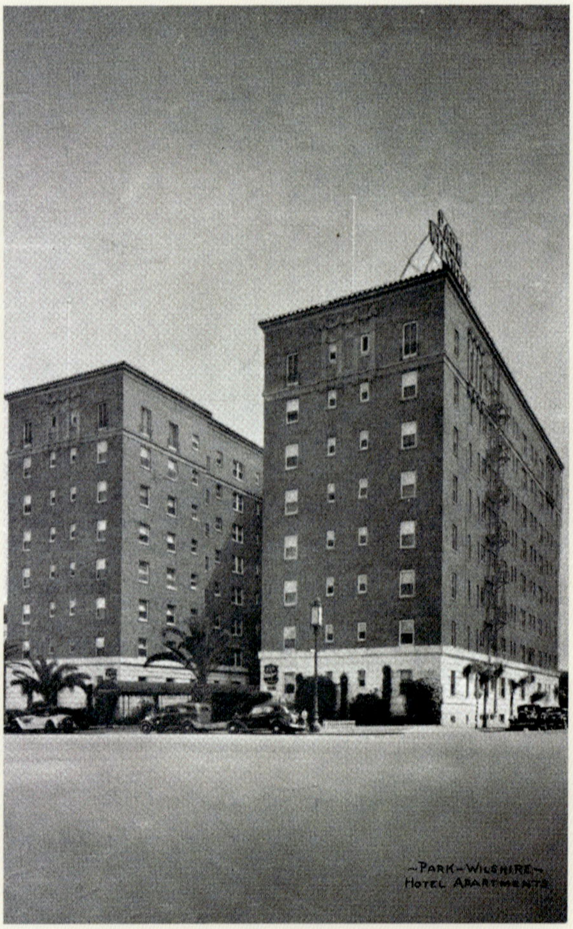

Park-Wilshire Hotel Apartments.

NOW

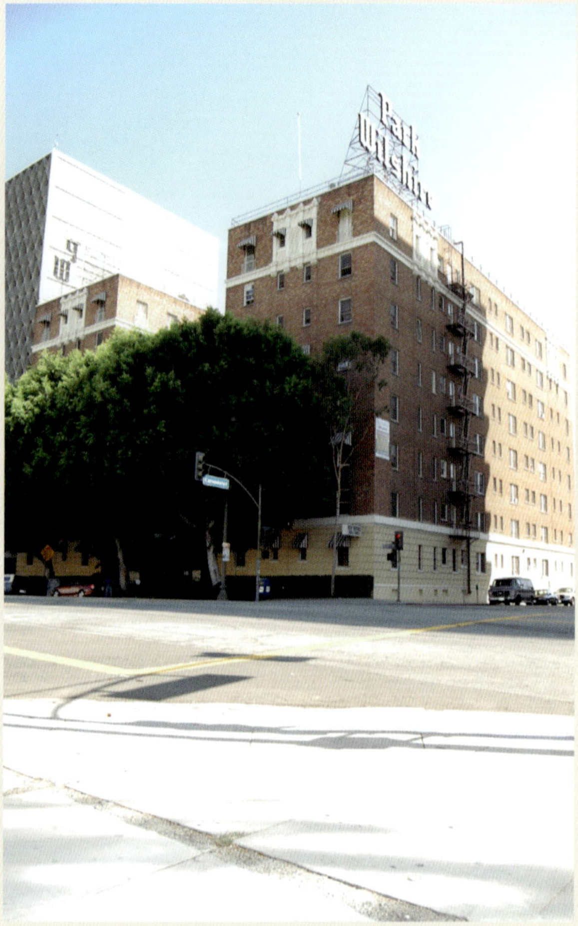

Park Wilshire, formerly Park-Wilshire Hotel Apartments, is an apartment complex located at 2424 Wilshire Boulevard.

Anna May Wong, the first Chinese-American actress to become a star, lived at Park Wilshire.

THEN

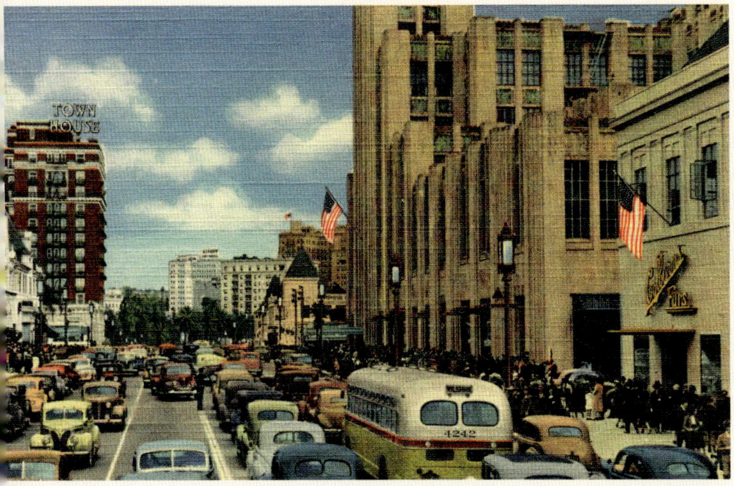

Busy crowds on Wilshire Boulevard.

NOW

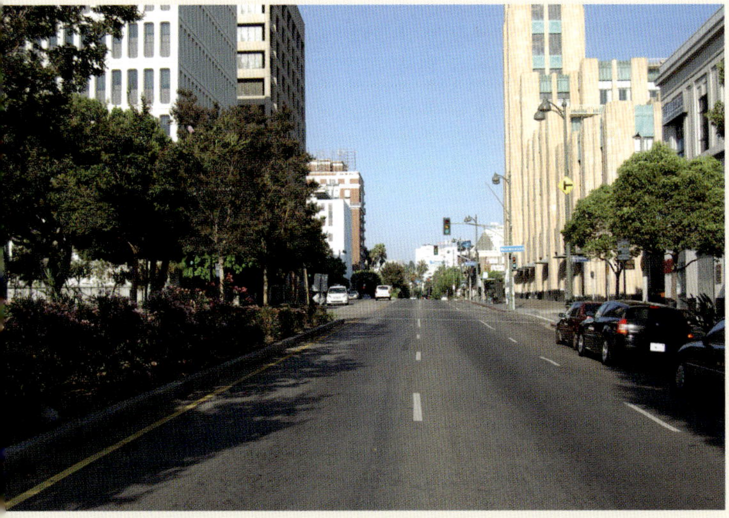

Looking east on Wilshire Boulevard just past Shatto Place, Bullock's Wilshire building, shown on the right, is prominent on the corner of Westmoreland Avenue and Wilshire. The Bullock's building is no longer a department store. The Town House, the prominent and tallest building on the left side in the postcard view, still stands. This historic structure has had a few names throughout its history.

Decades ago, Wilshire Boulevard was referred to as the "Fifth Avenue of the West."

THEN

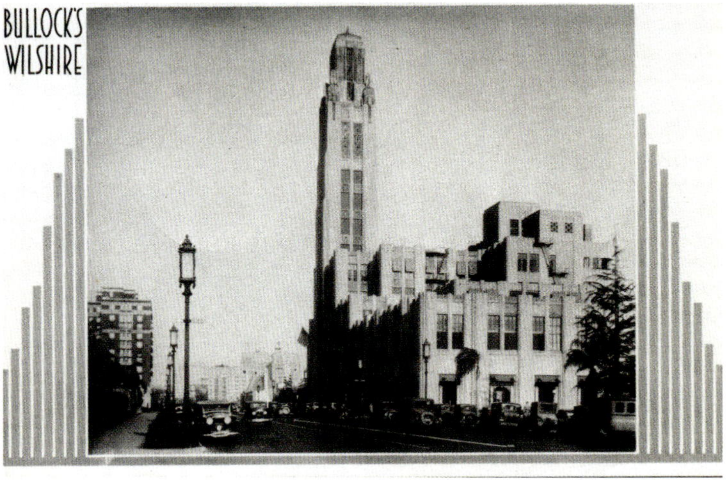

Bullock's Wilshire.

NOW

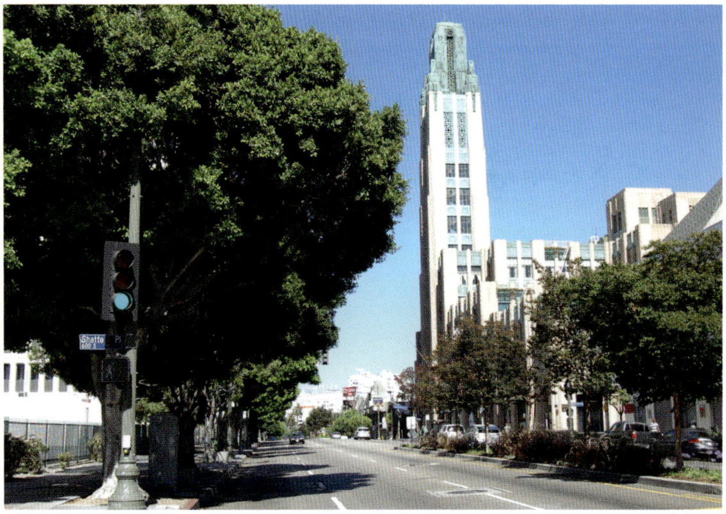

Looking east on Wilshire Boulevard from Shatto Place, the Bullock's Wilshire building continues to stand guard over Wilshire, despite its namesake no longer operating.

The Art Deco-style Bullocks Wilshire building has been gracing Wilshire Boulevard with its presence since 1929.

THEN

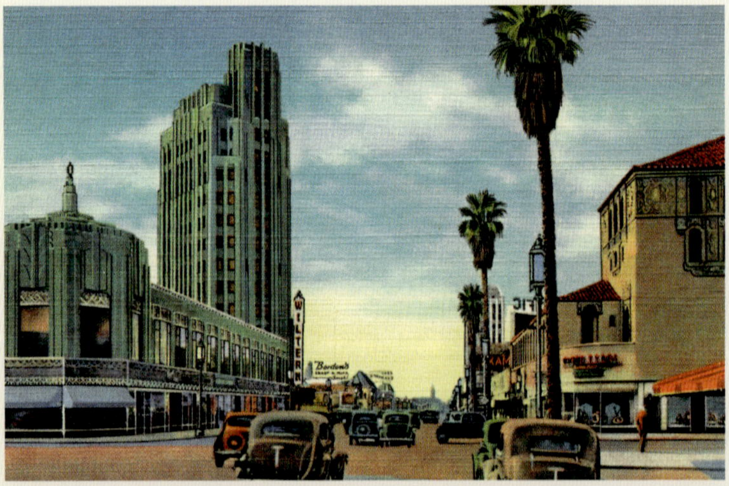

Wilshire Boulevard near Western [Avenue].

NOW

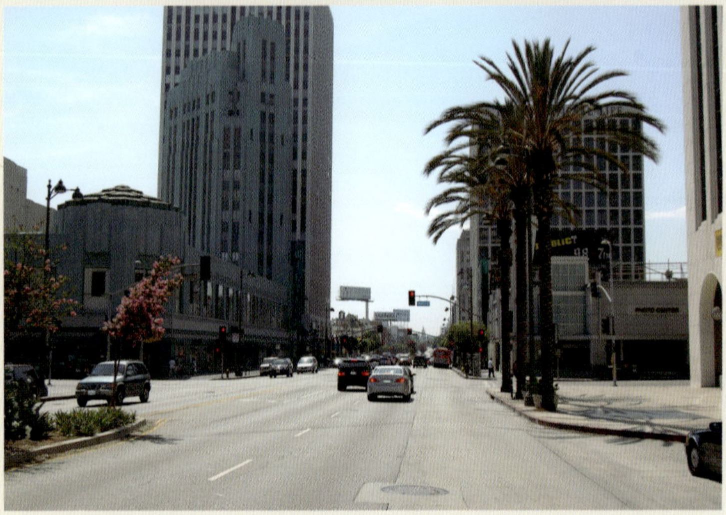

Wilshire Boulevard near Western Avenue. On the southeast corner of Wilshire and Western sits the Wiltern, historically known as the Wiltern Theater, and the attached Pellissier Building towering over the Boulevard. View is looking west on Wilshire, which connects with Oxford Avenue in the foreground intersection.

Wilshire Boulevard is home to the Wiltern Theater and the attached Pellissier Building. The Art Deco-style structures were built in the early 1930s.

THEN

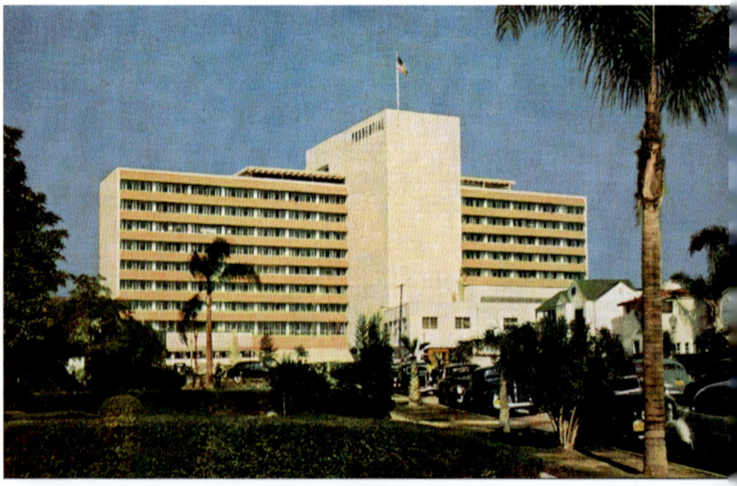

Prudential Square.

NOW

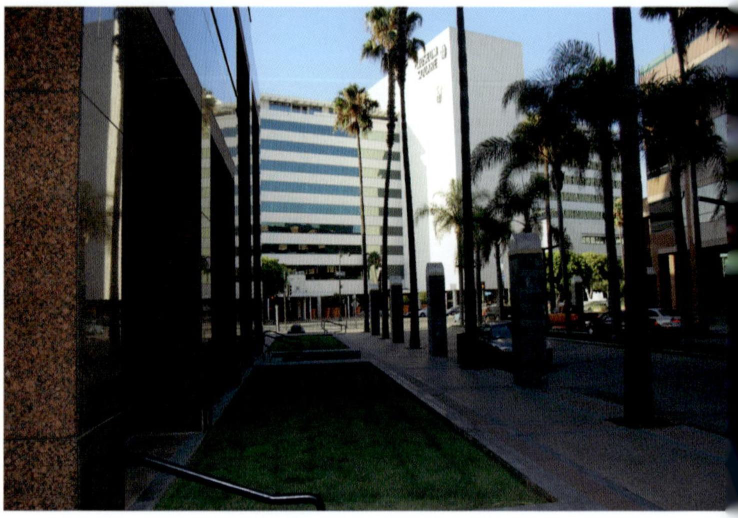

Museum Square, formerly called Prudential Square, stands at 5757 Wilshire Boulevard. The building is an office complex with retail space on the ground floor. Buildings have sprung up across Wilshire from Museum Square since the time of the postcard.

Museum Square, formerly called Prudential Square, was built in the 1940s, with further additions constructed in the 1950s.

THEN

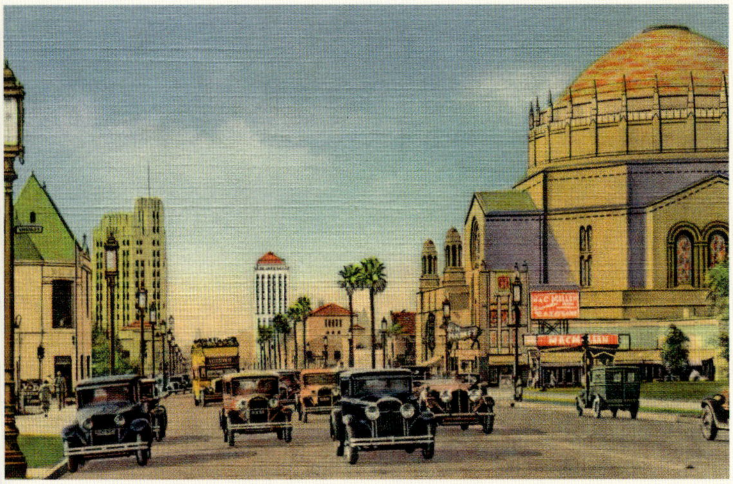

Scene on Wilshire Boulevard.

NOW

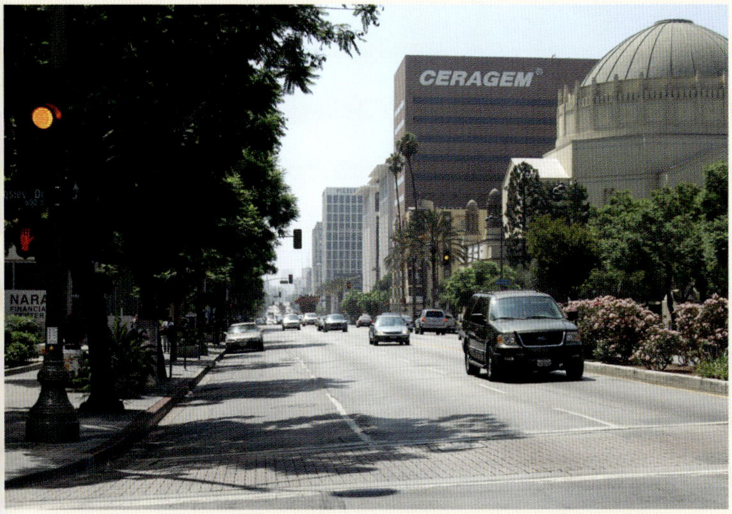

Scene on Wilshire Boulevard. The Wilshire Boulevard Temple, seen on the right, is prominent in the foreground here. View is looking west on Wilshire from Kingsley Drive.

Wilshire Boulevard stretches from downtown to the beaches of Santa Monica.

THEN

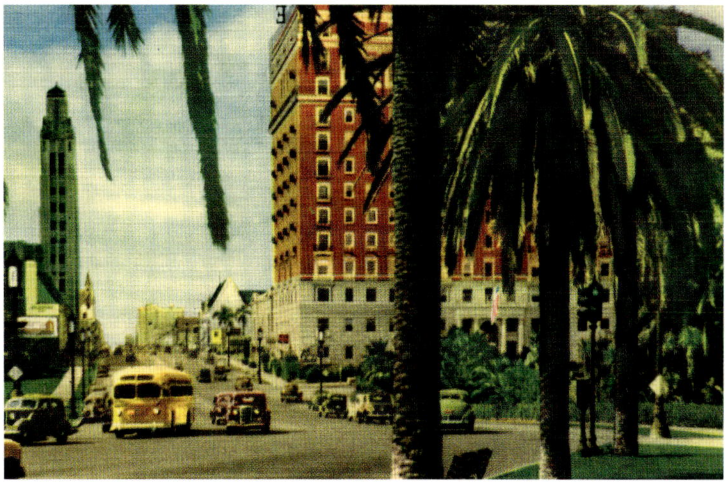

Wilshire Boulevard [showing] Bullock's Wilshire [and the] Town House.

NOW

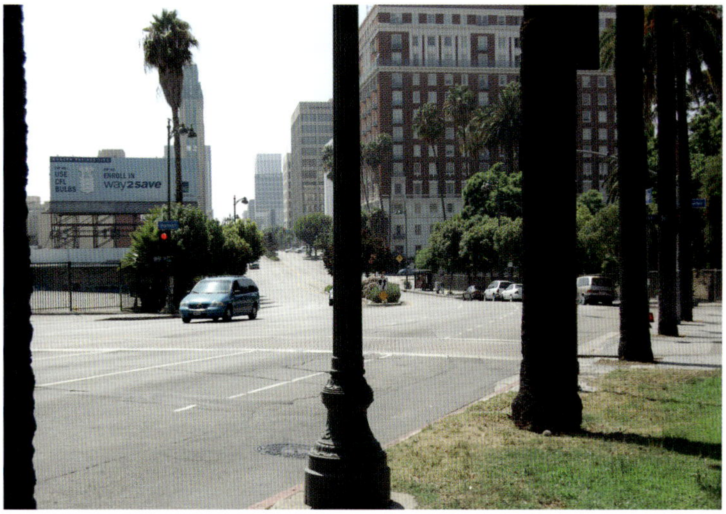

Wilshire Boulevard showing Bullock's Wilshire (tallest building on left) and the Town House (building in foreground on right). Bullock's Wilshire is no longer a Bullock's and the Town House building has been called a few other names throughout its history. View is looking west on Wilshire; Hover Street runs into Wilshire in the foreground.

A drive along Wilshire Boulevard offers visits to, among others, the Mid-Wilshire District, the Miracle Mile, Beverly Hills, Westwood, and Santa Monica.

THEN

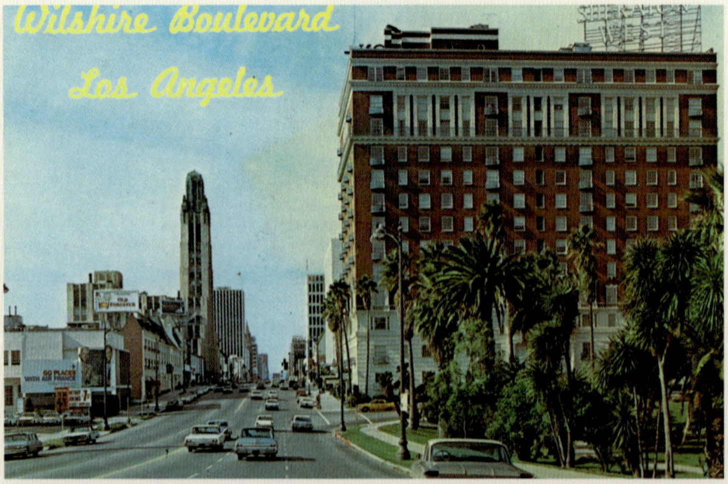

Wilshire Boulevard.

NOW

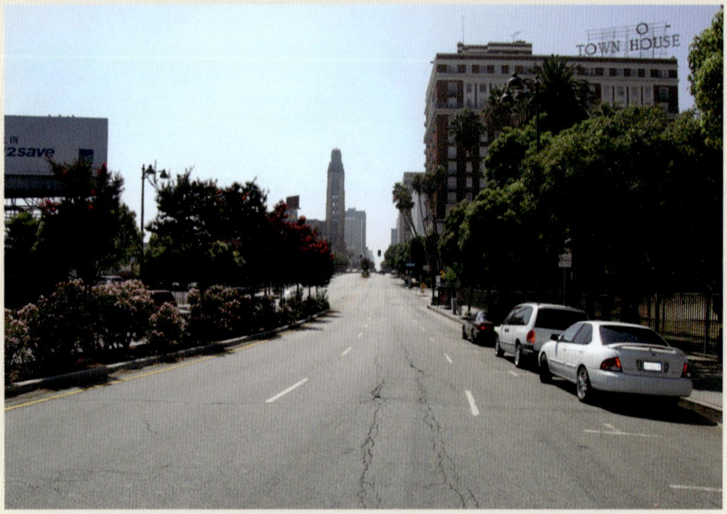

Looking west on Wilshire Boulevard from where it runs alongside Lafayette Park, the Bullock's Wilshire building is on the left in the distance. Dominating the right foreground is the Town House, a historic building. The "then" postcard view of this building has the Sheraton West name on it, reflecting that the building has at times been a hotel.

Wilshire Boulevard was named after millionaire socialist Henry Gaylord Wilshire (1861–1927).

THEN

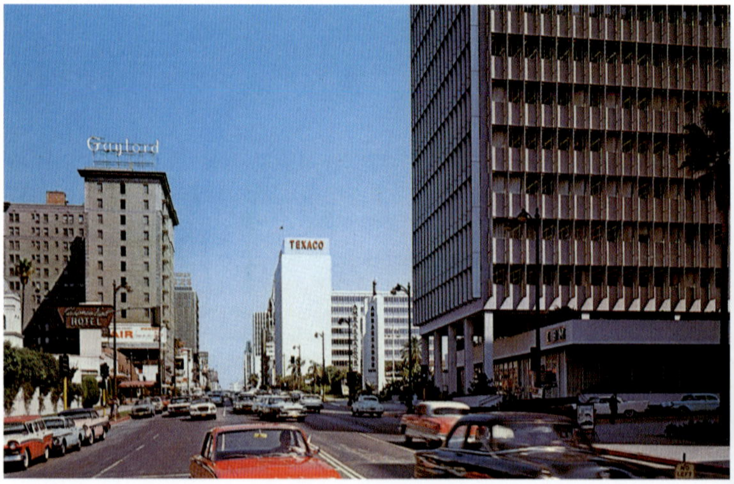

Wilshire Boulevard.

NOW

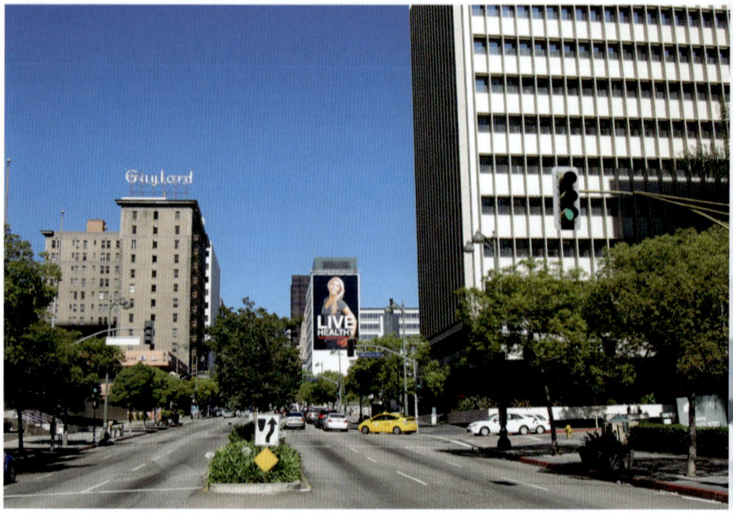

Looking east along Wilshire Boulevard just before it meets Mariposa Avenue, the Gaylord building can been seen on the left. Located at 3355 Wilshire, today it houses the Gaylord Apartments.

It would take a huge number of books to study all the historic and architecturally significant buildings that Wilshire Boulevard displays.

THEN

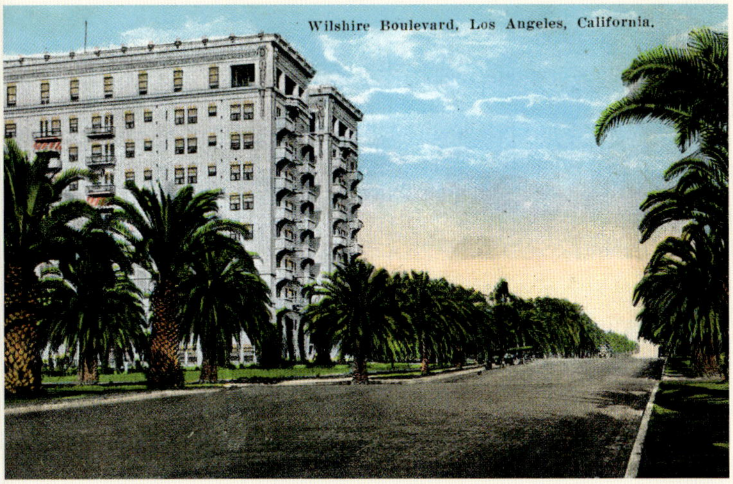

Wilshire Boulevard.

NOW

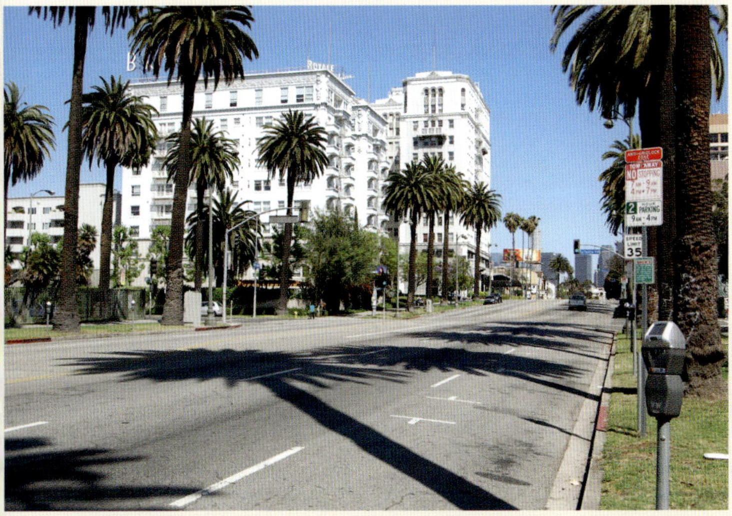

Looking east on Wilshire Boulevard, the intersection of Wilshire and La Fayette Park Place is in the foreground. Dominating the view is the Bryson Apartment Hotel, a historic building that has experienced business and name changes over the years. The building has recently been called the Bryson Apartments.

Among the big-name streets that Wilshire Boulevard intersects are La Cienega, Beverly, Westwood, and Lincoln boulevards.

THEN

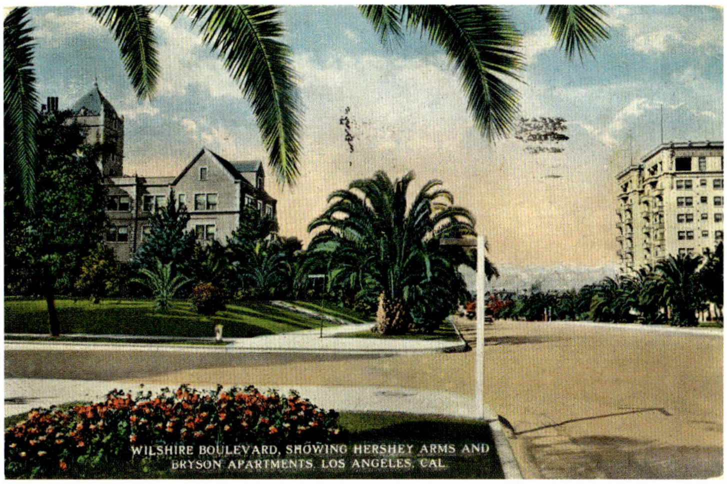

Wilshire Boulevard, showing Hersey Arms and Bryson Apartments.

NOW

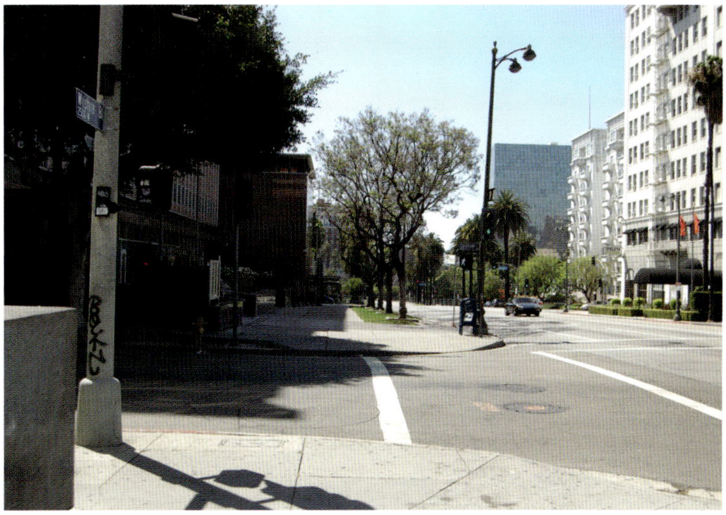

Wilshire Boulevard with Bryson Apartments, the second building on the right. The Hersey Arms Hotel, left side of the postcard view, no longer stands. It was located at 2600 Wilshire. View is looking west on Wilshire from Coronado Street.

Taken from the message the sender wrote in 1917 to the recipient on the back of this postcard: "Things are just as this picture shows now." The same message applies to the now view of Wilshire from Coronado Street.

THEN

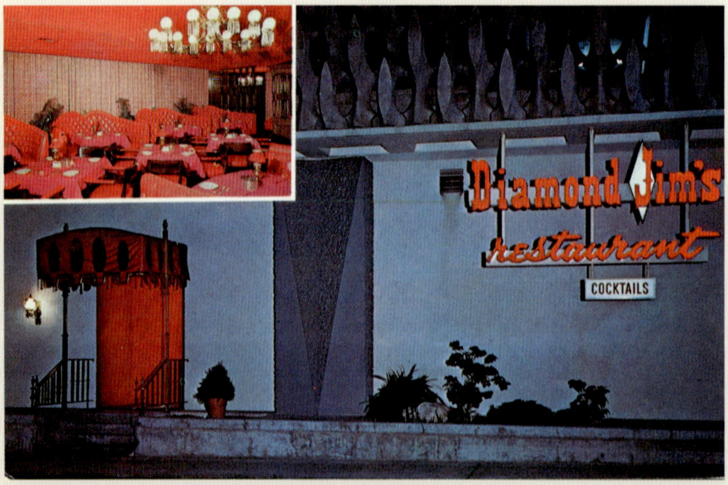

Diamond Jim's Restaurant.

NOW

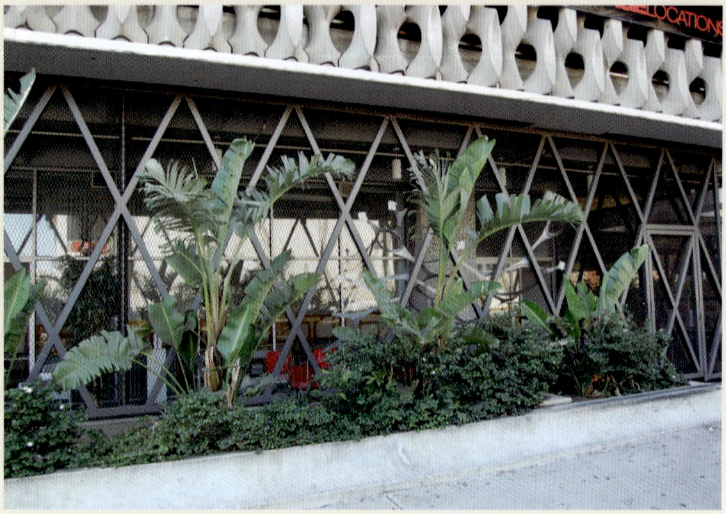

Diamond Jim's Restaurant listed its address as 2400 Wilshire Boulevard. (Author notes that this photograph does not attempt to align with the view the postcard offers. It was not possible to determine the exact spot of Diamond Jim's door since the building has been modified.)

The sender of the postcard wrote in 1964 to the recipient: "Had some fun here plus some work. Will be home tomorrow. Love xxx Charley."

THEN

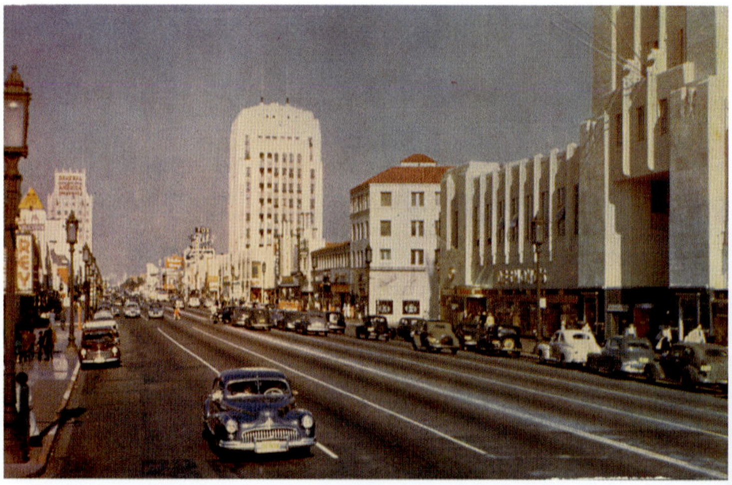

Miracle Mile on Wilshire Boulevard.

NOW

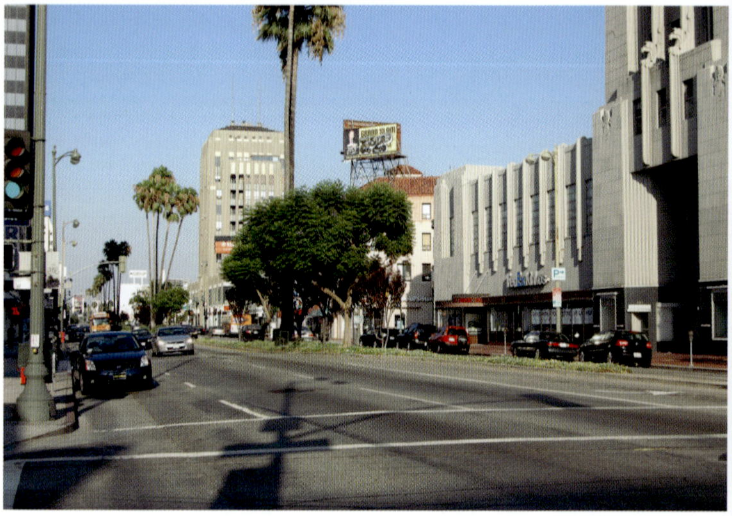

Looking east on Wilshire Boulevard from Burnside Avenue, Miracle Mile is on display here along Wilshire.

The Miracle Mile runs along Wilshire Boulevard between La Brea and Fairfax avenues.

THEN

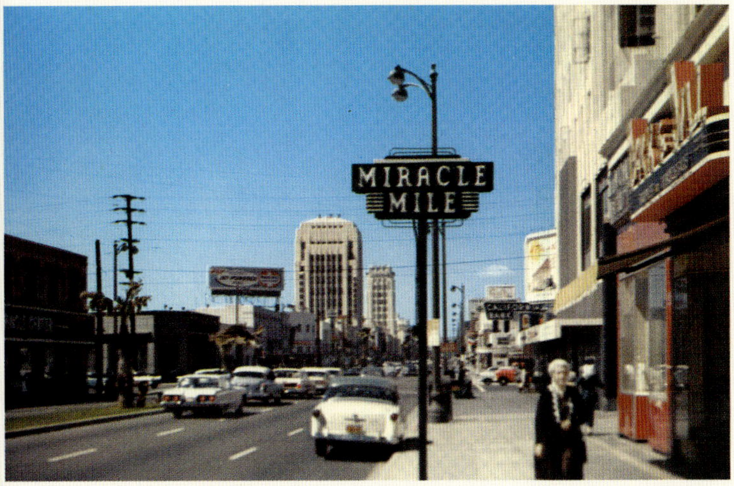

Miracle Mile, along Wilshire Boulevard.

NOW

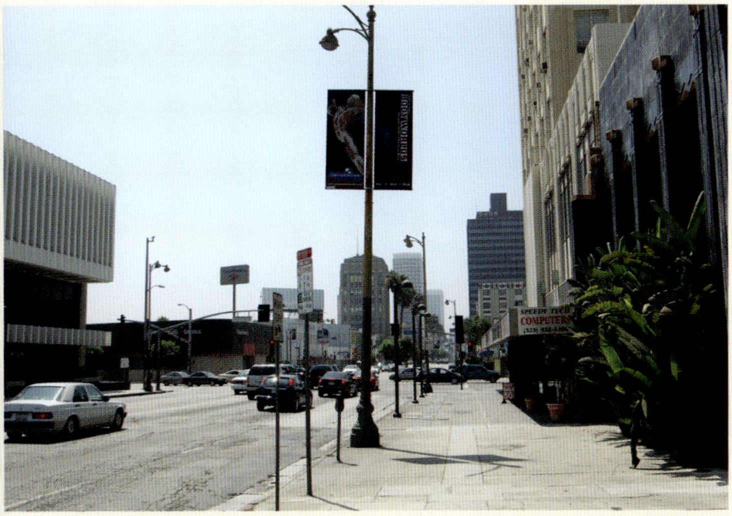

Miracle Mile on Wilshire Boulevard. Many prominent buildings in the "then" postcard view remain along Wilshire today. This view is looking west on Wilshire before it intersects La Brea Avenue.

The Miracle Mile got its name in 1928, and by 1929 it had become a retail shopping destination.

THEN

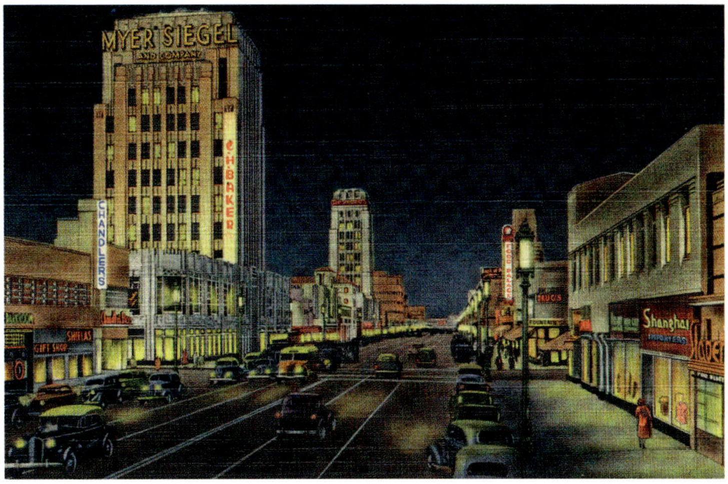

Miracle Mile, Wilshire Boulevard.

NOW

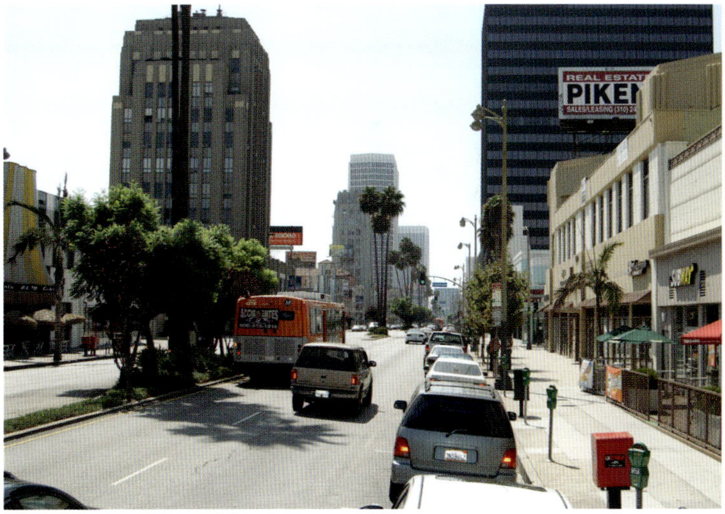

Miracle Mile on Wilshire Boulevard. View is looking west on Wilshire, a half-block short of Cloverdale Avenue.

Today, the Miracle Mile is less about shopping and more about museums and Art Deco-style buildings.

THEN

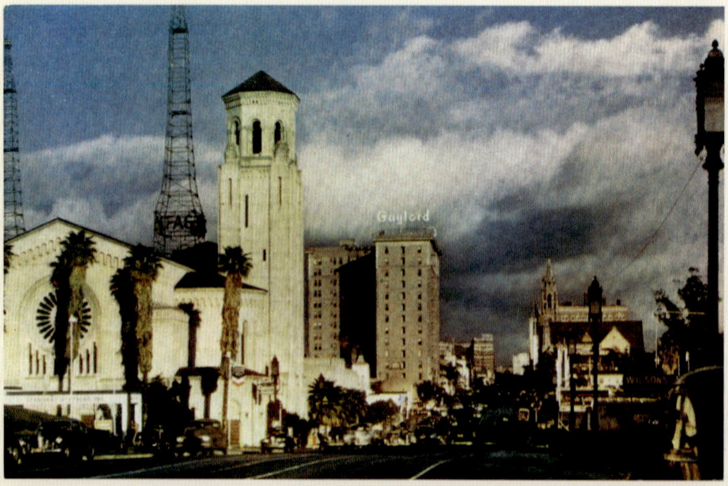

Wilshire Boulevard Christian Church.

NOW

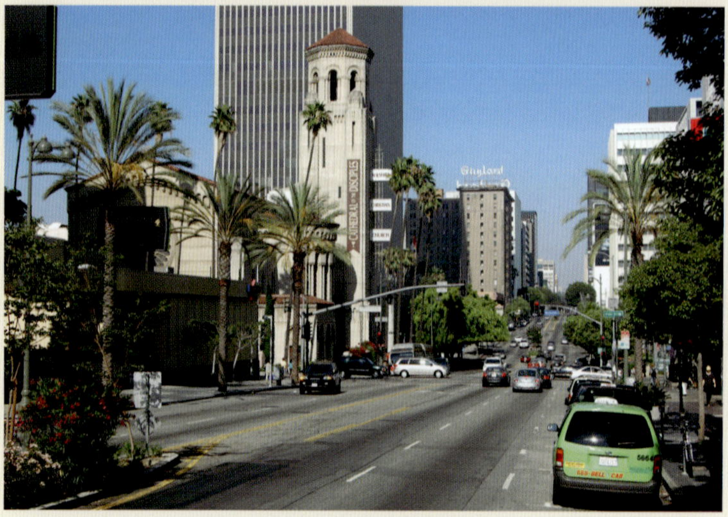

Looking east along Wilshire Boulevard, Wilshire Boulevard Christian Church is now called Wilshire Christian Church.

The back of the postcard tells of the Wilshire Boulevard Christian Church (now Wilshire Christian Church) as being "distinguished by its west façade cartwheel window, based upon that of the Rheims Cathedral in France."

THEN

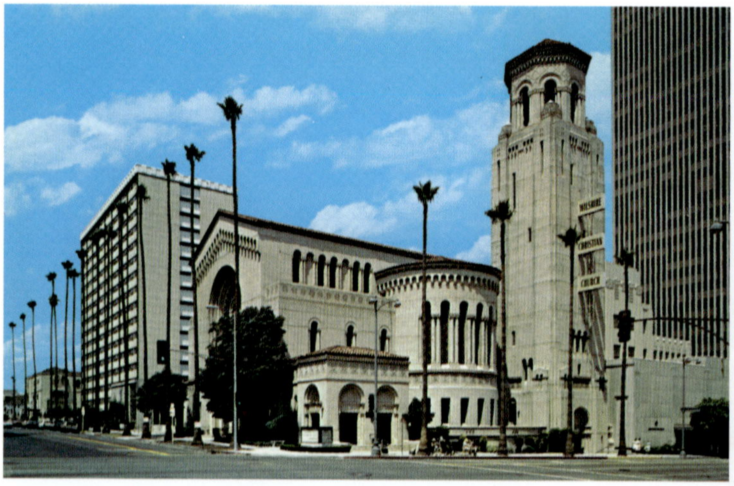

Wilshire Christian Church.

NOW

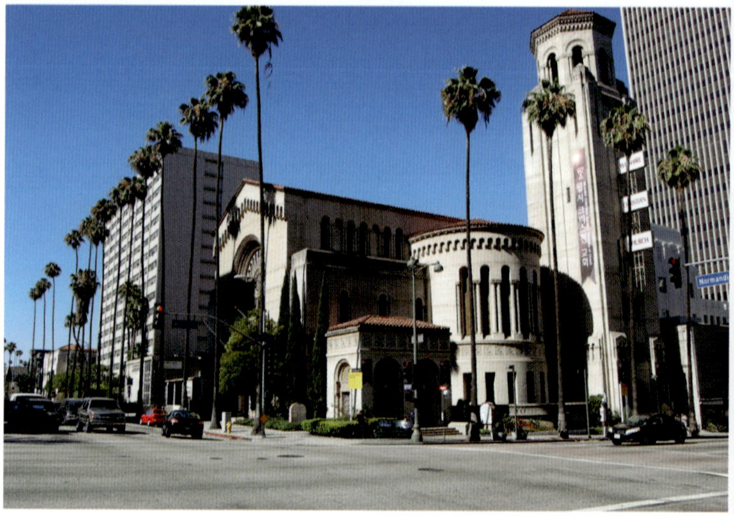

Wilshire Christian Church is located at 634 South Normandie Avenue. The church resides on the northeast corner of Normandie Avenue and Wilshire Boulevard.

Wilshire Christian Church, designed by Robert H. Orr, was built in the Northern Italian Romanesque style.

THEN

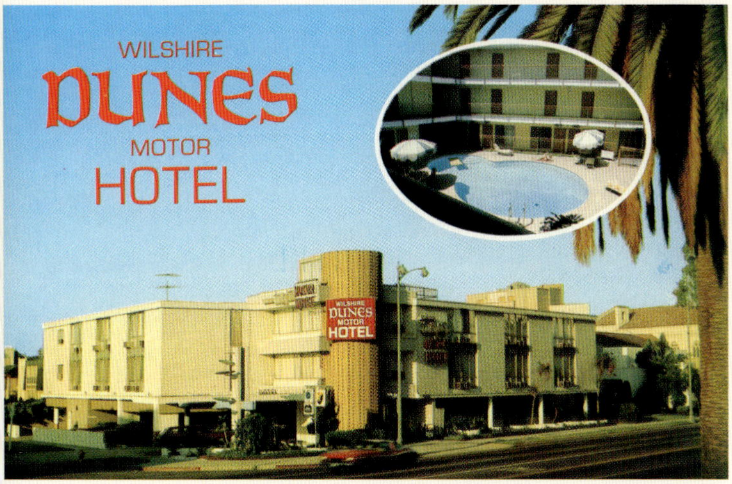

Wilshire Dunes Motor Hotel.

NOW

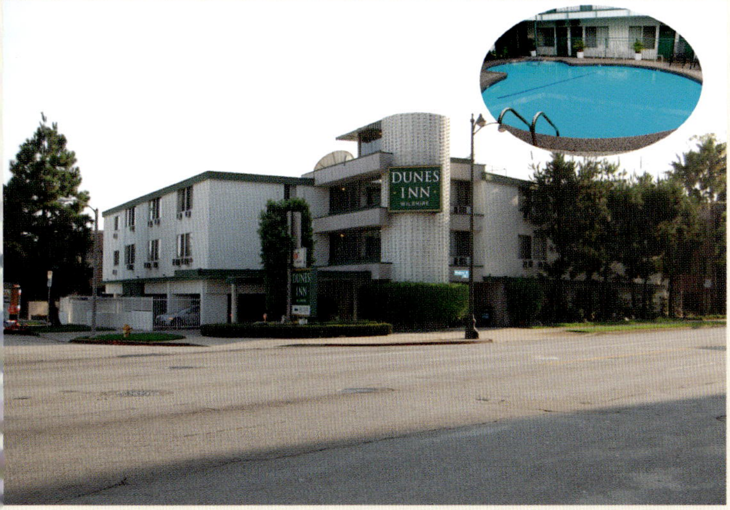

The Wilshire Dunes Motor Hotel building remains nearly identical to its postcard view. The property is located at 4300 Wilshire Boulevard and carries a different signage. Its pool shape has also remained the same. (Note: Postcard views are recreated by the author, not by the hotel.)

When the Wilshire Dunes Motor Hotel postcard was printed, it was advertising its location as "Midway between Beverly Hills, Hollywood, and Downtown Los Angeles."

THEN

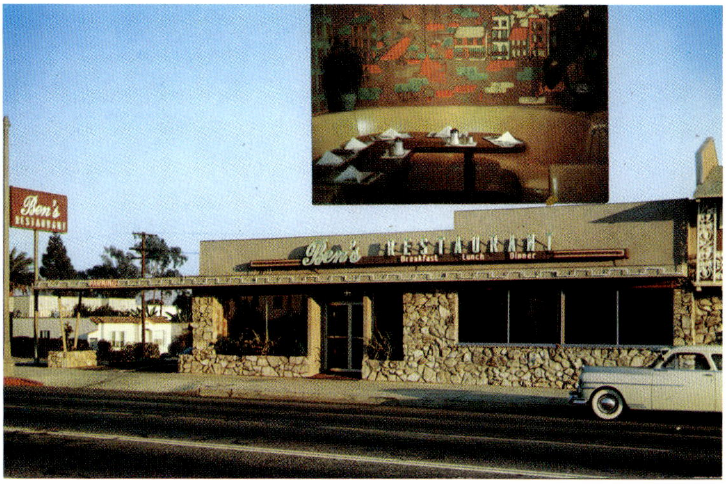

Ben's Restaurant.

NOW

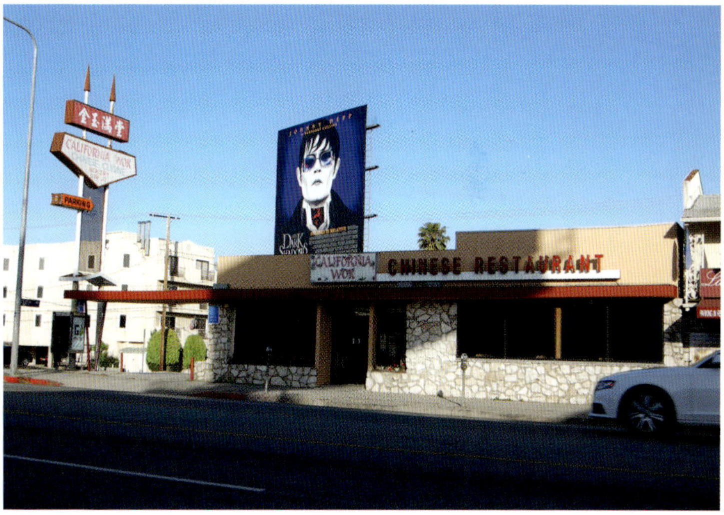

Ben's Restaurant stood at 12004 Wilshire Boulevard. The property is now a restaurant of another name. Rocks continue to decorate the building.

The parking meters in the "now" view speak of the increasing premium placed on parking spaces in Los Angeles.

THEN

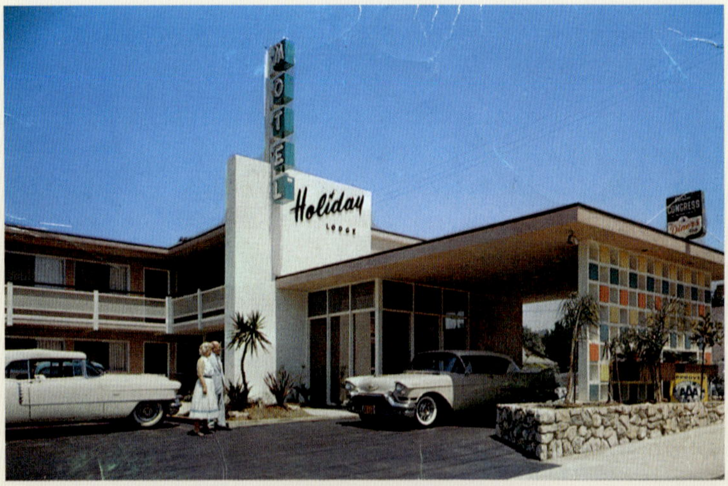

Holiday Lodge.

NOW

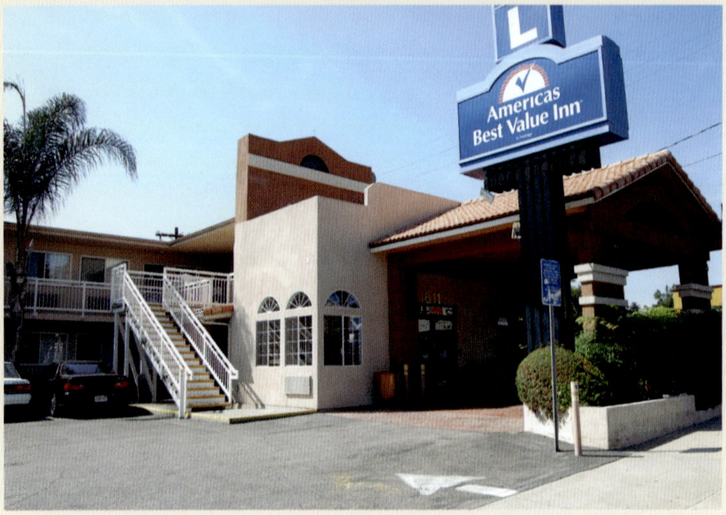

Holiday Lodge was located at 811 North Alvarado Street. The property operates as a hotel, but is no longer called the Holiday Lodge.

The Holiday Lodge postcard harkens back to a time when "Private Telephones" and "Personal Television" were amenities that motels would advertise to attract room guests.

THEN

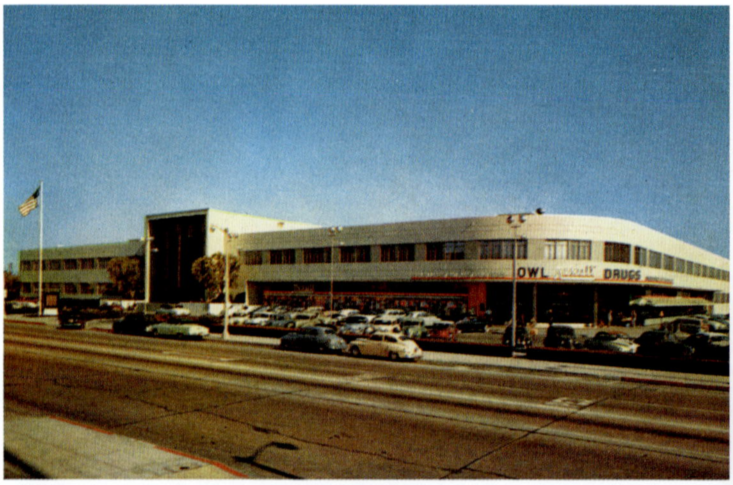

Rexall Drugs.

NOW

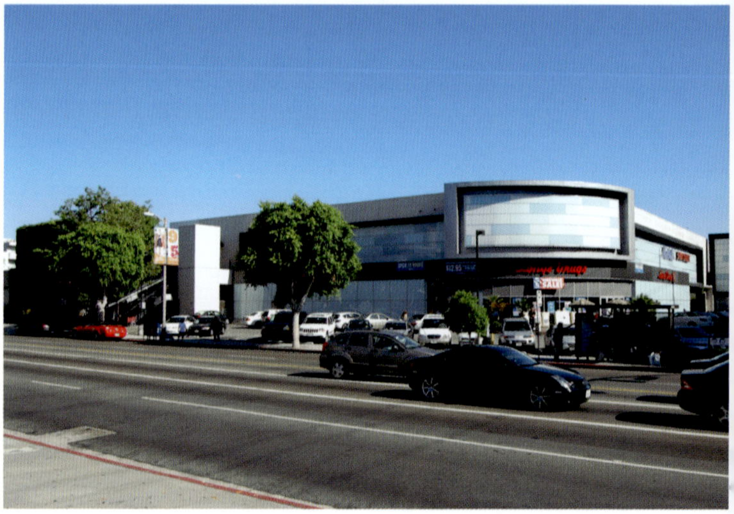

Rexall Drugs was located at the southeast corner of Beverly and La Cienega boulevards. The curving building remains, but it houses another drugstore business.

Parking lots can speak to societal trends. The nearly full parking lots in both the "then" and "now" views attest to the continued popularity of drugstores.

THEN

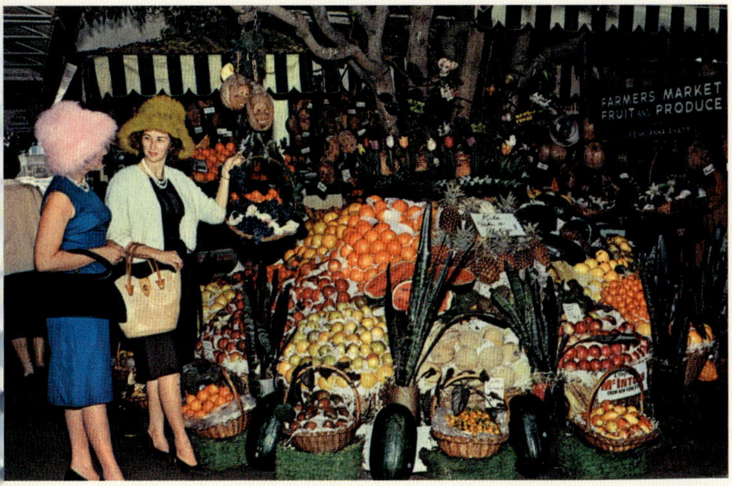

THEN

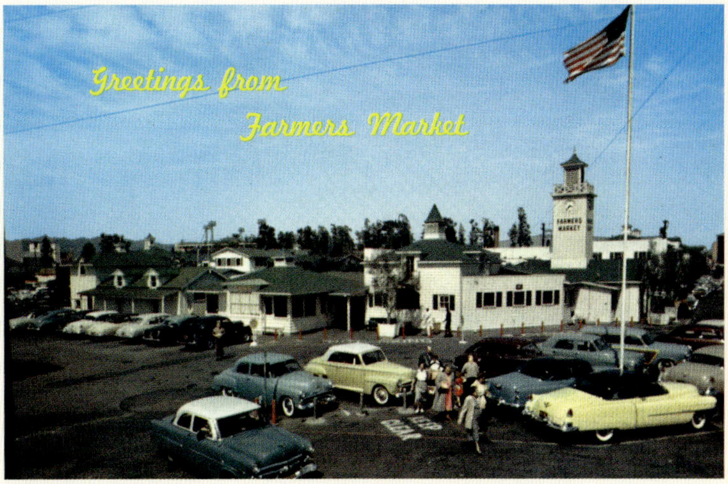

Farmers' Market.

NOW

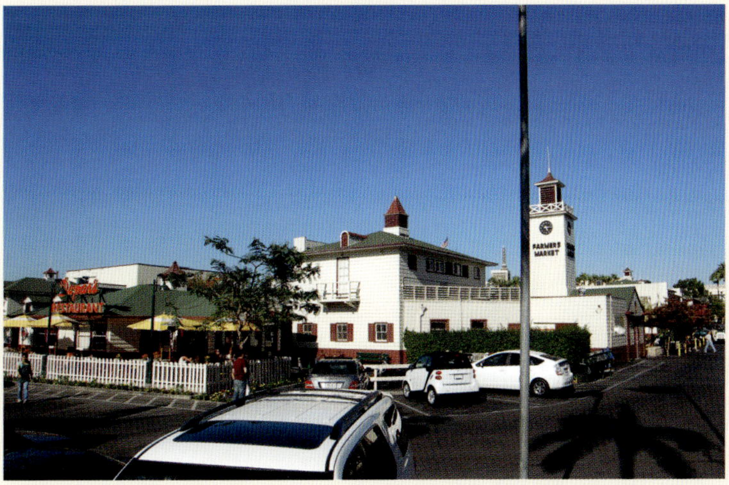

The Farmers' Market remains located at the northeast corner of Fairfax Avenue and 3rd Street.

The Farmers' Market dates back to the 1930s. At the start, it was a bunch of farmers selling their fresh produce from the back of their trucks and this humble atmosphere appealed to consumers. As back then, it is best to arrive hungry at today's Farmers' Market.

THEN

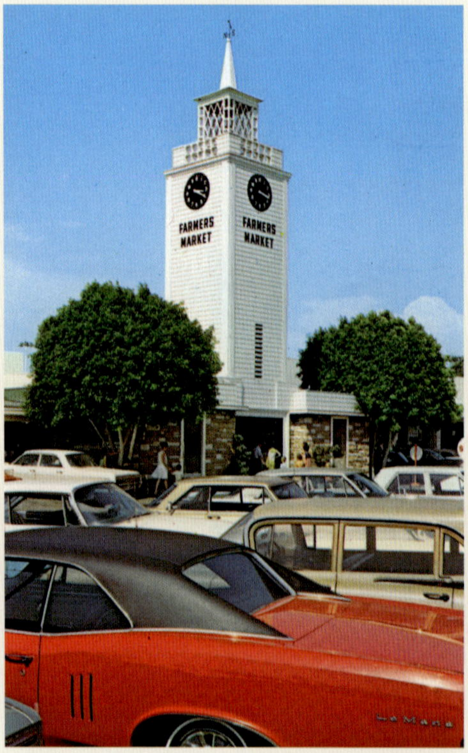

THEN

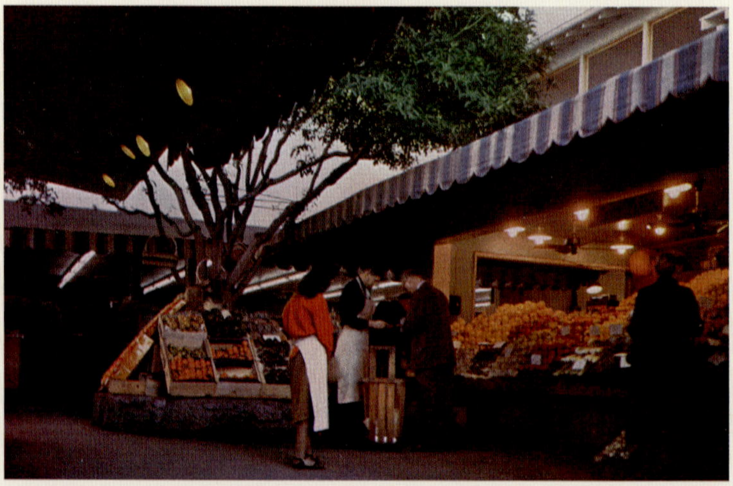

Farmers' Market. Colorful fruit and produce has been a constant at the market from its beginning.

NOW

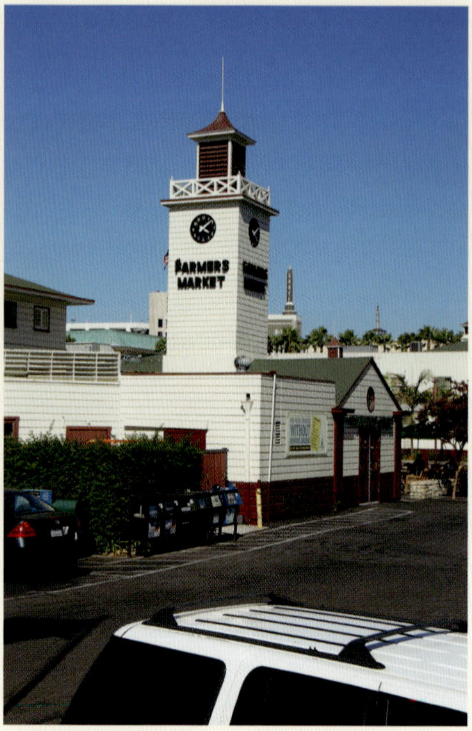

Farmers' Market continues its operations today. Since 1941, the clock tower has been a landmark of the market, standing guard over its parking lot.

THEN

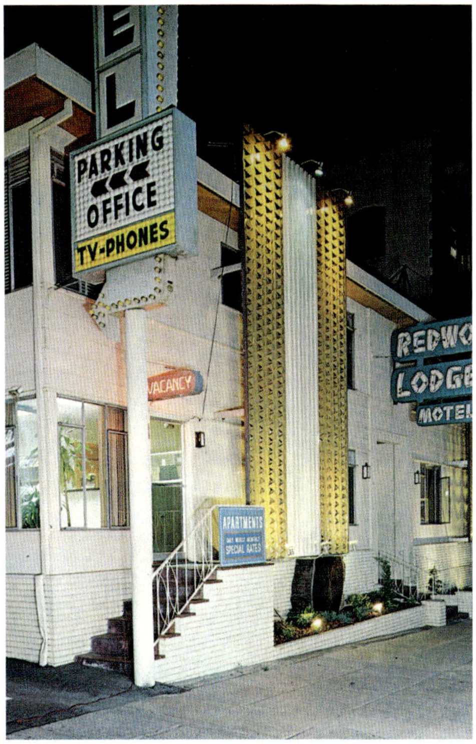

Redwood Lodge Motel and Apartments.

NOW

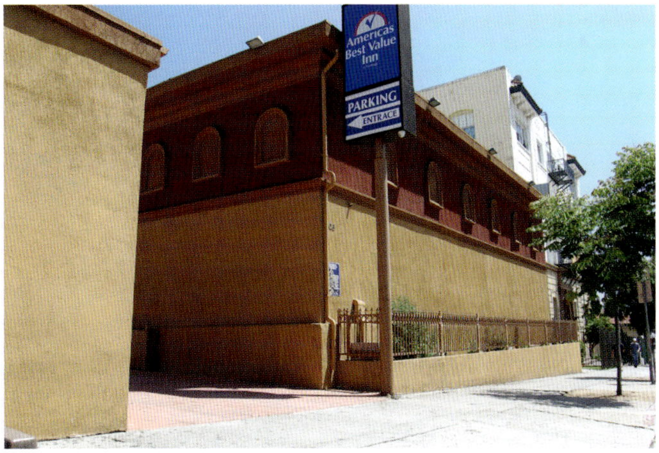

Redwood Lodge Motel and Apartments was located at 906 South Alvarado Street. The Redwood Lodge is no longer operating.

Per the back of the postcard, the Redwood Lodge Motel and Apartments offered such features as wall-to-wall carpets, Panelray vented heat, full-tile showers or tubs, and telephones in each room.

THEN

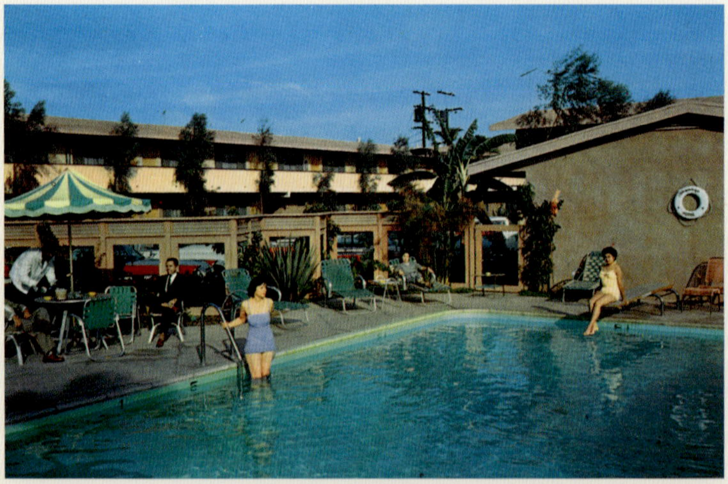

Skyways Hotel.

NOW

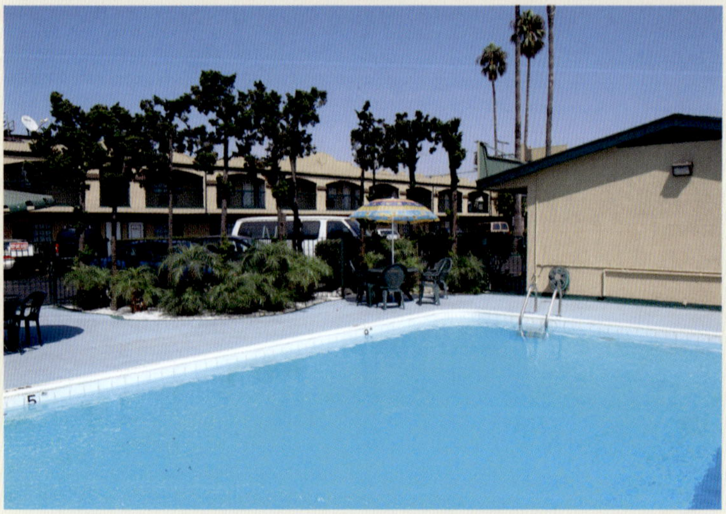

Skyways Hotel was located at 9250 Airport Boulevard. The property remains a hotel, but under a different name. A pool area here seems nearly untouched since the time of the postcard view.

In the "then" postcard view, the ladies in or over the pool are either cold or the men by it are hot. The suits and ties on two of the men imply cool weather while the bathing suits on the aforementioned ladies speak of warm weather. Perhaps the Skyways Hotel desired to produce a postcard for all seasons.

THEN

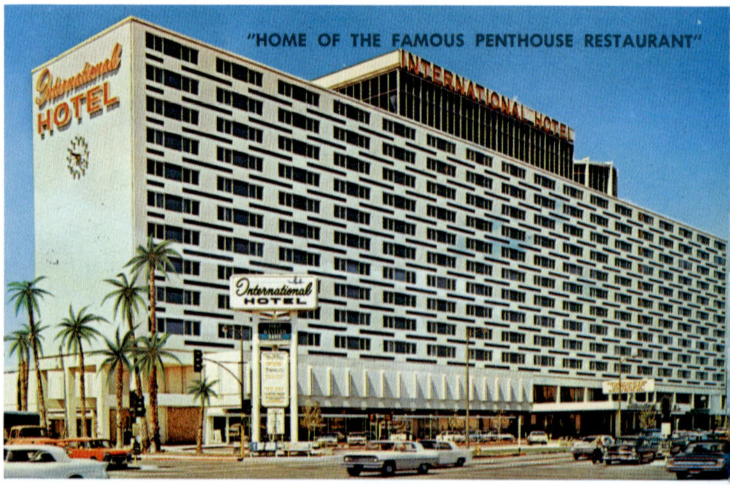

International Hotel.

NOW

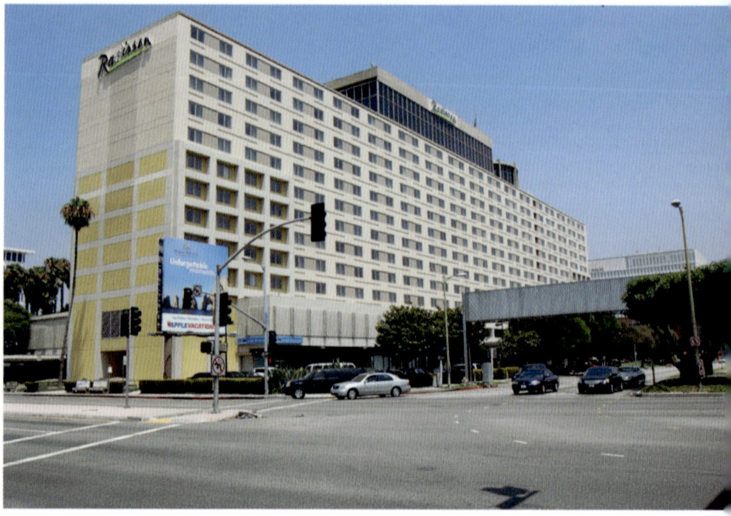

International Hotel was located at the northeast corner of Century and Sepulveda boulevards. The building remains a hotel, but with a name change.

This hotel property was built in 1963 and sits close to the Los Angeles International Airport.

THEN

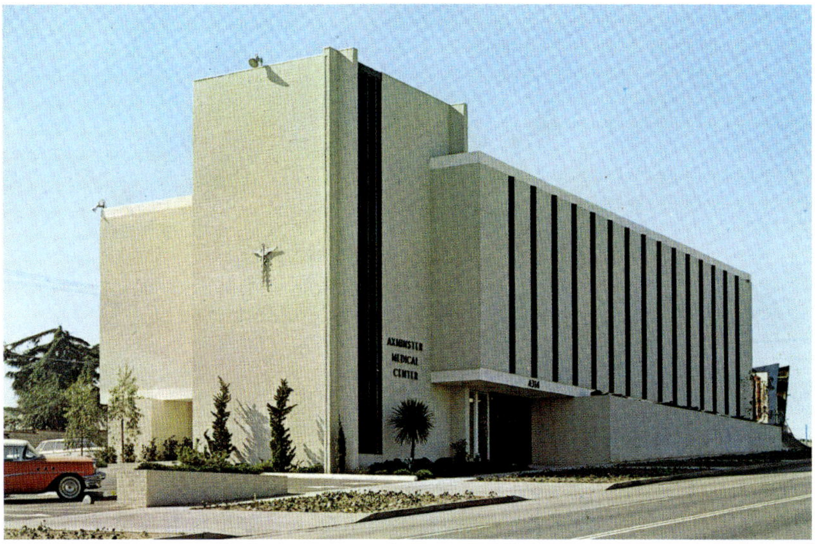

Axminster Medical Center.

NOW

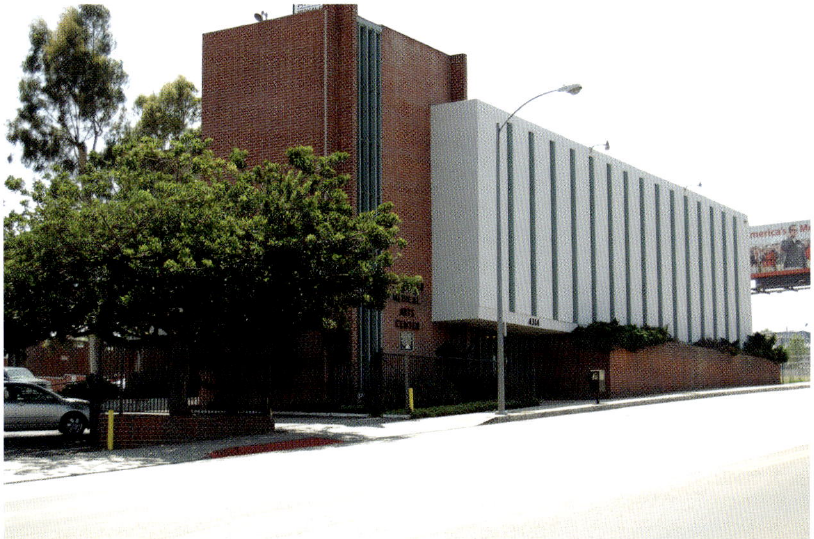

Axminster Medical Art Center is located at 4314 West Slauson Avenue. Besides the paint change, the only other obvious change to the building is the word "Art" added to the signage between "Medical" and "Center."

Even if a building in the "then" postcard view is nearly identical to its corresponding "now" view, something indefinable makes the comparison interesting.

PHOTO CREDITS

The author attempted, without success, to locate the below postcard photographers/publishers. He would like to thank and recognize them. (Note: There were more photographers than listed below, but they were credited on vintage-like, aged postcards, so attempts to reach them would have been thought not feasible.)

8. Yahei Komatsu (The Century Plaza Hotel, taxis in front)
10. David Rubinoff and card publisher Columbia Wholesale Supply (Century Park East)
39. Charles Van Pelt (Harbor Freeway)
73. Ryck Von Quedens (Fisherman's Village, Marina del Rey, docks on water)
74. Vicki Allred (Marina del Rey, hotel and water)
75. Levertt Bradley (Marina del Rey)
78. George Elton Watson (Sunset Boulevard, Pacific Palisades)
121. Vladimir Novak or card publisher Kolor View Press (Wilshire Dunes Motor Hotel)

ACKNOWLEDGMENTS

Jennifer Marie Savage, of Schiffer Publishing, was easy to work with as my editor. That makes doing a book pleasurable.

Judy Artunian got me into the book business by not only co-authoring my first two efforts, but also teaching me the ropes of writing. She and my Aunt Patty also helped me with what shopping in downtown was like (see Postcard: J. W. Robinson Company store building and its accompanying captions). Judy told me about going to town with her mother for shopping days. Aunt Patty told me a shopping day with her mother (my grandmother) would include "gloves and high heels" and a stop at Clifton's Cafeteria, where, she recalled, as a young child fearing its intimidating interior.

I would like to thank a Mike, who I met on a lazy weekend afternoon in Lincoln Park while doing research for this book. He told me cool stories and spoke about living in Lincoln Park all his life, saying (and I'm paraphrasing), "pretty much, [Lincoln Park] has been my whole life."

A girl was strolling Ocean Park with a camera. When I asked her what she was photographing, she replied, "Just taking pictures." This gave me an idea that I didn't end up using, but I believed help get this book to publication.

My appreciation goes out to the nice couple strolling along Rodeo Drive in Beverly Hills who agreed to take the "now" photo of me for "About the Author."

As a two-year-old, my niece Ava encouraged me to keep writing by flipping through a book of mine and pointing at each page she turned (her way of reading). I'm sure she will inspire her younger brother Ayden to love books!